I AM THE SECRET WAG

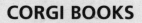

CORGI BOOKS

TRANSWORLD PUBLISHERS
61–63 Uxbridge Road, London W5 5SA
A Random House Group Company
www.transworldbooks.co.uk

I AM THE SECRET WAG
A CORGI BOOK: 9780552171137

First published in Great Britain
in 2014 by Corgi Books
an imprint of Transworld Publishers

Addresses for Random House Group Ltd companies outside the UK
can be found at: www.randomhouse.co.uk
The Random House Group Ltd Reg. No. 954009

The Random House Group Limited supports the Forest Stewardship
Council® (FSC®), the leading international forest-certification organisation.
Our books carrying the FSC label are printed on FSC®-certified paper.
FSC is the only forest-certification scheme supported by the
leading environmental organisations, including Greenpeace.
Our paper procurement policy can be found at
www.randomhouse.co.uk/environment

Typeset in 11/14pt Palatino by Falcon Oast Graphic Art Ltd.
Printed and bound by CPI Group (UK) Ltd, Croydon, CR0 4YY.

2 4 6 8 10 9 7 5 3 1

I AM THE SECRET WAG

Foreword

*M*y wife will no doubt take great pleasure in my stating that behind every good footballer is an even better woman. I can safely say that I would not be the player I have become if it wasn't for her being in my life. A footballer can only be happy on the pitch if he's happy off it, and that's me down to a 'T'.

I knew from the moment I saw her that she was the one for me. I liked her a long time before I was even on her radar. When we finally got together, I couldn't have anticipated how much she would grow as a person. She is today unrecognizable from the over-sensitive, naive and sheltered young girl I first met in a club many years ago.

She has become wise and worldly, in no small part because of the trials and tribulations she has experienced as a result of being married to me. She came from such a privileged and carefree upbringing that our relationship would have nose-dived in the early days if she hadn't shown such resilience to the pressures of football. At times, she probably wanted to run a mile from me, but she didn't: she became my rock; the love of my life.

I remember breaking the news to her about a move that meant we'd have to relocate hundreds of miles away from her home, her friends and her family, who have always meant so much to her. I literally turned her life upside down. After that first move she had many down days when she felt incredibly homesick. I felt terrible that my decision had made her unhappy. I sometimes wondered whether she would be happier if she moved back home, and I constantly asked her if she wanted to, but she was always adamant that she wanted to live with me.

Sometimes I feared she'd resent me for living a life that she didn't have much control over. I was all she had for a while; the only person she trusted and the only person she could turn to. I felt that all I could do was to reassure her, make her feel secure that I was there for her, and keep her motivated about the future. Thankfully, with time, I saw her form friendships and take up hobbies, and eventually she found her feet. She adapted to our new life and became happy again. In fact, she became a strong and independent woman and that is how she has remained.

From a footballer's point of view, because of all that goes with the job, there are many things that we look for in a potential partner. Discretion and trustworthiness top the list. I can safely say that I trust my wife one hundred per cent. I trust her with even my deepest, darkest secrets. She knows too much and she has witnessed things that, if I had my way, she would never have seen, things that could quite easily cause a lot of trouble for me and my team-mates. However, she has remained tight-lipped. She keeps everyone's secrets.

If a girl is married to a footballer, she's also got to have an understanding of the game itself. It was a real bonus for me that my girl knew the game inside out. She watched matches as a kid with her dad and, while she can't quite articulate the offside rule, she gets the dynamics, the demands and the lifestyle that accompany football, all its evils and all its blessings.

My wife is the type of person to count her every blessing. She is very gracious and humble, traits that, too often, people I come across forget to show. After all these years she still thanks me for taking her for a meal, to the cinema, and even for the lattes that I buy her in our local coffee shop. My wife doesn't take anything for granted and she has never asked me to buy her anything extravagant.

I see many of my team-mates constantly spending on their partners to keep them happy – or quiet. Some guys I know wouldn't dare arrive home after a stint away with the team without an expensive present in hand for their 'missus'. The birthday presents they 'have' to buy their women are often pretty outrageous too: tens of thousands of pounds on diamond jewellery, cars and trips abroad for her and her girlfriends. When I ask my wife what she wants for her birthday, I always get the same response: 'Just a card will do.' Even though I would give her the world if I could, she would never expect it, or take it, and that is rare behaviour in the circles we mix in.

My wife is also fiercely loyal. Just as I am often overwhelmed by the constant support and loyalty that fans show towards me, my wife wows me in how she stands by me. She has watched me play matches in the most horrendous conditions and in locations that have meant her having to travel hundreds of miles. I've never asked or expected her to do that, but knowing she's watching in the stand fills me with pride and great peace of mind.

My wife has looked after me when I've been ill or injured, boosted my morale if ever the game has got to me, dealt with press intrusion and scandals with dignity and decorum, and given my home life an order and calmness that it never had before. Additionally, I could not have wished for a better mother to my children; she has shown me great forgiveness in that I've not always been able to be the most hands-on father.

I feel such guilt that my wife's loyalty to me has prevented her fulfilling her own dreams. She's not been able to pursue her own full-time career, despite the years of studying she did in preparation, and she has had to relocate all over the country, often at the drop of a hat, because of my job as a footballer.

I appreciate how hard it has been for her to live in my shadow. Maybe after I retire, when I'm around more consistently, it will be her turn to pursue her career dreams. Perhaps the tables will turn and it will be my chance to support her and follow her in whatever decision she chooses to make. Until then, I thank God that she is right beside me wherever my footballing

career takes me, and that she will withstand whatever
life throws at us.

The Secret WAG's husband
March 2014

Chapter One

*L*ike most human beings, WAGs occasionally tell lies. I particularly enjoy listening to their 'How I met my man' fables. Perhaps the most amusing I've heard thus far is: 'He picked me out of the thirty-thousand-capacity stadium one Saturday afternoon and asked one of the stewards to pass me a handwritten note, on paper scented with his aftershave.' I've also told a few whoppers on this front, mainly to fellow WAGs. 'I met him before he was famous' and 'I didn't know who he was' have both featured in my bullshitted 'memories' of our first meeting.

The truth is that my relationship with my husband began where many relationships begin: in a nightclub – when we were both wasted. The saying 'No great story begins with a salad' is true: our great love story began with copious amounts of Budweiser and a line of tequila slammers.

Many WAGs seem to be in denial about how they got together with their man. I imagine such myth-making is an attempt to elevate themselves above other women, a signal for potential temptresses to back off since 'Only a goddess like *moi* could win *his* affections.' However, denial is not just a river in Egypt.

The fact is that most WAGs met their footballing fellas when they were drunk as skunks and hanging around the VIP areas in a nightclub. I'd even go as far as to say that many a WAG probably had her sights fixed on her man way before he'd registered her bumping and grinding in her skimpy dress and stilettos. There's no shame in that either. I can't see anything wrong with women being the hunters, identifying their target, covertly stalking them and then pouncing. Usually the guy doesn't even realize he's prey. More often than not, *he* thinks *he's* made the kill in the form of the pretty lady he just kissed. Us women are good.

I predict that ninety-nine per cent of WAGs meet their footballers out on the piss. If a footballer isn't at the training ground, or at home playing Xbox, then he'll be painting the town red. The remaining one per cent probably met their footballers at school, were childhood sweethearts who grew up together, if it can be said that footballers do grow up.

I wasn't much of a grown-up when I meet my man. I was eighteen years old and had just started university . . . and binge drinking.

Unlike most of my girlfriends, who would spend their weekends drinking cheap cider on recreation grounds, I spent most of my teenage mornings playing sports and my evenings relaxing with my boyfriend. I had two serious boyfriends. When, at eighteen, I realized that my current beau wasn't 'the one', I broke up with him and unfortunately broke his heart in the process. I also realized that I'd been missing out on a lot of fun. My friends had been partying throughout their college years while I'd been far too healthy, sensible and settled for a normal teenager.

So, as summer was beginning, I found myself single and very much ready to mingle. I was determined not to waste any more of my youth on a boyfriend and was desperately excited at the prospect of going to university. I'd studied conscientiously for my A levels. I had been accepted by a nearby university, one of the top-rated in the country, and the course I had applied for was one that could lead me into my dream job. I'd also still be close to many of my best friends.

I'd had an older sibling go through the higher education system so I had an inkling of the hard work and hard partying that was involved in full-time student life. So I was a girl with a plan. I also made it my mission to have a good time and use my university years as the last blow-out before real adult life began.

'Two serious boyfriends' translates as: 'I'd only ever had sex with two men', so I figured that I needed some more experience of the male kind. I wanted to kiss as many boys as I possibly could and play the field with-out tying myself into a serious relationship. I felt that I'd been a devoted girlfriend for far too many of my youthful years.

Home became a tiny room that I rented for fifty-five pounds a week in one of the university's halls of residence. The move from my parents' sprawling five-bedroomed house in the countryside, complete with indoor swimming pool, was a culture shock to say the least. The room was dire. I made a note to self: regardless of the mission, no bloke would be visiting me within these walls. It'd be far too shameful.

Unlike my friends and hall-mates, I didn't pull anyone during my first weeks at university. There were hardly any guys on my course and none of them were hot – in fact most of them were gay, or as immature and annoying as the ones I'd left behind at college. In the evenings when we were out drinking, I was approached by lots of sweaty students and lechy locals, but regardless of how drunk I became, I didn't feel attracted to anyone I met. The man mission was failing at the first hurdle.

However, I did make a lot of acquaintances with the bar staff and doormen at the clubs. I'd often find myself drunkenly chatting to them instead of my friends, who'd be playing tonsil tennis on the dance-floor with random guys they'd ensnared. On a few occasions kindly door staff rescued me from obnoxious men who'd been hassling me for a dance or kiss, although I'm sure their kindness was partly to do with how I used to dress. My choice of evening attire didn't leave much to the imagination – and men will be men.

Soon my friends and I were regulars at a few choice venues in the city where we were let in for free. The city we lived in was relatively small and there was a familiar night-time community. It was easy to predict who would be where. We went to student bars that played cheesy music and had a 'Pound a Pint Night'.

Once the DJ ordered 'lights up', we'd walk half a mile to the biggest nightclub in the city where, on a Saturday night, the Premiership footballers could always be found.

Footballers attract pretty girls, pretty girls attract single men and single men attract single women, so the club was always packed to the rafters. It had a huge dance-floor, flanked by long, neon-lit bars and a few sofas and tables. There were several rooms off the main area, all accessed by mirror-lined corridors, that played different types of music. The venue could hold thousands and it was one of the few places in the city where all cliques of night-clubbers partied together.

There was no VIP area, and that was probably why I failed to notice the group of footballers who frequented the club. Neither could they be identified from their choice of tipple – this was a place for drinks that cost a pound not Cristal champagne. I imagined that the footballers relished the fact that they could blend in with the crowd and get away with acting like morons. The irony was that people went to the club in the knowledge that the footballers were there, but unless you were a hardened fan, it would have been difficult to pick them out of a line-up.

On a few occasions, gaggles of girls would nudge and whisper to each other and gesticulate in the direction of a group of men who *could*'ve been the footballers, but because I didn't know or care who they were or what they looked like, I didn't register their presence. So the footballers were inconspicuous, and that was how they remained to me, until my cousin started dating one. She was at a university eighty miles away, but we took turns in visiting each other whenever a free weekend surfaced.

One such weekend when she was visiting me, we were ending the Saturday evening in the same way we usually did, in our girl pack on the dance-floor, when an inebriated guy slapped her hard on her backside. She swung round and slapped him hard on the face. The guy put his hand on his smarting cheek and said, 'I think I'm in love.' He then grabbed her hand and bent down on one knee in the middle of the packed dance-floor, looked up at her, with a puppy-dog expression on his face, and said, 'Please forgive me? Then come on a date?'

On their first outing together she discovered that he was one of the rising stars of the local team. She reported that he showed enough charm to warrant a second date. In the weeks to follow, they went on a handful of dates but their relationship would be short-lived. According to her, the footballer would boast about how much money he earned yet would accept her offer to split the bill whenever they ate out . . . and she was the broke student! She said his conversation was infantile and that he couldn't even name the prime minister – 'thick as shit' was how she actually referred to him.

The final nail in the dating coffin was that, despite his boasts about his sexual prowess, he had a small penis and no idea of how to get a woman in the mood. She found this out not from having sex with him – my family and I have been better brought up than to sleep with a man after a few dates – but from the one occasion that she visited him in his lodgings to watch a film. Halfway through the movie she made a trip to the bathroom and on her return found that he had stripped naked and was lying on the sofa. She said that he rocked his hips backwards and forwards, with his tiny erection on full show, and said, 'You're a good-looking girl, darlin', but you'd look a lot better with my balls on your chin . . .'

She didn't return his calls after that.

Unbeknown to my cousin, the footballer had simul-taneously been dating other girls too, and was the worst 'cheater' on the team. We found this out a few weeks later on another Saturday night out together in the same nightclub. Ladies' toilets are often the places where the juiciest gossip can be overheard and we happened to eavesdrop on an argument between two girls – about him and which of them was his girlfriend.

My cousin and I are not people to suffer fools gladly, so we made it our mission to find the philandering footballer before his warring lovers confronted him. It was a fateful decision to make since this was the spark that led to the chain of events that resulted in me meet-ing my man.

We found my cousin's ex-date standing with a huddle of other footballers at one of the bars. Apart from the freakishly tall goalkeeper, they all looked super-hot and were dressed to kill, but as we were introduced to them, I began to feel very intimidated. I managed to stutter a weak 'Hi' to the handsome faces that surrounded me but then grabbed my cousin by the arm and walked her back to our group of girlfriends.

I didn't want to be seen talking to the footballers. I thought ill of girls who hovered around rich and famous men, and I didn't want to be judged by my own standards. Moreover, going by my cousin's experiences, I had no interest in gaining a footballer's affections. I certainly wasn't interested in sharing a prospective boyfriend with other girls, and I was definitely not in the game for having any testicles on my chin.

However, I did look out for the footballers whenever I returned to that club. I felt a little intrigued and, if I'm honest, it did feel quite cool to know that they knew me. When I saw them I'd give them a friendly nod or say a meek 'hello', but that was where the familiarity ended.

Despite their good looks, they often behaved obnoxiously – they were rowdy, boozy and leery. They acted as if they were invincible: they would grind their bodies against girls on the dance-floor, knock back shots at the bar and lord it over any fans who dared approach them.

I also noticed that every time they left the club it'd be with a different girl, or different *group* of girls, and I soon homed in on the rumours about them circulating among my student friends. Their reputation was not good. I learned that they were renowned for sleeping around and often swapped 'girlfriends' in the process. As much as I was on a mission to 'snog about', I certainly wasn't a one-night-stand kind of girl and was not willing to become a used piece of footballers' meat.

However, a few weeks later I found myself at the club for an eighteenth birthday party. I was dressed in tartan hot pants and a lace backless top with no bra. I teamed my outfit with black pointy stilettos and a black leather bag covered with metal studs. I can only recall this because recently my husband and I were reminiscing about our fateful meeting and he described in detail my ensemble. Apparently it had made a lasting impression on him and helped me to stand out from the crowd, who were mostly in ra-ra skirts and boob tubes, probably straight off the rails of Bay Trading. I've never followed fashion, and on that occasion at least my rebellion against current trends served a purpose.

The footballers were surrounded by a group of scantily clad girls, otherwise known as 'hang-ons', who were bumping and grinding with each other in a sorry attempt to get their attention. I presumed that they would be the footballers' last-resort-shag if they hadn't bagged anything better before two a.m.

Over the years since, I've learned that many girls want to have one night of sex with a footballer to tell their friends about or to sell the story to a tabloid. I'm sure the reality is that such women would have liked a one-night stand to amount to much more, that they hoped to become a WAG and live a stereotypical life of luxury. But such dreams aren't reality, and even if they were they certainly wouldn't become so via a quick fuck.

When it was my turn to buy a round of drinks, the bar was at its busiest and the tunes were pumping. I was in my own world and bounced to the beat. When I finally made it to the front of the queue, one of the footballers got there at exactly the same moment. It was the team's star player, no less. His face was always splashed over the press and even my father had talked at the dinner table of his prowess.

At that moment we were shoulder to shoulder, so close that we almost rubbed noses when we turned to look at each other. He was absolutely gorgeous, a fact that the media regularly exploited. He was wearing a light-weight casual jacket over a T-shirt, dark-blue denim jeans, bright-white trainers, and his hair was spiked-up. Every item of his clothing sported a designer label and his look was streets ahead of how most of the chavvy blokes in the club chose to dress. I thought he looked cool, a bit preppy for my usual type, but most definitely sexy.

It would have been impossible not to speak to each other while we were being served; in fact, it would have seemed rude if we hadn't, given our proximity. I wish I could recite the exact words we exchanged but they've been lost somewhere in time. I know we didn't discuss anything intellectual since he was a footballer and I already had a negative impression of his kind, and more to the point, I was trolleyed, thus not at my smartest.

As we bought our respective rounds of drinks, we engaged in light pleasantries. Then, to my surprise, he invited me to do a tequila slammer with him. It wasn't a romantic gesture, but I appreciated the sentiment; I'm not sure I turned down any free drinks in my student days. So he ordered two shots of tequila, we clinked them together, banged them in unison on the bar, then threw them down our throats. Then we had another, and another.

Breathless at the strength of the alcohol, after the 'third-time lucky' shot, I thanked him and moved to walk away. Before I could, he asked me for my phone number and I gave it to him. It was rare for me to give out my phone number, the correct one, but he caught me off guard and the tequila might have weakened my feminine defences.

As I returned to my friends, I felt flattered at what had just happened, but I didn't feel excited at the prospect of his phone call. I didn't think it would actually materialize, given the reputation those boys had for taking girls' numbers and not calling. I forgot about the incident quite quickly and I didn't even tell my friends that I'd given my number to the local football team's star player.

The remainder of that evening passed in an alcohol-infused haze and I barely remember returning to my student accommodation. Although I do remember that after I flopped onto my tiny single bed, my thick Nokia mobile phone beeped to signal that a text message had arrived. It was the footballer.

The message read: 'So glad you gave me your number. When can I take you out?'

I remember that I closed one eye to read and re-read the message. I drunkenly squinted at it and swayed from side to side. The shock of receiving the text must have given me momentary clarity as I recall concluding that the text signalled that, first, he couldn't have gone home with another girl, and second, he must be alone and thinking of me. I smirked but decided to play it cool. I wouldn't text back until the morning. In all honesty, if I had texted back immediately, the message would probably have been incomprehensible and thus made me look like a drunken twat.

The next day I had an awful hangover, but I also felt the giddy excitement that can only be brought on by new romance. I re-read his text countless times. I felt unsure when or how to respond to it because, although I've always been a firm believer in 'Treat him mean to keep him keen', I also didn't want him to lose interest in me. That itself made me realize that I liked him. I remember thinking, Shit. I like a bloody footballer. This is not good.

Throughout that day I agonized about when and what to text back; whether to wait another day; whether to phrase the response as funny, serious, sexy or nonchalant; whether to ask a question or, so I wouldn't be disappointed if an answer didn't come, whether to make it cool and indifferent. Even when the evening arrived and I sat on my bed with my phone in my hand, I wrote and rewrote at least ten different messages until I arrived at the one I was content to send.

It read something along the lines of, 'Nice to speak to you last night. I'm really busy this week. How about next Tuesday?' As I pressed 'send', my inner goddess high-fived herself. Approximately one minute after the little envelope icon had appeared on the phone's small screen to indicate the message had been delivered, my phone beeped. It was his reply. 'You're going to make me wait that long?' Seconds later another text arrived: 'Send me your address and I'll pick you up next Tuesday at 7 p.m.'

Chapter Two

When date night Tuesday arrived, I felt nervous, not because I was due to go out with a footballer but because my first date for months was with a guy who was probably a Lothario, a philanderer and a dating pro. I anticipated that he would be rehearsing the lines that would sweep a girl off her feet . . . and into bed. With that in mind I resolved that I would not fall for any of his potential faux charms or clichéd conversations. I was not prepared to take shit from any man, sexy footballer or not.

I spent the day in lectures although my mind was not focused on anything academic. As our seven o'clock date approached, I began to worry about potential situations, and questions raced through my mind. What should I do if he tries to kiss me? Shall I eat in front of him? Shall I keep my compact mirror in my pocket for covert bogey and make-up checks? What will we talk about if he's thick?

In search of reassurance, I called my parents. They are the only people in the world to whom I tell everything, even now. This time their advice was limited.

My mother's response was, 'Ooh, be careful, darling. I remember what footballers were like when I was younger. I wouldn't have touched them with a barge pole,' while my dad said, 'Great! Can you get me his autograph?' I had hoped for some comments along the lines of 'He's just a normal person, stop fretting', but their replies brought me no peace of mind.

I showered in record time, straightened my hair and applied light make-up so as to appear as near to my natural self as possible. Then I had to choose my outfit. Tiny as my wardrobe was, I packed a lot of clothes into it. I couldn't decide whether to dress sexy, sophisticated, sassy or sweet for my date. I wanted to make a lasting impression on him and I thought that, regardless of how I might feel at the end of the evening, I wanted him to want me. Since I believe men are visual creatures, I wanted to wear an outfit that he'd feast his eyes on and not forget in a hurry.

Eventually I decided on dark-denim flared jeans, high black ankle boots, and a black, shimmery, high-necked sleeveless top. For quirkiness, I completed the ensemble with a black bowler hat. I must have been the only person in the city in that era to own one. I love hats: they hide a multitude of sins and in my opinion add a little glamour and mystique to any outfit.

At seven on the dot the front-door buzzer sounded loudly in my room. It was him! I swiftly applied another layer of lip gloss, then grabbed my handbag and leather jacket. When I opened the front door he was standing confidently, legs astride, with a wide smile on his face. He wore jeans, a matching denim jacket, and a pair of ridiculously white trainers. Double-denim cannot be worn well by many but he made it work. His eyes sparkled. He held out his hand to me – I didn't take it – and said, 'Shall we go?'

My date led me to his black Porsche and opened the passenger door for me; a gentlemanly gesture I duly noted. I tried my best to manoeuvre myself gracefully onto the cold, hard cream leather of the front passenger seat, but failed miserably when I hit my head on the low door frame. 'Idiot!' I whispered to myself.

His expensive sports car didn't impress me at all. I was brought up in a well-off family and my parents have always owned 'posh' cars. At the time of the date, my father drove a Mercedes and my mother a brand-new Range Rover. I remember musing, If you think I'm turned on by being sat in your fancy car then you're very much mistaken!

As we drove out of the halls of residence car park, with a rip-roaring rev of the Porsche's engine, he announced that we were headed to the cinema. I was relieved at our destination as it meant there wouldn't be the pressure to make idle chit-chat. I dreaded awkward silences or shallow conversation. However, as we drove there, I discovered that my fears had been misconceived: conversation flowed. He asked me about my university course, my friends and my hobbies, which I decided was a good sign of his interest and respect.

We also spoke about our upbringing. I found out that he'd been raised in a traditional working-class family by hard-working and loving parents, who had done everything they could to ensure he had a good education and access to all he needed in order to follow his footballing dreams. He said he'd had a happy childhood, and there were no proverbial skeletons in his family's closet. I was a little taken aback at his educational achievements: he'd got better results than I had at school – and I'd been considered clever!

We also found that we had additional common ground in our musical tastes and social interests: Pound a Pint student nights and dancing to Bon Jovi. I felt at ease in his company almost immediately and most of my dating worries disappeared, although I allowed my doubt about his intentions to remain.

After he'd parked at the cinema, he darted out of his door and over to mine to open it. It was another small, chivalrous, gesture and I was impressed. He didn't attempt to hold my hand while walking in: my frostiness at his first hand-holding invitation must have put him off, but I probably would have taken it had he made a second attempt.

He told me that he hadn't booked seats because he wanted us to watch a film of my choosing. I feigned indifference and passed the decision back to him. It was a test, and he passed it with flying colours. The romantic comedy was precisely the movie that I would have chosen, although I did wonder if he'd picked it based on what he thought a girl would like to watch.

After he had gorged himself on a man mountain of snacks – not behaviour that endeared him to me – I waited for him to make some sort of move. I waited . . . and waited. I completely lost track of the film, as I questioned why my date hadn't tried to hold my hand again, put his arm around me or kiss me. I began to conclude that he could not be interested in me, or that perhaps the cinema was simply a precursor to 'Let's go back to mine.'

I began to feel a little disappointed. Even with food and drink falling out of his mouth, I found him immensely attractive. Also, he was interesting to talk to and not stupid in the slightest, so I began to think of him as a real catch. Not because he was a footballer, but because he seemed like a decent human being.

After the film, as we drove through the city centre and passed the bars and clubs that we both frequented, I watched people turning their heads to look at his car, or to wave at him. I remember thinking it was incredible that so many people knew him.

When we eventually returned to my halls of residence, my inner goddess silently screamed, 'Say thank you and get out of the car! Go on! Just get out of the car,' but I couldn't bring myself to do that. Instead, I remained in the passenger seat and we chatted for what seemed like an age. He was not sleazy or arrogant, but normal, polite, articulate and interesting. I liked him, I realized that much, and the more I looked into his eyes, the more I wanted him to kiss him. His eyes were kind and alive; they were inviting, mysterious and, I thought, promised much excitement.

When I noticed the Porsche's clock flicker to two a.m., I decided to return to my room. I had lectures the next morning and I couldn't allow my adrenalin to pump any longer in the hope of a goodnight kiss. As I began to say goodbye, he asked quickly, 'Would you like to go for a bite to eat tomorrow night?'

His invite took me by surprise and gave me a buzz. However, I kept my cool and, in an attempt to play hard to get, I answered, 'I'll think about it.' Then he leaned over to the passenger seat, drew my face to his and kissed me, gently yet firmly. His lips were noticeably soft and we lingered in that kiss for slightly longer than would have been normal.

As I walked away from his car, I had to stop myself skipping. Despite the late hour, I felt the excitement that can only come from romance, attraction, love, or whatever 'it' begins as. But a barrage of questions still raced through my mind. What would I be letting myself in for if I dated him? Would I be seen as one of those detestable girls who were desperate to bag a footballer? Would my friends have less respect for me? Would he prove the rumours right and just want me for sex?

Thankfully, the human brain is the greatest and fastest computer in the known universe and mine came to my rescue. It drew a quick conclusion to my rising doubts. 'Just say yes!' it told me. 'After all, part of your mission is to date boys . . . and he's a gorgeous specimen.'

I had difficulty sleeping that night and the next day dragged. Lectures felt long and tedious, and I couldn't concentrate on anything aside from planning what I would wear in the evening. I opted for my trustworthy little black dress; trustworthy because it had never failed to make a good impression on those who had seen me in it. I still have that LBD in the attic in a box marked 'Special Memories'. I had also decided to wear stockings and suspenders; less for him since he wouldn't see them, but more for me. If my underwear is sexy, then I feel sexy.

My date picked me up on time and looked as handsome as he had the night before. We chatted in the car like excited teenagers and the chemistry between us became even more apparent. He took me to a family-run Chinese restaurant in the city, where we were treated like royalty and he was on first-name terms with the waiting staff.

The restaurant was busy for a week night and it was obvious that we were the centre of many of our fellow diners' attention. During our meal two people tentatively approached our table and asked for my date's autograph, and a photo, which he duly and happily agreed to. Thankfully, such adoration did not seem to go to his head. He obliged his fans immediately but quickly excused himself from them so as to not neglect 'his beautiful date' – his words. His words! The LBD had not let me down.

The food was delicious and my date's manners throughout the meal were impeccable: he pulled the chair out for me to sit on, poured my wine before his and complimented me whenever the opportunity arose. We remained at our table, conversing over candlelight, until the waiting staff locked the doors.

The night had passed quickly and I was disappointed that the time had arrived for me to return to my student digs.

As we walked back to the car, my date gently clasped my hand in his and adrenalin surged through my body. It was the most innocent form of physical contact but the feeling it produced in me was far from innocent. It was electrifying. As he drove me home, he held my hand whenever the journey allowed and only released it when he had to change gear. My heart pounded in my chest whenever his skin met mine. I'm sure the blood rushed around his body a lot faster when he rested his hand on my thigh, over my suspender clips – he looked at me with a shocked yet mischievous grin when he realized what he had found.

Once we had arrived back at the halls of residence, he turned to look at me intensely. For the first time that evening we were in silence, although it spoke a thousand words. I returned his gaze and for a few moments we just sat looking at each other, our faces illuminated in the moonlight. If eyes are windows to the soul, then at that moment we saw the essence of each other – at least, that was how it felt to me.

He raised his hand to the back of my neck and tenderly caressed the nape, then gently eased my head towards his. Then he kissed me. First he let his lips softly press into mine, and then he kissed my top lip and bottom lip separately in what felt like an exploratory tease. Our breathing quickened and it was erotic to feel his warm breath on my face. Then our mouths locked together and our tongues met in what I still define as the best kiss I have ever had in my life.

We kissed passionately. He caressed the back of my hair and the sides of my face and brought me closer into him until we were locked in a tight embrace. I ran my hands along the muscular outline of his back and clasped his face as our heads moved from side to side, held together by our frantic tongues and lips. It was a breathtaking experience, one that I will never forget.

It seemed that the kiss had sealed our affections, for we saw each other every night for one month. It was intense and obsessive behaviour, but we could not stay away from each other. Even if we had to go out independently, we'd ensure that we spent the end of the evening together; he would arrive at my room in the early hours of the morning after a night out with his friends or I would drive to his apartment after I'd been out with my girlfriends. We were spending whole nights together but just to kiss and cuddle. It was blissfully innocent.

He passed many 'boyfriend tests' during that period of time. He had met my friends and impressed them with his bad jokes, with his normality and his generosity. He even slept on the disgusting scratchy carpet of my room with no complaint. I broke my rule about having boys back to my room: I'd realized that they just don't care, especially when the scantily clad girl they fancy is in it.

Staying over at his place was a treat for me. He lived in a gated apartment complex, complete with its own exclusive shopping parade, private gym and indoor swimming pool, which had the best changing-room power-showers I'd ever experienced.

The apartment my footballer rented was modest for the wage he commanded. It was on the second floor, with two bedrooms, a living room and a small galley kitchen. The bedrooms and living room opened onto a balcony with beautiful views of the city. He furnished his home minimally: there were the stereotypical framed pictures of him with various super-famous footballers and managers of the past fifty years perched wherever would be most obvious for people to view them, and there were a few more personal family and friends' photographs.

Aside from expensive electronic equipment, such as the television and stereo system, and the wine rack full of fine wines and vintage champagnes, his furnishing and decor were basic: cream walls, cream curtains and cream leather sofas. The place desperately needed a woman's touch! Each visit I made, I subtly added a little femininity to his surroundings, and he didn't object – a vase of flowers on the windowsill, a framed piece of colourful artwork produced by my university friend. It all made a difference, and the fact he kept them in place was a signal that he wanted me around.

I didn't have sex with my footballer until five and a half weeks into our relationship, which he later confessed felt like three years in comparison to what he was accustomed to with girls. I'm proud that we waited. Although I wanted to have sex with him, especially when we were in bed together and our spectacular kissing reached fever-point, it felt like we were both waiting for the right time. It was as if we were teenagers secretly planning to lose our virginity to each other: we knew it would happen eventually so there was no haste or pressure.

I think the waiting was at times frustrating for him, for I did notice that when things got heated between the sheets, while I could cool down relatively quickly and go to sleep, he would always have to go to the bathroom for a significant amount of time before he could drop off. There must have been a lot of tension in his boxer shorts.

That tension spilled over once, literally. We were out with my friends from university in a late-night cafe bar, when we both felt a little amorous. I had been perched on my man's knee on a comfy sofa-chair, and on the occasions when I slipped into his lap I could tell that he was turned on. The knowledge of him being aroused had a knock-on effect and I suggested that we venture outside for 'a little air'. We headed to the terrace at the back of the cafe, sneaked into one of its dark corners and began to kiss passionately. As I pressed myself against him I could feel his erection pushing into me. It was rock hard, begging to be touched . . . and I couldn't resist!

Rather than groping his manhood in full view of anyone who wished to take interest in us, I slyly released two of the top buttons on his jeans and touched him through his boxer shorts. In my mind it was meant to serve as a tease, a 'taste of things to come later'. However, given the erotic nature of our public passion, unfortunately the pressure got too much for my man. As I was rubbing his private parts, he suddenly whispered in my ear, 'Oh, shit!'

He had come. He had come for England! And predominantly over the groin area of his light-blue jeans. When we moved into the floodlights of the terrace to examine the damage, it was a funny sight to behold! There was no way out from the terrace, so he had to take off his long-sleeved shirt, wrap it around his waist, hiding the 'evidence', and walk back into the cafe in the white T-shirt he had on underneath. In winter.

We left with the lie that he was burning up with a case of the flu and needed to get home to rest. We got into a taxi and both cracked up with laughter, although he had the last laugh since I rather stupidly promised to 'make up for it' when we got back to his place. I'm sure it's not difficult to imagine what he ordered off the proverbial foreplay menu.

Like our first kiss, our 'first time' together was unforgettable. It was midweek and I was due at his apartment to watch a film. Despite there being no indication, no hint or suggestion, that there was to be a night of passion ahead, I had a feeling that there would be. I felt ready for it and I wanted it.

It seemed that our feelings were in synchronicity for as soon as I walked through his front door, he looked at me lasciviously then pinned me against the wall and kissed me deeply. I welcomed his pounce. There was a new urgency to our kissing and soon we began to rip off each other's clothes. We tumbled and stumbled from the entrance hall into his bedroom and left a trail of our clothes behind us. We fell onto his bed and for hours we caressed and explored every inch of each other's bodies. It was intense, hot and extraordinarily passionate.

From the way he touched me I could tell that he was experienced – I'd arrived at that conclusion even before we had gone on our first date – but he wasn't over-confident. He was the perfect combination of tender and strong, passionate and controlled, and he was significantly blessed in the groin area. I had felt his rock-hard erection pushing through his clothes against me many times, but seeing and touching it directly was a thrill. He was a fine specimen of a man! His body was amazing: he was muscular and toned, and his six-pack was a work of sculpted art. I traced my fingers along each and every muscle contour as I allowed his hands unrestricted access to explore me.

After what seemed like hours of unadulterated pleasure, we began to have sex. It was slow, deep and felt more natural and 'right' than any other sexual experience I'd had before. It felt like more than a physical act: we connected emotionally and spiritually through it. He was on top of me, his warm body bore down on mine and he leaned on his forearms while his hands held the sides of my head. He looked directly into my eyes as he moved slowly and gently inside me. It was mind-blowing. He controlled his animal instinct, which I'm sure was just to fuck as hard as he could, and preserved the tension and passion in his tender yet strong movements. We didn't speak throughout it. I was too overwhelmed to do anything but feel and I guessed it was the same for him. As I looked into his eyes I saw emotion, not just of the sexual kind, but in his beautiful and intent stare I could see that he felt as I did. We were in love.

After perhaps twenty minutes of romantic, sweaty and emotional sex, our first time came to an end with both of us reaching orgasm. Satiated, we lay in the afterglow with our bodies entwined together, trying to regain our breath, not from our physical exertions but from the overwhelming feelings that had taken it away.

'I love you,' I whispered to him, between my shallow panting. I'm not sure what possessed me to allow that line to leave my lips for I hadn't before considered whether I loved him or not. It had felt like 'too soon' to know. In that moment, though, I had little control over those three words falling out of my mouth. It was as if my subconscious saw its chance to burst into my consciousness at a moment of vulnerability, as if it needed to make him and me aware of what my heart knew.

Thankfully, I didn't have a chance to regret those words or fear his response because he immediately replied, 'I love you too.' Then he added, 'And I've wanted to say that to you for weeks.' My inner goddess performed cartwheels.

We fell asleep in a tight embrace and remained tangled in each other's limbs until the morning. When we woke to the sun that beamed through his balcony doors I felt heavenly: we had sealed our relationship. It was love!

He had to get up for his early-morning training

schedule but I remained dozing in his bed after he left. I didn't want to go back to my halls of residence. I didn't want to leave his presence or his home. Being in his world made me feel more complete than I had ever felt.

When I left his apartment, I posted his key back through his letterbox. I got into my car and felt a sudden sense of sadness. Doubts began to surface again. Would things be different now he had bedded me? Was I just a challenge? Would I hear from him again? At the prospect of not seeing him, tears pricked my eyes. I was 'in' deep.

As I gripped the steering wheel, I realized I had to pull myself together and that there was actually no indication that anything was wrong. In fact, everything was right. I was perhaps in disbelief that everything seemed so perfect – who really believes that the fairy-tale romance will happen to them? Even when it's staring you in the face, it's difficult to comprehend that life can, sometimes, be a dream come true.

I drove home praying that things would be OK, and I believe that my prayers were answered. A text message arrived on my phone even before I left his apartment complex. It read: 'I had an unbelievable night. Miss you already. Love you x'. My heart skipped a beat when I read that message. Then I cranked up my music and drove home singing, 'It's A Beautiful Day'.

From then on, our relationship went from strength to strength. What I didn't realize until years later was how much my man liked me from the start. He said he had noticed me even before my cousin and I were introduced to him that fateful night in the club. He said that whenever he saw me out he used to wish that I would come and talk to him, and that sometimes he'd try to say hi to me but I would blank him, which made him feel like shit. I had no recollection of him ever making any attempt to speak to me, and I certainly hadn't noticed that I had him as an admirer. The devil in me does find it amusing to think that I made him feel like shit without even trying – if only I could wield such power today.

On reflection, I should probably have been a little less judgemental of footballers: by date two, my man had trounced all the stereotypical views I'd held about them. He'd certainly challenged my assumption that all footballers were thick because, while alcohol had helped in that first encounter at the bar, my man scored me because of his intellect. If he hadn't had the clever foresight that a student would never refuse a tequila slammer then I would probably not have been drunk enough to give him my number!

In all seriousness, it's perhaps obvious to conclude that I scored my man because I didn't shag him at the first opportunity, but in reality, I think that our meeting was simply 'meant to be'.

I believe that the story of the game was already written before play had started.

Chapter Three

When I became a WAG I thought, This is how Alice in Wonderland must've felt. I went from being a normal girl with a sensible life to having many strange experiences. I have met some Mad Hatters and Queens of Hearts in the Players' Lounge. I have eaten strange foods and drunk potions that made my head spin. I have travelled to exotic lands and been to exclusive places where only a bite of a magical cake, or a footballer's salary, could ever have taken me. The difference between me and Alice is that she woke up and escaped Wonderland.

My previous boyfriend was the same age as me, worked part time in a men's clothing shop for seven pounds an hour, lived at home and borrowed his father's car at the weekends to take me to the pub or to the cinema. One year later I was dating a famous footballer who was a few years older and more experienced than me, drove a Porsche and earned nine thousand pounds per week. He had press and women stalking him, enough friends to fill a football stadium, and a football stadium full of people who wanted to be his friend.

Our relationship took some adapting to.

Initially, the biggest lifestyle change was not having to think about money. I was a broke university student when I met my man. The only money I had was what my parents subbed me each month for my rent, my student loan and what I made from working two or three nights a week in a bar. When we first started dating I didn't know what my boyfriend earned; I didn't ask and he didn't tell me, although there was much speculation among my family and friends. That astronomical nine thousand pounds a week was low compared to what he has earned since.

I was wined and dined by him almost every night of the week. We rarely spent an evening indoors and he would never allow me to contribute financially. If I ever reached for my purse to pay for something, even an item as insignificant as popcorn at the cinema, he would push my hand away, look at me disapprovingly and shake his head. He would genuinely have been offended if I'd paid for anything. I would always offer, despite his silent protests, and I would always feel uncomfortable at having to accept his generosity. I sometimes imagined that he felt obliged to fund our lifestyle, or wondered if it was his way of controlling what we did together. Although most of the time I was relieved because I rarely had more than twenty pounds in my bank account, and that wouldn't have bought two drinks in some of the places we went to.

After we had been together for about a month, I decided that it was time for him to meet my parents. My mother invited us for Sunday lunch and was delighted when I accepted. I was slightly nervous about how my father would receive my new beau. He loved football but was very protective, and I was nervous about the silent scrutiny that might occur given my man's unwarranted reputation with the ladies. The negative stereotype of footballers frustrated my man because he was not as hedonistic as his peers, and he detests people prejudging him. Also, while he lived and breathed football, he left talk of football at the training ground, unless he had to entertain a fan. I didn't want my father to seem like a fan.

As soon as we arrived at my childhood home, the front door opened and my parents appeared, dressed to impress, with nervous smiles. I remember thinking, Oh, shit, here we go . . . However, as we walked into the house, they welcomed my man with such natural warmth and friendliness that I felt proud of them. Over an exquisite roast dinner, they didn't embarrass me or tell any humiliating stories. They were at ease. They didn't put on an act, and conversation flowed between us all.

I could tell my footballer was nervous because he was so quiet. It was quite endearing that he was on his 'best behaviour' since it signalled that he wanted to make a good impression on them. He had not got as far the 'meet the parents' stage before. The furthest he used to go with girls was to have a slice of toast with them the morning after, then see them out of the front door. The only blunder he made that day was to sit in my father's chair. No one sits in my father's chair.

However, I figured my father must have liked him as he allowed him to stay put. My partner had passed the boyfriend test.

I failed the girlfriend test when I first met his parents. I was introduced to them when they came to watch him play, a couple of months into our relationship. I was terrified. I knew how much they meant to him. The respect he had for his father was clear from the way he talked about him and also because his father dealt with all of his financial issues. He called his father daily for advice.

We had planned to have dinner at his apartment after the game, and as the hour approached, I began to feel very scared and not even my foundation could hide my flushed cheeks. I didn't want to say the wrong thing and I desperately wanted them to like me. My man had obviously told his parents about me and how he felt, but I was worried that I wouldn't live up to their expectations or be able to quell their concerns that I was just another wannabe WAG looking to jump on a footballer's gravy train.

Everything was fine to start with: we ate, we watched television and in an attempt to show my hosting skills I made hot chocolate for everyone. I loaded up a tray with the mugs and walked into the lounge. His mother stood up from her seat to assist me. I politely refused, but as she sat down again, I tripped on the rug, propelling a mug of the hot drink onto her lap.

She froze in shock for a few seconds before jumping up and dancing around the room, shaking her skirt in an attempt to get the boiling hot chocolate away from her skin. She dashed to the bathroom and stripped off her clothes. I remained standing, with the tray in my hand, my mouth gaping wide open in horror. I couldn't believe what I'd done! It was like something from a comedy film, only no one was laughing. As far as I knew, she could have received three-degree burns and it would have been my fault. My eyes filled with tears. My boyfriend took the tray from me and led me to the sofa. 'Sit there. Don't worry. I'm going to check on Mum,' he said. I sat with my head in my hands and sobbed. I was devastated. It was not exactly the impression I had hoped to make.

Eventually they came back into the room. His mother was dressed in a new outfit and she wore a faint, forced smile. She said that I shouldn't worry, and recognized that it had been an accident, but I still felt terrible. I tried to get over it but as everyone else turned their attention to the television, I couldn't beat back the shame I felt. I wanted to leave. When a little more time had passed, I made my excuses. After saying goodbye and sorry for the millionth time, I left.

After I had arrived back at my halls, I must've sent ten text messages to my man apologizing for Tray-Gate. He replied to each one with something along the lines of 'It's no big deal' and 'Forget about it', but even now I cringe when I recall that moment. I couldn't think of many worse things I could've done on my first meeting with his parents, apart from throwing up the dinner she had made for me onto her lap.

His parents are the 'salt of the earth' type people,

however, it was years before I felt accepted by them. For a long time I felt that they thought I wasn't good enough to be with their son. I knew it wasn't because I'd spilled hot chocolate on his mother: there were deeper issues at work. He was their beloved son, with the world at his feet, and they were probably fearful of losing him to his first real relationship.

Looking back, I can sympathize with how hard it must have been for his parents to have a professional footballer for a son. He'd left home at the tender age of sixteen to live in digs. He didn't go to college or university even though he had the brains to. His parents had travelled hundreds of miles across the country to watch him play and they'd had the worry of not living near to him when things got tough. They'd had to witness the abuse he got from fans when he made mistakes on the pitch, and they had seen his name and reputation slaughtered in the press.

They also watched his wages increase and must have worried about how such vast quantities of money might corrupt him. They must have had countless sleepless nights thinking about him speeding about in his Porsche, possibly wrapping it around a lamp post. He'd been eighteen when he'd got the first.

As far as his parents were concerned, their son's whole future depended on him being good at football . . . and remaining focused. They probably perceived me, or any serious girlfriend, as a potentially destructive distraction; a threat to his career. The fact that I was at university, had come from a good family and had career goals of my own may not even have

47

registered on their radar. Neither did they recognize that I had become the one and only person that their son trusted, confided in and received support from.

I learned not to take their attitude towards me personally. Gradually I saw their defensiveness as protectiveness. They were so proud of him, placed him on such a high pedestal for achieving his dreams, and didn't want anybody to hurt him or affect his career. As time passed, they began to realize that I was with their son for love, not money, and became a little more relaxed, but their full acceptance only arrived once we got married. On our wedding day I finally, and officially, became a member of their family.

We had become almost inseparable and spent on average five nights a week together. Even when I was working at the bar, he would come to see me towards the end of my shift and wait until I was finished. I noticed many of the locals choke on their pints when they realized who was seated on the bar stool in 'their' pub.

My man's parents weren't too impressed, though, when he asked me to move in with him, for obvious reasons. In all honesty, initially I wasn't too willing either. I felt unsure about the morality of moving in with a boyfriend I'd been dating for less than a year. For him, it was easier and not much would change: he would have company, help with the chores and sex on tap.

I felt too young to move in with a boy, and although my student room felt increasingly claustrophobic, it was my space and no one else's, and I hadn't had my independence for very long. I didn't want to surrender it on a romantic whim. Also, I was worried that, if it all went wrong, I would have to start again. He wouldn't. He was the one with all the security and I had none.

Fortunately, love doesn't allow rational or pessimistic thinking to continue for too long. As time passed, the frequency of the cohabitation conversations increased, and my man cleared two of his drawers out for me to store my overnight gear in. I found myself spending more and more time at his apartment, and each time I had to be on my own for the night in my student room, my heart ached for him. The yearning outweighed my caution. When he next asked me to move in with him, I said yes.

It was exciting to move out of my halls. My friends were sad to see me go, but before I had even walked out of the front door they were angling for a moving-in party invite.

My man has always loved to party. He will host a party on any excuse – 'won a match', 'first day of summer', 'took a shit' – and they were another concern of mine before I moved in, not without reason. My man's apartment would be full of his team-mates and some of their girlfriends (most of them had girlfriends, but not all of them were invited out on a Saturday night, no clues for guessing why), and the other guests were always his mini-skirted and pouty-lipped entourage, all desperate to bag a footballer, and the wide boys from the city – the 'I wanna be in your gang' category of footballer friends.

The parties were always loud, raucous and cost my

man a fortune since everyone, including his good friends, took advantage of the free booze he offered. Unfortunately, people often do not think the 'bring a bottle' etiquette applies when going to a footballer's party. The partygoers often took the piss out of my man, generally because they could as he was usually drunk before anyone else. His guests would crank up the stereo system to blast music at top volume and they would raid his kitchen cupboards to devour any food or drink they could find. Sometimes things went missing: football trophies, pictures of him posing with famous people and designer clothes have all remained unaccounted for after a party.

Often the noise would prompt the neighbours to call the police, which I was usually grateful for as it would signal the end of the night. More often than not, though, the night only drew to a close when the sun began to rise and the last drunken acquaintance had slammed the front door. Sometimes there would be nowhere to sleep after a party since my man's team-mates would have barricaded themselves into the bedrooms with one 'lucky' female reveller. The beds would be made available if we banged on the bedroom doors until our fists hurt, or if a 'quickie' had just ended.

In the case of the latter, the girl would appear from the room looking bedraggled, the footballer would follow, generally topless, and he'd usher her to the front door, give her a goodbye kiss on the cheek and tell her he hoped she got home OK in the cab. Frequently he would have little recollection of her the next morning; the moment of the party that he would relive was the drinking game or the bottle of rum that he'd finished solo. I'm not sure the reflective fixation would be the same for the girl.

I would rather not have attended such parties. Before I lived with my man the main reason I went to them was because I couldn't bear to know that a group of sluts, as I used to fondly refer to his female followers, would be in his house and I wouldn't. In short, I wanted to keep an eye on the situation. When I moved in with him, the parties were on my turf, so I had to be there. I often felt like the parent at the party rather than a reveller; I frequently felt paranoid about what could go wrong, what might get broken or stolen and who would try it on with my man.

I didn't feel paranoid or territorial about the attention he attracted in any other setting: I was always quite confident that he had eyes only for me. It was different to see women in my home, in my man's home, blatantly flirting with him or someone else's man. I guess to watch such promiscuous behaviour at close quarters served to hold a microscope up to the situation.

Whenever I was present, my man would never chat to the chavvy girls. He claims that the girls were there for his team-mates, not him. His team-mates and the city boys took full advantage of the females who laid 'it' on a plate for them. They used to shag on the cushions I had plumped, in the bathrooms I cleaned and on the beds I made.

So, my man's apartment did not feel like a home to me. It was cosy and comforting when it was just the two of us in it, but at the weekends it felt like a shag-pad. I felt vulnerable having so many strangers around my possessions, especially given that if anyone had stolen my laptop I would have lost all of my university work.

I didn't tell my man how much I detested his house parties. I told him I didn't enjoy them and that I felt his friends took the piss out of him when they were in his home, but I didn't give him the full force of my opinion because I didn't want to seem like a witch of a girlfriend. I didn't want to move in and lay down demands, or scare him off. Everything else about our relationship was blissful, so I figured there was always going to be a compromise: his drinking and partying. If only I had realized then how big an issue that would turn into.

Another reason I bit my tongue was because I knew how influential his mates were. I knew that if I tried to ban parties at his house, they would tease him for being 'under the thumb' or perhaps try to put him off me.

One of his team-mates, 'Mr Cocksure', gave him endless grief for getting a girlfriend. Cocksure didn't want to lose his pulling partner and drinking buddy, and he let me know it. When I was in his presence he'd either ignore me, or talk to me like crap, or generally find ways to make me feel as if I was a she-devil who had stolen his mate away from him. Cocksure always used to make inappropriate jokes in front of me about my man's ex-girlfriends or women they both knew and thought were 'fit'. Fortunately I don't rise quickly to provocation, and I'm very good at pretending on the outside that I'm not hurt, even if I'm crying like a baby on the inside.

I'd not met characters like Cocksure before, but my man seemed to attract such types as friends. I had grown up around good people with decent morals, and while I wasn't naive, it was a change to be surrounded by people who had such hedonistic lifestyles. He went out with his team-mates after every game and on any week nights if they didn't have training the next day.

In the early days my social life calmed down. First, I had a lot of university work to do and I was finding my course demanding, especially as I was often trying to complete essays with a hangover. I lived in Party Central and there were always people intruding on our peace; the constant interruptions added many hours to my home study.

I'd also had a bad experience in a nightclub, so going out drinking became something that I began to dread. As soon as I started officially dating my footballer, the news spread around the city like wildfire that he was off the shelf and I was the 'chosen one'. It was great in some ways: I managed to get on the VIP lists everywhere and I was treated like royalty by the doormen of clubs.

However, one night in particular no one was keeping watch over me. It was a Thursday and I was out with a couple of friends from university. My boyfriend was not with us as he had training the next day and a game on the Saturday. He would never go out the night before training: any player who smelled of booze would get a royal bollocking from the gaffer and they would be fined a significant fee. For just one night out it wasn't worth the risk.

The only reason I went out that evening was because I had handed in a project I had been working on for months; I wanted to let my hair down and celebrate. We went to a club in the centre of town that played the best seventies and eighties music. We arrived around ten p.m., after a few rounds of hilarious tequila-based drinking games at my friend's house. We went out feeling tipsy, but we were not riotously drunk.

The club was rammed, and cheesy retro hits boomed out of the speakers. My friends and I were enjoying ourselves on the colourful lit-up dance-floor and laughing at each other's over-exaggerated moves. As Michael Jackson blared out and my friends attempted to moon-walk, I left them and went alone to the toilets.

In the Ladies, as I headed towards a cubicle, I walked past a group of girls at the sinks. One of them sniped at me, 'That's the slut who's going out with that footballer . . .' I bit my lip. I used the facilities, then washed my hands with my head down and eyes focused firmly on the floor as I endured listening to the group of women bitching about me. They commented on what I was wearing – my 'tacky' dress and 'bet your boyfriend bought them for you' platform shoes. Considering that my veins flowed with tequila, I have no idea how I managed not to explode in anger or retaliate with an equally bitchy remark. But I was on my own and I didn't want any trouble.

As I turned around to head to the door, one of the girls purposely blocked my way. She looked like a 'townie', as we used to say: she wore a cropped T-shirt, with her pot belly and pierced navel on show, a short denim skirt, which was far too small for her, and I remember that her lip-liner looked like eyeliner. I nervously asked if she would 'please' allow me to pass. This sparked her fury. With the speed of a horse-racing commentator and the voice of the 'street', the girl began to rant at me. Her face was so close to mine that our noses almost touched and I felt the odd spit-ball land on my cheek.

'If you don't fucking stay away from him, I'll 'ave you' was one of the lines I recall. 'He was talking to me before you came along, you fucking slag' was another. 'You're fucking minging' was an additional memorable line. She then shouted at point-blank range that if I were to tell him this had happened, 'bad shit' would happen to me. Then she spat in my face, pushed me over and dragged me by my hair into a toilet cubicle. She shoved me and pulled me as if I were a rag doll. It all happened so quickly that I didn't have the chance to defend myself. She slammed the cubicle door on my leg and swaggered out, with her entourage, who had passively watched the whole episode, in tow.

I remember sitting on the floor of the cubicle in a daze, wondering what the hell had just happened.

Fortunately one of my friends entered the toilets within minutes of the group of girls leaving and saw me, mascara running down my cheeks. I was immensely upset. I had never been in a fight before, let alone been attacked. My friend helped me to compose myself and clean myself up, then took me out of the toilets to the nearest bouncer. I reported what had happened but, unfortunately, the girls were gone. I tried to describe who they were, but since there was no CCTV in the toilets, my descriptions could have matched any number of females in the club. I felt it wasn't worth reporting it to the police because I wasn't seriously hurt, and since I had no witnesses, I had no proof. I had been attacked and she had just got away with it.

I thought that the only person who might have had a clue as to her identity was my man, given what she had said. Although I really couldn't imagine him being interested in a girl like her. It was too late to call him that night, but the next day, he was angry, shocked and sympathetic when I told him what had happened. He felt responsible. He called the club and later spoke to the doormen, but still no one knew who the girl was, and he could not think of who she might be either – he professed not to have been seeing anyone before we began dating. He believed the reason I was attacked was simply jealousy, and that all she had said was fabricated to wind me up.

Sadly, the girl who attacked me was never identified or reprimanded for her behaviour. I have not seen her since, although a part of me wishes I could because I'm a lot older and wiser now, and my tongue is distinctly faster and sharper in a war of words than it was back then.

I was traumatized for a few days after the attack. I kept finding small clumps of hair on my pillow where it had been pulled so hard that some of it had come away from the roots. I also had a bruise the size of an orange on my leg where the door had slammed on it.

So, my confidence in going to nightclubs was grossly damaged and it served as a rude awakening to the fact that women who date footballers are targets for verbal abuse or worse.

If I am in a bar or club now, I cannot completely let go. I scout the vicinity for people who might be potential threats and avoid them like the plague, and I will not go to the toilets alone. It's a known phenomenon that women go to the toilets in groups and I would encourage such behaviour. Women alone are vulnerable, and gone are the days when they only needed to protect themselves from male attackers.

Chapter Four

After the attack it took me about a month to summon the courage to go out in the evening again. Then I reduced my nights out to once every couple of weeks instead of two or three nights per week. I lost my mojo on the partying front, through fear and insecurity or perhaps because I had changed and wanted different things in life.

Unfortunately, my man had not changed his partying habits. He would literally have gone out every night of the week if he could have. There was always a lock-in at a club or bar, or an after-party at one of the footballers' houses too, and he was always a willing attendee. I absolutely hated this at the time.

The reason was not my possessiveness: I championed independence in everyone, including my man, or our relationship would have been dead and buried a long time ago. I didn't like the person he became when he got drunk. He could not stop at one or two drinks, or even when he felt tipsy; he'd always drink to get absolutely smashed. He would then become incoherent, irrational and arrogant. Indisputably, he's a good-looking man but alcohol could and does turn him ugly.

Shots of hard liquor would always make an appearance on one of his nights out. The boys used to drink champagne, vodka shots, tequila shots and even the lethal absinthe if it was available. The problem was that they had no financial budget to keep to. They didn't allocate fifty quid for the night, then stop when it was nearly spent: their money pot was bottomless. The number of drinks and rounds of drinks they bought were excessive.

Anyone standing at the bar, including the bar staff, would get a drink. That's probably one reason why my man and his footballer friends were always swamped with people around them when they were out. People soon realized that congratulating a footballer on winning a match or scoring a goal or just doing a bit of basic arse-licking generally resulted in a free drink. It's still the same now, to be honest. My husband is a sucker for a compliment at a bar.

Footballers are often approached in public. I have learned to deal with the amount of attention my husband gets. Boys, girls, grannies, kids: he is approached by all sorts of people. It's bizarre to walk into a bar, then watch its entire population turn their eyes to look at him. Once they've looked, the whispers begin: 'Oh, my God, it's . . .', 'You'll never guess who's just walked in . . .' Countless numbers of fans shake his hand or ask for a picture, while I just stand back and feel like a total loser. He used to grab my hand and pull me into him as an attempt to make me feel less uncomfortable; to give him his due, he did try. However, the attention he commands is at times annoying, especially when we want to have a quiet chat over a glass of wine and every Tom, Dick and Harry butts in.

I had to grin and bear the intrusions, and just prayed there would be a time when it would all get better. The odd girl who threw herself at him never failed to piss me off, more over the audacity than the action, but I learned very quickly that this was part of being with a footballer and that it was out of his control. As long as he didn't spend too long talking to the strangers, I kept my cool.

Going food shopping was and is an absolute nightmare. It takes three times longer to do the weekly shopping when my husband is with me. In every aisle he's stopped by fans for an autograph. Quite often I'll leave him to his public and do a supermarket-sweep-style shop and meet him at the check-out. However, I don't think I'll ever tire of watching a kid's face light up at seeing him in the supermarket.

If I'm envious of anything he does, it's that. It's truly amazing how much joy his presence can bring to a child; his scruffy signature on the back of their mother's till receipt seems to bring untold pleasure to a little kid. My husband knows it too, and he would never deny a child a minute of his time.

I've never enjoyed the attention that being a WAG has brought me, and it seems ironic that the first negative attention I received as a WAG was from other WAGs. When my man first invited me to the Players'

Lounge to watch him in a match, I was scared, to say the least. I was used to being in the stands, as a member of the general public, but I had no idea what to expect from the ominous WAG community.

I remember his line to me on the first Saturday I entered the hub of WAGdom: 'So, let's see if you can be my little lucky charm this Saturday.' I knew I'd have to go at some point, but I dreaded it. He'd briefed me about what would happen. He said I would be taken through a special door by the main reception at the stadium to the Players' Lounge where I would have some pre-match food and drinks, then watch the game in a specific section of the stand with all the other players' families. He assured me he would meet me in the Lounge at the end of the game.

I remember the panic I felt at the thought of being left on my own with a group of women whom he'd previously described as 'vipers'. It was like he was sending me into their pit without any anti-venom.

My first concern was regarding what I should wear. I was only a student and lived on my student loan and the minimum pay I earned from my part-time bar job. My clothes were quirky but I had nothing remotely expensive to wear; I didn't have the funds for designer gear. I imagined that the other WAGs would be oozing glamour and chic, and I feared I'd be the odd one out.

I hadn't been dating my man for very long at that point so I couldn't have asked him to buy me anything new or even tell him of my wardrobe worries. I reasoned that I'd just have to do the best I could. The ticket to the Players' Lounge stipulated 'smart-casual' and 'no denim' so I decided to wear the black trousers I wore for work, black boots and a pink stripy shirt. I figured it was boring but would fit the dress-code criteria. It wasn't my usual style but it was a safe bet, and it was a cold day so I figured I'd be hidden under my winter coat and scarf for at least some of the duration.

When the morning of the game arrived, I made an eleventh-hour telephone call to my father to come with me. I could have taken a friend, but I chose my father, because I knew how much he would love it, and there's nothing quite like a father's moral support. I also wanted him to experience VIP treatment at his home team's stadium. Unsurprisingly, he jumped at the chance.

We went to the match in his brand-new Mercedes and upon arriving at the ground we drove straight into the players' car park, through the barriers, past the crowds of fans, who peered into the car thinking my father must be a player, and past the burger van that he and I used to get our food from before matches when I was a kid. I must admit that the attention made me feel quite important. After I checked my make-up in the rear-view mirror, my father and I got out of the car and walked to the players' entrance of the stadium. My hand shook as I gave the guy on the door the tickets. He then escorted us up to the Players' Lounge. My stomach was performing somersaults as I went up the stairs.

The carpet in the corridor had the club's crest on it. Pictures of football legends who had played for the team flanked the walls, and all of the staff we passed on our route were dressed in identical uniforms. They all smiled at us. There seemed to be a real buzz in the air about the match: it was as if every employee worked at the stadium because they supported the team, not because of the job itself.

As our escort opened the doors to the Lounge for us, it dawned on me that this was an almost ceremonial experience: I was being shown to the other women. I began to pray that the other WAGs would like me, or at the very least be friendly. Even my father looked nervous.

As the doors creaked open, every head turned to look at us. Their gasps were audible. From their facial expressions it seemed they had been waiting for Victoria Beckham to enter but had got Ugly Betty instead. I quickly realized that they had not even considered I could be the girlfriend of the team's 'man of the moment'. My father and I weren't famous so were not worthy of a second glance. It was a horrible moment. I will never forget it. Their reaction to my father and me made me feel paranoid and self-conscious. Even now I hate walking into the Players' Lounge. I'm fine once I'm in, but I still fear opening the door for the reactions it may bring.

My father and I shuffled to the bar for refuge with our heads down. While he ordered me a Coke, I took the opportunity to survey the room. I couldn't tell who was a girlfriend or a wife. Everyone looked normal. None of the women was dressed outrageously. I noted a few designer handbags, manicured nails and straight-out-of-the-salon hairstyles but otherwise all the women looked remarkably un-WAG-like. They all had jeans on too. Damn it! I thought. I would have been much more confident in jeans. They all looked cool and casual, ready for a football game. I looked like I had just come from the office. My confidence level was at zero. I kicked myself for not having dressed in my usual style. I learned a big lesson at that moment: I should always be myself. What an idiot I was to think that I could compromise my dress sense in order to fit in.

The game we watched was great. I was surprised to see how much the partners celebrated the team when they scored. They jumped out of their seats, shouted at poor decisions by the referee and didn't seem to care what anyone else thought of them. I found it refreshing to see that the WAGs didn't sit quietly in a row. They knew the rules of football and appeared to enjoy the game. I realized it was OK to clap and sing along to the chants, so my father and I did exactly that. When the full-time whistle blew, my partner's team had won 2–0. It was a great win as the opposition were much higher in the league; a 'proper result', as my man would say.

No one spoke to me or my father throughout the game. No one introduced themselves, or even looked at us to smile, and I certainly wasn't confident enough to approach anyone. We just chatted to each other and watched the boys on the pitch. It was how we had always spent football matches, with the difference that we were warm and surrounded by a multitude of rude, insular women. I was immensely relieved when the ninety minutes were over.

As I waited for my man to arrive in the Lounge, there was a notable tension in the room. The WAGs seemed on tenterhooks. When the players walked in, the atmosphere turned to excitement and they were mobbed. It was as if they were gods who had just descended from heaven. Their wives and girlfriends fawned around them as if they'd not seen them for a decade, and the other visitors to the Players' Lounge, the 'day-trippers', clambered to get their autographs and photographs.

My partner was the last player to walk in; he's always the last out of the changing rooms. I remember thinking that he looked super-hot in his suit. After he had signed everything that was thrust under his nose and manoeuvred through the small crowd that he'd commanded, he joined my father and me. He first shook my father's hand, then gave me a big kiss on the lips. It was an amazing feeling to have that public display of affection in such an uncomfortable and unfamiliar setting. It felt good to give the other WAGs confirmation that I was 'one of them' and not a desperate fan. In fact, it was as if someone had made an announcement over the Tannoy that I was his new girlfriend, because the WAGs immediately started smiling at me. One girl even came up to me and introduced herself. I am still friends with her now.

At the next game my new friend introduced me to a small selection of the other WAGs in the Players' Lounge and they all turned out to be nice, ordinary girls who weren't dripping in designer clothes or living the life of wannabe celebrities. The WAG connotations did not fit them at all. In fact, those women made my subsequent Players' Lounge experiences pleasurable. I really enjoyed going to the home games from the moment I met them. I also adopted the comfort approach to Players' Lounge attire, and rather than abiding by the 'no denim' policy on the ticket, I flouted it. Jeans became my dress code.

I met a lot of other WAGs in the Players' Lounge who did fulfil the negative stereotype of a WAG, and I have met many since, but thankfully I had enough savvy to avoid them and stuck with my small group of 'normals'.

Despite the fast pace of our two lives becoming one, our relationship went from strength to strength. I'd known very early on that I loved him, and he never put the phone down without saying, 'Love you', and after all these years he still doesn't, unless I've really pissed him off. After a short while of us living together he put a stop to the parties at our house, thank God, and the most I had to put up with was to accommodate a few of his mates when the pubs had closed. They would drunkenly play on the PlayStation until the early hours of the morning.

When I started my third year at university, the demands of my degree led me to decide to quit my part-time job. My manager was gutted, not at the prospect of losing me, but because it would mean that my man would no longer be a regular: he had brought in a lot of new punters. I was sad to leave because it was a tiny piece of independence for me, but my boyfriend was getting frustrated that I was never around on a Friday evening. He used to say that he would rather give me the £6.75 an hour I earned at the pub and have me with him. He didn't like being alone in the evenings. He doesn't like being alone at all, which seems a little ironic given how much time I have since had to spend on my own because of his job.

I did feel a little suspicious about our future together. I thought that if he couldn't bear me to work even one night a week, what the hell would he be like when I got my degree and a full-time job? I resolved to cross that bridge when I came to it. I really wanted a career. My whole life had revolved around studying, revising, taking exams and completing coursework, so I was really looking forward to moving on.

In my final year at university I kept my head down, socialized very little, and spent most of my time with my nose in my textbooks and my fingers stuck to my laptop's keyboard. I completed my degree and graduated with a much higher grade than anyone had thought I would get. I was immensely proud of myself.

However, shortly after I received confirmation that I'd passed my degree, when I began talking about my future career, I didn't receive the encouragement from my man that I had hoped for. He made it very clear that he wanted me around; he didn't want me moving to another city to chase my dream job; he didn't even want me to work full-time. In fact, he didn't even like it if I was at the gym when he got home from training; if that happened, he'd phone me constantly to ask when I would be home.

I had so much ambition but he was like an anchor to it. I couldn't see myself as being a housewife ... especially not before I was even a wife! Furthermore, he wasn't pumping money into my bank account for me to live off. At that point we had been together for three years, but I still felt uncomfortable accepting money from him. He paid the bills, bought the food and paid whenever we went anywhere, which, I thought, was more than enough. I didn't want to carry on like that. I wanted to contribute financially to our life. I needed to for my own self-worth.

I had finished university in June and by September I had found the perfect job that I'd hoped would act as the first step on my career ladder. It was contractual, with a reputable company and in the heart of the city. I managed to strike a deal that allowed me to pick and choose my hours. The pay was great for what I had to do and the experience was priceless. I had landed on my feet without help from anyone.

The job didn't take me away from home regularly because I could complete a lot of my work remotely, but when I had to be elsewhere, especially in the evenings, my man felt it was a major inconvenience to him. I felt guilty, but I perceived it as his problem, not mine. We were still able to spend a lot of time together and I was enjoying what I was doing; I also relished that I could tell people I had a job and wasn't sponging off him.

However, my employment was short-lived. The transfer window saw to that.

January arrived and the transfer window hadn't been open for long. My man was doing really well at his club; he was a permanent member of the starting line-up and the fans almost worshipped him. Therefore, when I received a call from him saying that a big club had made an offer for him and his club had agreed he could go, I was bowled over with shock. In the few seconds of that conversation it was clear that my life was going to change completely. A long-distance relationship was never going be an option. My man's signing with a new club meant we'd have to relocate and leave my friends, my family and, of course, my job. The commute would have been too much for what I was getting paid.

That house move was the first of many. With almost every transfer my husband has made we've had to move hundreds of miles to a new area and start a new life. Wherever we have moved to, I've looked for a job, but often the location has been wrong for my trade, or my husband has lumped so much responsibility onto my shoulders, with regard to organizing his timetable and our new home, that my time has not seemed my own.

I can count on one hand the number of WAGs I have met who have a job. The majority of WAGs I know left their job shortly after meeting their footballer. It's unfortunate that WAGs have the reputation for being lazy and living off hand-outs because I believe that the real reason many don't have full-time jobs is the neediness of footballers. Footballers are an archaic species of man who want their woman at home when they return from work.

Unless a WAG had established a career for herself before she met her footballer, like Victoria Beckham or Christine Bleakley, climbing up a career ladder is almost impossible, and it's not because of choice of footwear.

Some WAGs have forged stellar careers for themselves off the back of their husband's fame and fortune. The likes of Coleen Rooney, Alex Curran and Abbey Clancy were catapulted to fame when they began dating their partners. These WAGs are now worth millions in their own right, but it is questionable as to whether they would have been if they hadn't had a Premiership footballer as their other half.

Those WAGs can do what they do because they can pick and choose what opportunities they say 'yes' to from the hundreds of businesses that want to capitalize on their public profile. If the opportunity doesn't fit in with their life as a WAG, they don't need to do it. The reality will not resonate well with hard-working souls: WAGs don't have to work. There's usually enough money in the bank for the family to live off the interest alone, regardless of who earned it.

Many people may be envious of the life changes that WAGdom brings. I cannot deny that there haven't been perks. I've been to many spectacular parties, I've had some amazing holidays and I've met some of my childhood idols in terms of the famous faces I've socialized with. The fact that I don't have money worries has alleviated a lot of the normal problems my peers face, and I probably take for granted that if I want a new dress, I can have it, regardless of its price tag.

But everything comes at a cost. My life changed because of my partner's fame and fortune, but I cannot say that the life changes have brought me unbounded happiness. My husband's love has given me great joy, but the lifestyle that was enforced on me by his profession has very often brought me frustration and sadness. I lost my independence at a young age and did not feel confident or knowledgeable enough to fight for it, or 'think outside the box' about how to lead my own separate life. I acclimatized to my man's neediness and became used to being at his beck and call. I reaped some rewards from not having to work, like being able to contribute my time to charity work, socializing and keeping fit, but my hopes and dreams for *just me* have always been on hold. I've lived long distances away from my family and friends because football has dictated our postcode.

It is only now, with my husband in the twilight years of his career, that I can begin to be a directional force on our family's life. Age and experience has brought me wisdom, and I've finally found my voice.

Chapter Five

There are some common misconceptions about footballers and WAGs. Supposedly, most high-earning players began life poverty-stricken in a council house, and kicked a ball around the slums until they were scouted. Most WAGs, it's assumed, grew up like Cinderella until they met their footballer prince who presented them with a glass Jimmy Choo slipper ... that obviously fitted perfectly.

WAGs have been turned into negative role models, 'what not to aspire to' celebrities. The term 'WAG culture' is used to refer to women's consumerism and narcissism. WAGs are blamed for sixteen-year-old girls wanting boob jobs and believing that being pretty can equate to not having to do a day's work.

Any girl linked to a footballer is almost automatically labelled a money-grabbing whore by the media and, due to the explosion in social networking, their lives are vulnerable to public scrutiny and intrusion. Luckily for me, there was less WAG stigma when I began dating my man, and the biggest objects of my fear were long camera lenses and gossip.

The bad press for footballers and WAGs concerns me, especially as a parent: I don't want my children believing the stereotypes. I don't want them growing up arrogant because they live in a world where they are above others simply because of who their parents are, or how much their father earns.

I was raised to value hard work, yet I don't feel I've been able to live up to that value, which saddens me. However, I work hard as a parent, and that in itself offers great compensation for having no career. WAGs' lives are akin to those of single parents, given the time their partners spend away from home.

My parents would not have allowed my somewhat privileged upbringing to dictate my character. In many ways, I am the antithesis to the WAG stereotype. I am fiercely independent and have always had my own objectives. I love my family and friends much more than my own reflection, and while I did view my man as a prince, it was more for his brains and banter than his bank balance and buying power.

I grew up in a traditional nuclear, cereal-box type of family. My father was the breadwinner and my mother was the full-time parent and homemaker. My father was born to kindly working-class parents. His intelligence and determination won him a place at a grammar school after which he went on to secure a place at a top university. Soon after he had graduated, he took the risk of starting his own business. He had no money and little vocational experience in his trade, but his self-belief and industrious nature paid off. The business went from strength to strength, and by the time he met my mother, he had three businesses. With my mother's support and natural buisiness acumen, my parents became self-made millionaires before they were thirty years old.

Football was one of my father's sacred pastimes, and we forged a very tight father–daughter relationship going together to matches. Saturday afternoon was the time of the week that we both looked forward to, whatever the weather. We had a routine to our match days: my mother would drop us off at a pub near to the stadium where my father would slowly drink a pint of Guinness and I would drink a glass of lemonade. We would then buy two hot dogs from the burger van that was always stationed opposite the stadium, in front of the players' car park. Once we'd finished our hot dogs we would enter the stadium via the heavy metal turnstiles and navigate our path through the throngs of people. We'd then ascend the concrete steps to my father's season-ticket seats. The stadium was huge: it seated well over thirty thousand people and usually every seat was filled. The crowds back then were mostly male so even from a young age I felt proud to be one of the few females at the game.

Growing up within a large network of family and friends instilled in me a strong sense of kinship, community and the need for camaraderie, which is probably why I cannot become accustomed to the somewhat lofty attitudes within WAGdom. My sociable upbringing is probably why I have so far survived it; like Darwin's theory of evolution, my skills in social adaptation and faux politeness have enabled me to live through many tedious and tense moments in the Players' Lounge. From my parents' dinner parties I also learned how to fake interest in someone and how to refrain from saying what I was *really* thinking, two very important qualities for a WAG to possess and rely on in WAG-to-WAG communications.

Furthermore, I have had fun as a WAG with an education in a Players' Lounge full of people without it. Multisyllabic words can cause great confusion and hilarity. For example: 'Louise, what you just said was so soporific! Amazing!'

'Thank you,' she replied.

Consequently, I have stood out in WAGdom as a WAG who doesn't fit the mould, but the reality is that there are many other WAGs like me. WAGs who have had a relatively 'normal' upbringing and who put their families before their finances. The sad fact is that many WAGs have bought into the WAG stereotype, so they tend to judge each other against false standards. For example, not to wear designer clothes puts you into 'the girl-next-door' bracket, also known as 'boring'.

I am fortunate to have a husband who was raised with similar standards to mine, and while he can on occasion fit the typical footballer stereotype, with regard to his sharp dress sense and drinking habits, his background is atypical.

He was raised in a small semi-rural village where everyone knew everyone else's business. CCTV has still not made its way to this part of the country, but even without Big Brother peering down a lens, Mrs Smith at number five would still know which lad had pissed on the church's welcome board at two a.m. the previous morning.

The stories my husband tells of his upbringing are happy ones that centre on how he played outside in the streets, fields and parks with other children from the community and, like me, went with his father to watch his home team play football every other weekend. He's recounted tales of getting into trouble with his parents for playing in unsafe, derelict houses, illegally fishing in the rivers and scrumping apples from the local farmer's orchards: outdoor fun that didn't involve the games consoles he seems to be addicted to these days.

Like me, my husband came from a traditional nuclear family where his father went out to work and his mother stayed at home to raise him and his siblings. He speaks of his parents as living for their children, and 'pillars of the local community'. Like my father, his father had to work his arse off and was rarely at home. His father's job earned the family enough money to survive, but not to survive comfortably. He earned overtime working away from home, so he spent weeks at a time separated from his family.

His father was the disciplinarian. Apparently, his father's verbal dressing-downs were worse than any dressing-room bollocking he has ever received, and he lived in fear of them. The worst-case scenario for him would have been a telling-off plus a strong clip round the ear. Knowing my husband's mischievous character,

I was not surprised to learn that he'd had enough clips around the ear in his lifetime to develop a twitch. His crimes were 'normal' ones and ranged from drinking so much vodka at the age of fifteen that he threw up into a fish tank, stealing penny sweets from the local corner shop and smashing his next-door neighbour's greenhouse with his football.

He's said that the worst punishment he received was being grounded for three weeks and having to watch all the other kids in his neighbourhood playing outside without him, opposite his bedroom window. He has always hated to miss out on a good time with his mates: it's one of the sources of our marital conflict today.

Throughout his childhood, my husband only ever lived in one house: a small three-bedroom semi-detached home that had an equally small back garden with a pond. His family owned one regular second-hand car and they went on one holiday each year, always to the seaside, to places like Hayling Island, Blackpool and Cornwall. They didn't holiday abroad as they couldn't afford it.

Unlike many of his peers, my man worked hard at school and excelled in sports, mathematics and science. He found football easy and his parents have said that every coach on every local youth team he played on said that he was their strongest player. They said he was effortlessly skilful. While he showed a lot of sporting promise, he didn't dream of being a famous sportsman. He wanted to be a teacher. And when he achieved ten GCSEs, this aspiration seemed within his sights. That was until one fateful Wednesday when he was playing for his school football team.

His father was approached after the match by a scout from the local Premiership team, who was a regular there, checking out the local young talent. The scout billed him as one of the most skilful players he had ever come across, a player with rare talent.

The scout spoke to his father and then to my man for a few minutes after the match, which culminated in an invite for a trial. My man said he was excited at the offer, and that he felt the recognition alone was flattering, but his father was not impressed. His father feared that his academic potential would be thrown away on the whim of a career in the competitive and cut-throat world of football.

At the trial, he made such a good impression that he was offered a Youth Training Scheme contract, but his father felt the risks were too high, and that if he didn't continue his education at sixteen, then he never would. He feared the YTS would not work out, that being a footballer was not a 'real' job. But my man now desperately wanted to play football for a living, especially for the team he had supported his whole life, and especially because of his father's opposition: he's always wanted to prove people wrong.

Eventually he won his father over: he promised he'd be a committed apprentice and that, if it all went wrong, he'd go to college at whatever age. He successfully persuaded his father to give his consent, and his father then resolved to support him. Ironically he became my man's biggest fan, his biggest critic and his biggest motivation.

The YTS contract paid him twenty-seven pounds a week and he got to live in 'digs', supported lodgings, even though his parents lived a stone's throw away. He's said that he was more than happy with the arrangement and has claimed that those years were the most carefree and exciting ones he has ever had. He relished cleaning the top players' boots, soaked up every bit of advice from the 'Big Dogs' and trained his arse off.

He put his stamp on the first team and his parents quickly realized that his decision had been the right one. Only months after he had first been scouted by the Premiership side, he signed a professional contract with the club. He was only seventeen years old and went from earning £250 a week to £1,000 a week after he had made his debut.

A few years down the line, without warning, he was sold to a Premiership club that was located far from his home. It was a fantastic career move, but it was daunting for him and his parents. He wasn't to move a few miles away, like I did when I first moved out, he was to move hundreds of miles from everything he had ever known. His mother was heartbroken. His father kept his cool but, according to my husband, he was distraught.

His move was swift, and he spent the first few weeks of his new life in a five-star hotel, all expenses paid by his club. After a few months of not having to make his bed and eating breakfast with a restaurant full of strangers, the novelty began to wear off. He went apartment hunting and within weeks had purchased a brand-new, luxurious, two-bedroomed penthouse apartment in a very sought-after area of the city. He was very young to have the sole responsibility of a mortgage, but he said the freedom he felt was worth it.

His parents travelled to support him at every game they possibly could, and afterwards his mother would often remain at his apartment for a few days to cook and clean for him. Apparently she used to stockpile his freezer with home-cooked meals, like lasagne and cottage pie, to see him through to the next week.

When my husband's wages increased to the point that he was earning thousands of pounds a week, he demanded that his father retired and that he become the family's bread-winner. He was determined to repay his parents for the sacrifices and risks they had taken because of him. Also he wanted to compensate his father for the long hours he had worked in order to put food on the table, and take the family on holidays.

At first his father refused, saying he didn't want to be dependent on his children: he 'didn't need a piece of his son's financial success because how proud he was of him was the real pay-back'. My man was adamant. He wouldn't take no for an answer, and even before his parents had fully accepted the idea, he'd set up a bank account for them and had started to transfer money into it every week.

Eventually his parents came round to his way of thinking and they accepted the arrangements he had made for them. His father retired and his parents began to live their lives together. They took up hobbies, they bought newer cars and they travelled abroad, to the places they had always wanted to visit but never before been able to afford.

There are distinct parallels in how my husband and I were brought up. We were both doted on by loving parents, we both worked hard at school, and family life came first. Part of the reason our marriage works today is because of our shared morality, especially our family values.

I have never been materialistic. Whether this is because, throughout my upbringing, I never wanted for anything, or because I was brought up with a grounded attitude, or both, I've simply never had 'things' as a focus. Throughout the years that I was dating my footballer, I didn't make any monetary or material demands of him. I paid my way as best I could, and didn't ever drop tactical hints when passing jewellery shops or designer window displays. I know some WAGs who, generally a few weeks before their birthday, would be shopping with their man and trip over the invisible carpet fold in the jeweller's to land conveniently on top of the diamond-ring counter, point and say, 'I want that one.' Not me. The simpler things in life make me happy, namely my loved ones.

However, my man made one purchase for me that made me happier than I had ever been before. An engagement ring!

As we approached our one-year anniversary we had decided that we needed more living space so we bought our first home together. Well, I contributed my minimal savings to the purchase, but life and finances are relative: it was all the money I had. Home became a three-bedroomed townhouse a block away from my man's previous apartment. The gated complex and all its luxuries proved too difficult to move away from.

The house was three storeys, with a garage and games room on the ground floor, a large living room, dining room and kitchen on the first floor, and three double bedrooms, all with en-suite, on the second floor. Each floor had outside access; there was a small courtyard-style garden off the games room, and large roof terraces off the lounge and master bedroom.

We needed the outside space because, as part of our togetherness, we bought a dog. She became our baby.

Our lives fell into routines whereby in the week he would go to training every day until the early afternoon while I would attend university lectures. In the evenings if I didn't have to study we would spend our time as happy couples do: we'd watch movies, enjoy dinners together, walk our dog, or spend time with our friends. Our existence was very simple, yet we were content. Conversations about marriage did not occur. I considered myself far too young to get married and I was immersed in my degree, so I certainly didn't initiate any wedding talk. I wasn't even thinking about marriage. At that stage I didn't even consider that he'd want to marry me. His career was flying: he was his team's star player, he was getting caps for England and the press were kissing his butt for what he was achieving. We were both making good progress in our respective dreams. Little did I know that another ambition of his was to make me his wife.

I realized his desires one Saturday in spring. I woke up at nine a.m., dressed, made the beds and breakfast, walked the dog and put the washing-machine on. It was an average Saturday morning. Before my man left for his football match he told me he planned to take me out for a meal after the game. That was nothing out of the ordinary. But he was very specific in how he followed it up: he said I would need to look smart because the restaurant he had booked was very posh.

I remember I said, 'That'll be nice, baby.' We often went to the best restaurants and ate expensive meals at the weekends. The strange thing was that he didn't usually remind me how to dress for them.

That Saturday afternoon, as normal, I went to his game. I found my select huddle of WAGs and spent the ninety minutes in the Players' Lounge inter-mittently chatting and watching the drama on the pitch. The match was an exciting one and my man's team came away with a good win.

Players go into the Lounge after they have showered and changed, received any treatment and had a bollocking, or praise, from the gaffer. Each time the door to the Lounge swings open, all eyes are on the person who comes in. Everyone wants to see their man walk through the door, or the most famous players on the team. When the players arrive they all head to the areas where their family and friends are seated, and in the process are usually interrupted for the odd autograph request or bit of football chat.

As I've said, my man is always been the last to enter the Players' Lounge. He's painfully slow at showering and drying. His primping and preening session is longer than most girls would take, let alone his team-mates. In fact it is often the case that half the Lounge will have emptied by the time he arrives in front of me to give me a kiss; he will always smell fresh, but his face remains the colour of a beetroot for a while because he's run around like a lunatic for ninety minutes.

When my man eventually arrived in the Players' Lounge after that match, he was not his usual jovial post-match self. He seemed distracted.

As we drove home I noticed that he was definitely on edge. I put it down to the intensity of the game, the comedown off the adrenalin coupled with exhaustion. He had played his football socks off, then had had to participate in the obligatory post-match television interview in the tunnel. He used to find the latter three minutes more nerve-racking than playing the full ninety minutes so I didn't question him – and barely had a chance to do so since we rushed straight home.

Once we arrived, on his repeated instruction, we both got dressed up to the nines. I wore a tight red Topshop dress and a big chunky gold necklace with gold strappy sandals, and he put on one of his most expensive tailored suits from one of the bespoke men's boutiques on Savile Row in London. Despite my persistent questioning as to his choice of swanky venue, he didn't give away any details of where we were going.

Before I was able to finish the glass of Dom

Pérignon that he had presented me with when I was halfway through my mascara application, the doorbell sounded. I darted through to the guest bedroom to see who our caller was and saw a black limousine parked on the kerb outside our house.

I tottered down the two flights of stairs and out of the front door, which my man gallantly, and impatiently, held open for me. The chauffeur driver was dressed in classic attire, complete with shiny buttons and hat, and he stood by the open rear door of the car holding a silver tray with two glasses of champagne on it. I remember thinking that my man had really pushed the boat out.

I climbed into the back of the limo, negotiating my glass of bubbly carefully through the door, and looked around. There was a lot of space for two people: the vehicle could have accommodated at least ten. I wondered if we would be picking up others en route and whether it was a surprise celebratory event that we were going to that he'd kept from me; a football awards ceremony or something of the sort. I began to guess that maybe the reason for his secrecy was that he wanted to surprise me with a major accolade he'd been given.

When he joined me in the limo, on the elongated black leather seats, which were up-lit by a string of yellow floor lights reflected in the mirrored ceilings, he appeared preoccupied and his skin looked clammy. He seemed to have the weight of the world on his shoulders. As the driver started the engine, my man suddenly decided he needed to go back into the house to use the toilet. Thus I began to think that maybe he had a stomach problem and that was the reason for his odd behaviour; it would have accounted for the sweating, at least. However, in response to my suggestion that if he was feeling ill we could abort whatever plans he'd made, he protested and repeatedly said, 'I'm fine, absolutely fine.'

He gripped my hand with his cold, wet palm as the limo pulled away. Then, when we'd driven through the city and passed all of our favourite haunts, he released my hand and produced a black piece of cloth from his trouser pocket. He raised it to my face and brought it close to my eyes. 'What the hell is that?' I asked.

'Just trust me,' he said. Then he pressed it over my eyes to block my vision and tied it at the back of my head. 'We'll be there soon enough,' he tried to reassure me.

I didn't feel reassured about being temporarily blinded, and anything but positive about my make-up potentially being smudged, although intrigue kept me from protesting. He held my hand and frequently squeezed it, especially when the limo made a sharp turn or came to a halt, I assume in an attempt to make me feel safe. His palm was now hot and slippery. At one point I felt for the button and opened the electric window to get some air circulating – I was slightly concerned that he was overheating. I quickly shut it when he whispered, 'People can see you, you know.' I would rather he roasted than have people see me blindfolded in the back of a black limo. It wasn't exactly the image I wanted to portray of myself!

The journey lasted about twenty-five minutes before the limo finally stopped. I heard the door open and my boyfriend untied the blindfold. When my eyes came back into focus I followed him out of the vehicle and registered where we were. We were parked in front of a renowned Michelin-starred restaurant. It was a well-known celebrity hang-out and it was notoriously difficult to reserve a table there. There was a waiting list of about three months. I had always wanted to go there: everyone I knew who had been lucky enough to get a reservation had raved about it.

It was in a central location, small, with ivy delicately climbing all over it. Grand pillars and fire pits flanked the entrance and a red carpet led to its front door. It oozed affluence. Although we lacked the toffee-nosed accents of its regular clientele, we didn't look too out of place when we walked in as we were dressed to impress. Heads turned; most of the diners recognized my boyfriend and at least realized that, while we weren't royalty or Arab billionaires, he could afford the menu.

The eloquent and well-dressed hostess led us to our candlelit table. The ambience was immensely romantic. To the rear of the room a grand piano was being played by a man dressed in a tuxedo, and the sound of fine glass chinking could be heard beneath the classical overtures.

I was a little bemused by the menus and the amount of silverware, plates and glasses that perched on our table was quite overwhelming. However, we rolled with it, and in our naivety we tried as best we could to look as if we knew what we were doing. I remember thinking, If this is how the Queen dines every night, then bugger marrying a royal.

My boyfriend took the plunge and ordered a very expensive bottle of champagne, £350 or something. I winced as I'm a cheap date. A bottle of the cheapest sweet rosé or a WKD was my usual tipple. My man knows much more about fine wines than I do, and wouldn't bat an eyelid at spending a couple of hundred pounds on a 'good vintage'.

However, spending hard-earned money on a good feed is something I wholeheartedly support! The food in the restaurant was exquisite. We were first served delicious canapés and then our starter of foie gras arrived. It was divine. Once I'd virtually licked my platter clean, my partner informed me of how geese and ducks are force-fed to fatten their livers. As an animal lover I resolved that, tasty as it was, I'd not eat it again. I didn't let my new knowledge put me off my main course, though, which was the most succulent steak I'd ever devoured. I love animals but I couldn't be a vegetarian.

Between each course we were served a palate refresher of some weird and wonderful concoction, and our banquet was rounded off with my favourite dessert: crème brûlée. The meal had been exquisite but I could tell that there was still something wrong with him. I just didn't know what it was.

Immediately after the waiter had cleared our dessert plates from the table, my man suddenly rose from his seat. He stood up so abruptly that his chair flew backwards and caused quite a stir in the quiet dining room. Almost everyone turned to look at him. I speculated that perhaps he was going to have to sprint to the toilet and that my previous assumption of an upset stomach was correct. When he took a few shaky steps to my side of the table, I began to realize how wrong I had been.

While he *did* look like he was going to shit himself, he gently took my left hand and then got down on one knee.

The voice in my head screamed, 'Oh, shit!' I heard fellow diners gasp, clap their hands together and coo in response to what they were witnessing.

My man was shaking. I quivered. With his free hand he reached into the inside pocket of his suit and from it produced a small wooden box.

He let go of my hand. He presented to me the box on the palm of his left hand and lifted the lid with his right to reveal a huge diamond ring. The diamond was less like a precious stone and more like a glittering rock.

My lip trembled. A lump gathered in my throat.

He continued to kneel and proceeded to tell me how he felt about me. He said that I made him laugh. Tears filled my eyes. He said that I was the most caring person he had ever met. I shifted nervously in my seat. He said that he loved me with all his heart and that he believed we were made for each other. I mouthed back, 'I love you too.' He said I was the most beautiful girl he had ever seen. I reached out and cupped his face with my hands. Then, trembling and with tears in his eyes, too, he asked me: 'Will you be my wife?'

I burst into tears. Then I leaned forward, kissed him through my salty tears, drew his face away from mine and nodded. 'Yes!' I said. 'Yes!'

The dining room erupted in applause. It was like a scene from a movie, and I felt like a leading lady. My man took the ring out of the box, nervously placed it on my finger and then he threw his arms around me in a tight embrace. 'Thank you, thank you,' he whispered in my ear. 'You've just made me the happiest man alive.' I wrapped my arms around his neck and cried. In fact, I bawled. My shoulders heaved up and down as if in spasms, mascara crawled down my face and my nose streamed, but I didn't care. I was overwhelmed with love and happiness.

We must have looked like a pair of overly emotional idiots compared to the stiff-upper-lip sort who graced the other tables, the wealthy businessmen and their wives dripping in jewels. As we held each other and sobbed into each other's shoulders, the room seemed to have muted and I didn't give a single thought to what our audience saw.

When we finally released each other, and my man returned to his side of the table, I gazed at my ring. It sparkled and twinkled in the ambient light. It was a large square diamond set in a thin band of platinum. It looked elegant on what I considered were my large man hands! I was relieved that I'd had a manicure two days before or perhaps it wouldn't have had the same visual effect set against my usually ragged and cracked nails.

We spent the remainder of that evening sipping our after-dinner coffee, gazing lovingly at each other and kissing as if our lips were attached by a bungee cord. I was elated. I couldn't believe we were engaged! Even though his proposal had taken me off-guard, I didn't need to ponder over my answer because love is love, and I had never felt the kind of love for anyone else that I felt for him.

We travelled home in the limousine as an engaged couple, and when we arrived back to our house, our celebrations continued in bed, of course!

Chapter Six

The next morning I couldn't wait to tell everyone our happy news. I called my parents first and they were overjoyed, although they weren't surprised. Unbeknown to me, my partner had kept with tradition and asked my father for my hand in marriage in advance of his proposal. In fact, my parents had known the entire proposal plan before it was put into action.

According to my father, my man had invited him out for a drink on a weekday two weeks before the Saturday he proposed. They had met at a country pub and while they were ordering their first pints apparently my father, who considers himself a bit of a joker, said, 'I take it you haven't invited me out on a date to tell me you love *me*?' then admitted he'd guessed my man's intentions.

My father already affectionately referred to my man as 'son', and set him to a number of DIY tasks whenever we visited, so he was elated to know that he would be his son-in-law and that he was going to make an 'honest woman' of me. Apparently my father followed up his approval with: 'Does this mean I can get box seats at *any* game now?'

My mother told me that when my father returned from the pub and relayed to her what had been said, he had punched the air in excitement. She then said she suspected it was not just because of the happiness a wedding would bring everyone, but that it was probably also because he would no longer be financially drained by his daughter!

My parents loved my man – at times I wondered if my mother loved him more than she loved me from all the attention she showered on him – and they were over the moon at our engagement.

My fiancé's family were lukewarm. 'That's nice' was the extent of their response. We only ever spent time with them on official occasions, like busy family birthdays and Christmas, and when they stayed with us they generally arrived, watched the match, had dinner and went to bed early. With regard to their feelings for me, I think it was a case of 'the jury's still out' since they hadn't had time to get to know me on a deeper level.

The other important people in our lives were extremely excited and happy for us. His team-mates and old school friends, my university friends and the girls from back home all reacted more than positively.

I loved to tell people that I was his fiancé. Even the WAGs at the club were full of genuine congratulations for me when I saw them, two weeks after the proposal. They gathered around me in the Players' Lounge and cooed and gushed over the bling on my ring finger. It seemed like the shiny rock encouraged them to take me more seriously; from then on, I was invited out by the older WAGs much more than I had been before, and a few WAGs I'd noticed could be bitchy now relaxed their tone with me when we chatted. If only I had previously known that a ring on my finger would ingratiate me to the other WAGs, I'd have bought myself one from Argos long before the proposal arrived.

In the first few weeks of our engagement we were bombarded with cards and gifts and demands for an engagement party. A party would have been a good excuse for merriment but we decided against having one. We wanted to get married sooner rather than later, so we figured we'd save our hosting skills for a big, blow-out wedding.

We were engaged for about a year, although our planning began with almost immediate effect. I knew what I wanted our wedding to be like from the outset. I imagine most single women have an idea of how their fairy-tale wedding would be. I wanted a ceremony in a church with our nearest and dearest in attendance, followed by a meal and big, no expenses-spared, party.

Next on my list of important-things-to-do was the purchase of my wedding dress. I had a clear idea of what I wanted my dress to look like. I wanted it to be princess-like, although not on the same level as Katie Price and not one that would remind people of those knitted Barbie dolls that are placed over toilet rolls. I wanted it elegant . . . but big. My mother and I scoured the local bridal-gown boutiques and attended numerous wedding fairs to no avail. We decided that we'd have to submerge ourselves in London shopping for an entire weekend.

We stayed for three nights at the Dorchester, a beautiful and elegant hotel in central London, dined out every night, went to a West End show and shopped-till-we-dropped. Literally: my mother fainted in Harrods – on the ground floor in the chocolate department, which was packed with people and distinctly warm. She fell into the arms of an Arabian tourist. His wife was shocked, to say the least. Thankfully, my mother came round within seconds, dusted herself off, and we progressed to the top floor for a glass of water and then a glass of wine to ensure that her shame was forgotten! I joked that she must have passed out because of the immense range of delicious chocolates on offer; she has a sweet tooth.

On our final day in London we found The Dress. We were at a designer-brand wedding boutique and on display within the shop was a gown that was almost the one I had dreamed of when I was a little girl, imagining my wedding day. It just needed a few alterations to make it exactly the dress I dreamed of, and I booked two fittings nearer to the wedding date. I would have to make two more trips to London, which wasn't really a problem!

We also managed to find the perfect bridesmaids' dresses in the boutique. Thank goodness for modern technology because we were able to photograph them and send the pictures to the bridesmaids for their immediate approval. It had been a productive mother-and-daughter weekend.

Then my fiancé and I had to find the venue for our wedding reception. The number of potential places that we visited went into double figures. We travelled hundreds of miles to peruse stately homes, converted palaces, renovated barns and exclusive grand hotels. We were deterred by the venues that didn't have a late alcohol and music licence because we wanted the party to be like a nightclub – big and loud.

Eventually we found the perfect place. It was a stately home situated not too far from the church and we had permission to use the grounds in any way we liked. We booked the venue, which included overnight rooms for us and a large number of our guests. The costs were mounting at a rate of knots.

We'd had a preliminary budget of fifty thousand pounds, but we soon realized that wasn't realistic. We had already gone over it with the venue alone. We'd been to a few weddings but we were the first to get married of our close friends and neither of us had any idea of what a wedding cost. The only party I'd ever organized was for my man's twenty-third birthday, complete with roly-poly stripper. He still hasn't forgiven me for that.

Once the church and reception had been booked, and the invoices had been issued, I began to panic. I wrote lists of what we needed for the day, then searched for each item online in an attempt to investigate how best to keep costs down. There was too much to search through, too many people to call, too much adding-up to do and it all became a little overwhelming. I was failing miserably at playing wedding planner for my own big day and I needed help.

Fortunately, help came from the Players' Lounge, in the form of advice from one of the other WAGs. I confided in her that my wedding planning was pushing me towards an emotional melt-down. Without saying a word, she simply reached into her Stella McCartney handbag, produced a small crystal-studded diary, turned to the back of it where hundreds of numbers were written, and pointed her long, manicured fingernail to WEDDING PLANNER. 'Just call her,' she said. 'She's amazing. She'll sort everything out.'

When she told me the other celebrity weddings the planner had put together, I became sold on the idea. I typed the number into my phone, scurried off into the Ladies', pressed 'call' and booked an appointment for the next day.

When we met her in her lavish office, which was full of enough plants to rival a Victorian orangery, I instantly warmed to her. She was a mature and sophisticated woman with a friendly face and lots of charisma. After we had exchanged pleasantries and finished our first cup of delicious coffee, delivered by her personal assistant, we were introduced to her 'Wedding Showreel'. It was a DVD compiled from many of the previous celebrity parties, weddings and events she had organized. It was an impressive presentation and we were newly inspired by what we saw.

She then questioned us about what we ideally

wanted for our Big Day and made a note of everything we said; she listened to our every whim and intermittently nodded and said, 'Of course' or 'No problem'. We were in her office for two hours unpacking our wedding wants and we booked in for another meeting the next week, to give her time to digest our ideas and develop some appropriate suggestions.

She became my very own Fairy Wedding Planner! Over the next few months she took all of the stress out of our wedding preparation. She researched all of the options and alternatives for the items and services we wanted, then made a short-list of the 'best' options. She presented the short-list to us and we had the easy job of making the final decision. Getting to the final decision involved sampling food and wine, perusing invitation designs, watching YouTube clips of wedding bands and the like. Needless to say, we looked forward to our meetings with our wedding planner!

In addition, she suggested things for our wedding that I would never in a million years have considered. She suggested personalized ice sculptures, plasma screens inside the church so that everyone was ensured a good view, a champagne fountain, a six-foot-tall wedding cake and helicopter transportation to the reception! Despite some of her outrageous ideas, we booked a lot of these 'frills'.

She even arranged my hen night. Twenty-two friends and I travelled to the Spanish island of Mallorca for what we deemed a 'retro weekend'. We embraced my last holiday as a single woman true to the stereotype of British hen dos. Our three days in the Spanish sun were spent sunbathing on the beach and in the evenings we dressed up in the shortest skirts to show off our tanned legs. We drank sangria day and night; it's a bit of a blur if I'm being really honest. I do remember it being a fun weekend and thankfully, albeit surprisingly, given the all-girl group, passed without issue.

Once I'd returned from my hen weekend, I checked into my husband's bank account and was shocked to see the list of wedding-related outgoings. It became apparent that to have what you want comes at a great cost. If my fiancé hadn't been a high earner, we'd have had to re-mortgage our home, take out an additional bank loan and sell a few body organs to pay the final bill. Our fifty-thousand-pound budget grew to an obscene £250,000.

I feel sick with guilt now that we spent that much money on just one day. On more than one occasion I've thought of what we could have done with it, the people and the charities we could've helped. But we got carried away. We were young, loaded and naive . . . We couldn't see further than the tips of our noses.

Furthermore, we didn't actually end up fronting the bill. On the day that we had to make another sub-stantial payment, and as my fiancé searched the house for his cheque book, his agent called. A well-known glossy magazine had swooped in at the eleventh hour with a substantial financial offer for the exclusive photographs of our wedding. They wanted to feature us in a six-page spread, including the front page. It was a lucrative opportunity, but it would come at a cost. We had to guarantee that we'd have a substantial number of famous faces at our wedding.

Our guests would not be allowed to take any photographs and we would have to ensure that no outsiders would capture or share any images of our wedding before the pictures were published in the magazine. Also, we would have an entourage of photographers, people we didn't know, at our wedding from when we opened our eyes in the morning until the party finished.

We called our parents and some high-profile friends to gain their opinions, since it would in some way affect them too. They were supportive. Despite the restrictions the magazine wanted to impose, our loved ones reassured us that all of our guests would understand, and that they would probably enjoy the novelty factor of potentially appearing in a magazine.

Ultimately, we wanted professional images of our wedding, from every perspective possible, and we knew the magazine would be all over it, so that would be a bonus. We also knew that we wanted to share our big day with as many people as possible: since the magazine's readership was several million people worldwide, we figured that was also a box ticked.

Our decision was a resolute 'yes' and our wedding guest list grew from 120 close family and friends to 260. To cover our backs with regard to the magazine's demands, we invited some celebrities we had only met a few times, thinking, the more the merrier.

To some people, it might have seemed narcissistic that we agreed to effectively sell our otherwise price-less wedding images, or as if we were making our nuptials a commodity, but we didn't perceive it in such a negative light. I felt more than flattered that a magazine was interested in *my* wedding! I didn't think I was worthy of it, but it wasn't about my worth: it was my man's . . . and the high-profile people we knew.

Having endured a nerve-racking yet smooth rehearsal on the eve of the wedding, my man made an emotional departure to stay with my father at the best man's house, while I stayed at our house with my mother, my close female relatives and a few of my best friends. We drank champagne, ate Chinese and indulged in a little girly pampering. It would have looked like a classic 'night before the wedding' scene.

My best friend shared the bed with me and we chatted nervously under the covers about the next day. She seemed almost as nervous as me! She panicked about tripping up the aisle in her bridesmaid's dress, about not being able to vet the photographs being taken and about the audience of famous faces. I remember thinking that if she was worrying about such things then I should start making a list for myself!

The butterflies in my stomach rested in the early hours of the morning to allow me a few hours' sleep, but when I awoke, they were back with a vengeance. I had never been so nervous, so excited and so appre-hensive. It felt surreal to wake up with the knowledge that I'd be marrying the man I loved! We had been planning that day (well, the wedding planner had been planning it) for the best part of a year and the fact that it had finally arrived was almost unbelievable.

I was out of bed and eating breakfast before the daylight broke, but I wasn't the first awake. My mother was pottering around the kitchen and had already made cups of tea for the security men who patrolled the perimeter of our property. They were on guard to detect and deter any stealthy paparazzi who might try to get a picture of me in my bridal gown. The idea that we had to have security seemed a little ridiculous to me. I realized that, because my fiancé was an international footballer, pictures of me in my wedding dress would hold value, but it seemed a little over-the-top to have a pre-dawn patrol of our house. However, the glossy magazine was footing the bill and wanted to ensure that our wedding photographs were their exclusive scoop, so I couldn't allow myself to be too bothered. We had signed up to it, after all, and if I'm being really honest all the attention made me feel like royalty!

Before dawn four photographers arrived at our front gates and began taking pictures almost as soon as they stepped over the threshold. They were extremely polite and courteous but they photographed my every move. I felt I had to ask for permission to have a shower and go to the toilet for fear that they would assume they could follow me *literally* everywhere! They took photographs of my bridal gown and the bridesmaids' dresses on their hangers, of the make-up artist applying make-up to the bridal party and me, of the hairdresser curling and straightening and pinning, of the colourful bouquets of fresh flowers when they arrived, even of my mother in the kitchen, in her self-appointed galley-slave role. The bridal party and I drank from our pretty pink champagne flutes, posing for the cameras inside and outside the house, and every face-to-face conversation I held felt like it was being recorded, frame by frame.

The photographers made sure they snapped each and every emotion on the faces of everyone who scurried around my home that morning. The moment I did not need a picture for, although I am very glad that one exists, is when my father walked into my bedroom to see me in my wedding dress for the first time. He's not an emotional man; I've only seen him cry three times and that moment was the second. The image was etched into my mind for ever, and the photographs of his reaction are truly beautiful.

That morning passed in what seemed like a heart beat, the hustle and bustle of the getting-ready process seeming to speed up time. When the cars arrived at the gates I could not believe that it was time to leave for the church. The wedding transportation for us ladies was expensive classic cars that gleamed in the daylight, despite the blanket of grey clouds that covered the sky.

The bridesmaids and my mother departed in the first two cars. I was shaking with nerves as I made one final hair and make-up check in the hallway mirror. 'We have to go, darling,' my father said to me. I suddenly became desperate to pee. I couldn't go to the toilet without assistance since my dress was far too large and heavy for me to lift alone, but my brides-maids and mother had already gone. To my great embarrassment, the only option I had was to ask my dad to help me. We made our way into the large family bathroom together and reluctantly my father helped hitch up my cumbersome skirt while I discreetly relieved myself. I was cringing as the urine tinkled against the toilet pan and my father twisted himself around to face away from me. If there was ever an awkward-dad moment, that was it.

Once my father and I were inside the wedding car the electronic gates began to open and the car edged forward out onto the road. Then, to my utter bewilderment, about ten paparazzi appeared. They swarmed round the car, poked their camera lenses up against the window and began taking pictures. I hadn't believed there would be one waiting pap, let alone a huddle of them. I turned away and cuddled into my father's shoulder in an attempt to hide my face and he put a protective arm around me. For those few minutes, the multiple camera flashes illuminated the car interior like a strobe light and I had a minute insight into what it must be like for the royals, or the super-celebrities, who probably face such intrusion at every outing they make.

As the car gained speed, we looked out of the rear window and watched the photographers scramble for their bags of equipment, then run in different directions to their cars. It seemed that they'd be on our tail. Fortunately our driver took a lesser known back route to the church, and we arrived in a timely fashion without any pursuing paparazzi. However, we had a welcome party. Upon our arrival at the church, there was to be yet another military-style operation as another horde of photographers, and a large group of local people, surrounded the entrance, cameras poised at the ready.

However, the glossy magazine already had the church covered. The heavy oak entrance door was set back from the pavement, accessed by a fifteen-metre long cobbled pathway. From the pavement to the front door, a white tent with drop-down sides had been erected. The cameras snapped, clicked and flashed in our direction as our car disappeared into the covering.

Once the tent's front entrance had been zipped shut, a member of the magazine's security team opened the car's back doors for my father and me. We heard him say, 'Mission complete,' into a wire that was clipped to the lapel of his bomber jacket and led to an earpiece. Goodness only knows who he was talking to – Tom Cruise perhaps? Nothing would have surprised me at that point.

My father climbed out of the car, walked around to my side, took my hand and helped me out. He almost had to drag me, given the size of my dress. After we'd posed for a few father-and-daughter images, we stood in front of the doors, ready to walk down the aisle. When I heard the organ begin to play Wagner's 'Bridal Chorus', I gripped my father's hand and my heart beat so hard that I thought I might drop dead of a heart attack there and then. I actually imagined the tragic scene as I stood waiting for the back of my dress to be straightened. At least I'd die happy I thought . . . and the glossy magazine would make a killing with the photographs.

A security man with an earpiece then gave us a thumbs-up and the church doors slowly opened. The organ immediately became louder and resonated through my body; the low notes reverberated off the high stone walls and sent shivers down my spine. The pews were full of our well-dressed guests, who turned their heads to watch us. Then my eyes fell on my husband-to-be, who was standing in front of the vicar at the end of aisle facing the altar, apparently not yet ready to look at me. My legs shook and I thought for a moment that they might give way, until my father gave me a little nudge, as if to signal 'Let's go.'

We walked gracefully along the aisle, making sure that each of our footsteps was in time with the organ's music. We looked left to right as we passed the rows of guests, and we returned their smiles with our own. My fiancé turned when I was halfway along the aisle. He looked every bit as handsome as he had done on the first day I'd met him. His face was awash with emotion as he stood waiting for me. His eyes were a little bloodshot and his lip clearly trembled.

When I arrived at the end of the aisle, my father kissed my forehead, let go of my hand and took his place behind me to the left. It was a symbolic moment that meant he had let me go, that he'd entrusted me to the care of another man. I then faced my fiancé. He was and is a beautiful man, inside and out, and at that moment, I felt engulfed with love. The moment had finally arrived: I was going to become his wife.

We exchanged loving smiles and the vicar started the ceremony. We had chosen a traditional service, with an operatic interlude of 'Ave Maria', and three of our loved ones took to the pulpit: one read from the Bible, another recited a poem, and the third read their personal tribute to us and our future together. When my auntie read 1 Corinthians 13, a classic and beautiful interpretation of godly love, I could no longer hold my tears back. I wept subtly throughout the rest of the service, through our vows and the ring exchange. I was so emotionally charged that I temporarily forgot my left and my right and spent a few seconds trying to force the wedding band onto my man's right finger, much to the amusement of him and our guests.

I regained my composure for the signing of the register as the photographers' pose requests ensured my thoughts switched from an overwhelming 'I'm so in love' to fretting about how my waterproof mascara and lip gloss were holding out.

When the ceremony ended, we walked down the aisle as man and wife to cheers and whoops from our guests. We then waited in the internal doorway of the church to thank everyone as they passed out into the white tent. We were not allowed to leave the church with our guests. We were required to walk *back* up the aisle to re-create some crucial scenes in the ceremony: the photographers claimed that the lighting hadn't been good and that they didn't have the shot they wanted. We had to wait behind at the church for over an hour to stage those shots – it was boring and draining. At least in the re-enactment I remembered which finger I was supposed to place the ring on.

By the time we arrived at our reception most of our guests were tipsy on the gallons of Cristal champagne that we'd provided, and the canapés were in short supply. The miniature fish and chips, wrapped in minute pieces of newspaper, were my personal favourites and I was relieved to have got there before they'd all been polished off.

There was very little time for us to circulate among our guests before we were whisked away for more photographs. I found that aspect of the day quite embarrassing because not only did we have very little time to speak with our guests immediately after the ceremony, but the magazine's photographers made it their priority to pose us with our famous guests; our respective families were last on their list. We spent the first hour of the reception standing against a light-blue backdrop behind a screen that had been erected in the corner of the room, posing with celebrities. The photographers allowed just twenty minutes for photographs with our close friends and family, although at least we had images of absolutely everyone present, and there was still a chance that our family members would make the magazine's 'final cut'.

The agreement that neither we nor our guests could have cameras at our wedding was a downside of the deal we'd made with the magazine. We hadn't before realized that people would be searched on entrance to our wedding. The security team had searched the bags of our guests and reminded each one that under no circumstance would photographs be allowed. They had said that if the rule was broken, the relevant equipment would be seized and wiped. The ban included the use of mobile phones as cameras; anyone seen to be using their phone for anything other than a call was personally challenged by a member of the security team. It brought an air of formality to the day and slightly depersonalized the event for some of our guests. Some people took offence at the restriction and my father had to be recruited on more than a few occasions to explain that if even one photograph was leaked to the press we would lose the magazine deal . . . and the financing of the wedding.

Furthermore, I was relieved that no one would be able to take any pictures and then capitalize on our nuptials. There were some people at our wedding whom I didn't trust.

The WAGs, most of whom I knew, although some were strangers to me until that day, stuck together in their wolf-like pack. Their clique behaviour unnerved some of our other guests, who felt as if they were being scrutinized for what they were wearing or who they were. My close friends commented on how the WAGs seemed to spend a lot of time looking other women up and down and chatting in that 'gossiping schoolgirl' way. The WAGs didn't make any attempts to socialize outside the group they'd formed. At any opportunity, though, they were all over me like a rash. They gave me compliments and fawned over the details of the wedding: the cake, the diamonds on my dress, the designer of the men's suits, the ice sculptures; few of the 'added extras' had escaped their attention. They all seemed impressed. Also, many of them questioned me about the publication date of the magazine, which, no doubt, meant they relished the thought of appearing in it.

When the five-foot-high gong was struck, our guests took their allocated seats at their tables and we retreated to the entrance of the room for the Master of Ceremonies to announce us. I felt like I'd won the Nobel Peace Prize for the rapturous applause we received as we walked in and took our seats. The food we had chosen in the tasting sessions with the wedding planner was executed perfectly, and when the last dessert plate was cleared away the speeches began.

My father kicked off the proceedings with a few stories about my childhood. He enlightened everyone to the fact that when I was a young child I had refused to wear knickers; I'd secretly remove them whenever the opportunity presented, then flash my private parts to anyone and everyone, which regularly included the postman. Apparently I became known to him as Miss Knickerless, which I had always heard as Miss Nicholas and thus always wondered why the postman thought I was a boy.

After all the jokes, which were mainly at my expense, although my husband's lack of DIY skills featured more than once, my father made most of the women in the room cry with his description of his love for me. I felt humbled to have been born to such wonderful, loving parents. My father must have felt such pressure to speak in front of so many people, especially since most of them were strangers to him and a significant percentage were well-known celebrities, but he did an awesome job. He touched all the right nerves and spoke with the perfect balance of humour, emotion and honesty.

The best man's speech was next. My husband's best friend can make a joke out of the worst situations, and isn't afraid of controversy, so he had people literally falling off their seats, laughing. My cousin's husband laughed so hard that he tipped himself backwards in his seat and almost knocked over the baby in the highchair behind him. That, too, was caught on camera, to our later delight!

My husband was metaphorically ripped to shreds by his best mate's words: there was an eyebrow-raising ex-girlfriend story, constant sarcastic references to my husband's anatomical blessings, and a few anecdotes from drunken nights out with the lads. The best man also had to read out the messages from those who couldn't be with us. One that I particularly remember was from the then England manager, who said something very clichéd about marriages being like a football team, that from kick-off to the full-time whistle, which I presumed meant death and not divorce, a husband and wife have to work together, continually discuss tactics, and always make sure there are oranges at half-time. I'm still unsure what he meant!

The final speaker was my husband. He's never been a confident public speaker so I half expected that he'd have downloaded something from the Internet and inserted the relevant names where appropriate. I had underestimated him. After he'd offered the obligatory and deserved thanks to all those who had contributed to making the wedding so fabulous, and personally delivered huge bouquets of flowers to our mothers and the bridesmaids, he gave the most eloquent and heart-warming speech I'd ever heard.

By the time he had finished, most of the ladies in the room were wiping their faces with tissues and half of the men had tears rolling down their cheeks. He spoke of the people he'd lost in his life and how our love had healed some of his wounds. He talked about the importance of family and how he'd sacrifice all that he had and owned if it meant it would better the life of someone he loved. He expressed his gratitude to my parents for welcoming him as a son from almost day one of our relationship, and he rounded his speech off by telling me how much he loved me, and how I'd made his dreams come true. Rewind a few years and I would never have believed that an international foot-baller's dream would be to find a normal girl and get married!

My husband was and is 'a bit of a lad' and showing overt emotion in public is not a habit of his, but when he spoke, his emotions were raw and there for every-one to see. His speech was astounding.

Then it was time for the party. It was no ordinary wedding disco with 'DJ Dave' spinning some retro classics from behind his multi-coloured spotlight and decks set-up. Our party had been crafted to rival a top nightclub. It was in the large ballroom next to where we had dined. It had a large stage and a balcony level that overlooked the dance-floor. There was ample armchair and sofa seating and a 'chill-out' area for those who would need it.

We had hired a temporary bar structure that was positioned in the centre of the room. It was mirror-lined and illuminated by UV up-lights, completed with bar stools, six bar staff and a vast range of drinks, all served with glow-in-the-dark ice cubes. The dance-floor was large enough to accommodate all of our guests, and we had hired four different caterers, which included my husband's favourite Chinese takeaway, to provide the evening food. There was an ice-cream van outside the side entrance, an oxygen bar on the balcony, and a small cocktail bar made out of ice off the side of the dance-floor. Two circus hoops on long wires hung from the ceiling for the contortionists who would later perform, and there was a cage for dancers at either side of the stage. We had booked magicians to circulate and entertain those guests who chose not to dance, and fire-breathers to literally add a spark to the proceedings.

A band took to the stage and began to belt out a unique adaption of Michael Jackson's 'Don't Stop Til You Get Enough'. They had been recommended to us by our wedding planner and we had flown them in from Spain. They were well known in some European countries, but not to us, although I'm sure all present recognized their talent; most of our guests were on the floor within minutes.

The evening continued in perfect form: the drinks flowed and the music was amazing. Even the super-famous footballers could be found cutting shapes on the dance-floor. My husband and I partied the night away with our guests and forgot about the glossy magazine's photographers, who were probably panicking about which scandalous moment they might have missed.

I hadn't noticed any catastrophes or controversies at the wedding, although there were some. A friend informed me that she caught some WAGs taking cocaine in the ladies' toilets. Apparently three WAGs crammed themselves into a cubicle to snort the drug but had neglected to secure the latch. The door swung open to reveal their behaviour to everyone else in the room. Not a good look. Not that I can believe they were WAGs since I sincerely do not know any who would admit to taking drugs.

There were a few alcohol casualties. One well-known footballer over-indulged and was found comatose on the croquet lawn of the stately home's grounds. One of our teenage guests had to be taken back to her hotel early by her disgruntled parents because she'd been caught, by them, kissing one of our married friends. My great-aunt, who was in her eighties at the time, became so merry that she went to walk up the steps to the stage, apparently to compliment the singers, and tripped. She had only twisted her ankle but she was taken to A & E that night by my cousin because they feared she'd broken a bone.

Thankfully, the alcohol on tap didn't spawn any

fights or fall-outs, other than those that probably occurred in private between the footballers and their WAGs.

When two a.m. arrived and it was time for the music to stop, I was devastated. I hadn't wanted it to end. I couldn't believe that my wedding day was over.

My husband and I made sure that we were the last people to leave. As the staff cleaned up, we stood in the middle of the dance-floor and leaned into each other, our foreheads touching, and simply breathed in the last moments of our wedding day. It had been an absolute dream and we had both loved every single minute of it. But the bridal suite was calling us and we thought it imperative to consummate our marriage.

The next day, as well as nursing hideous hangovers, we met our guests for breakfast, then left the reception venue in a taxi headed for the airport. Our honeymoon was spent in a warm and exotic location that was not a tourist trap. It was a relaxing and romantic break and we did very little with our time other than spend it together. Every day we reflected on how phenomenal our wedding day had been, sipped piña coladas, sunbathed and swam in the sea. The evenings were reserved for moonlit walks, dinners on the beach and steamy sex wherever the mood took us.

When we returned to the UK, I dashed to WHSmith in the arrivals hall and there on the front cover, in full glory, was a picture of my husband and me on our wedding day. We were on the front page of a shiny, glossy magazine on the shelf. I could hardly believe it.

I loved the pictures that had been published. I loved the interviews that were used, and I loved the tone of the article. It was perfect. Also, to my great relief, my teeth, something I've always been conscious of, did not steal the show; the pictures were very flattering of everyone. The knowledge that there was a cheque for a quarter of a million pounds waiting for us was also a burden lifted.

We sent all of our guests copies of the photographs and we also made a pact. We decided that on our tenth anniversary, we would go to Gretna Green and renew our wedding vows, just the two of us and our iPhones . . . and perhaps a couple of glow-in-the-dark ice-cubes.

Being 'Mrs' and no longer 'Miss' was a very strange concept to comprehend, let alone becoming an official 'footballer's wife'. It was like I was now a member of the hierarchy and those beneath me, who were just engaged or a girlfriend, should bow in my presence. OK, so I'm exaggerating, but that was how I was made to feel by the married WAGs in the Players' Lounge. Undoubtedly, the queen WAGs didn't take the single WAGs seriously; they tended to stick together in their circle of football matrimony groups. However, I had transitioned. That shiny ring on my finger meant that I'd passed into their circle. I was duly accepted by the women who had previous dismissed me as 'just a girl-friend'; I was in it for the long haul, as far as they were concerned. I could be trusted.

I had a new surname, new acceptance and a new title: 'official footballer's wife'.

Chapter Seven

When I was a student, I had a reason to get out of bed in the mornings. If I didn't have to attend a lecture, there was always a book I needed to read or an assignment to work on. I had aims, direction and an ultimate goal to work towards each and every day. That was, of course, apart from the days when I was nursing a hangover and would lie about watching soaps.

I only went shopping when I desperately needed something, and if I had the money for it. I shaved my own legs and bikini line, had never had a facial and hadn't even heard of colonic irrigation; I later found the latter to be less enjoyable than the former.

When I had to resign from my job to move hundreds of miles and follow my footballer's career, my motivation for getting out of bed changed dramatically. I became a sort of 1950s housewife. As is almost customary for a WAG, I planned my days around my footballer; he expected it of me and I was too naive and obliging to consider that I could have it otherwise. I cooked, cleaned, dealt with his paperwork and business interests, entertained his friends, kept up communications with his family and was generally at his beck and call.

If he was scheduled to be home at two p.m. from training, I would be at home waiting for him. I can't count the number of times I had to change my after-noon plans with a WAG friend due to my partner's training being rescheduled. If he had an away game, I would travel to wherever it was in the country to watch him. If he had a weekend off, I would be ready to dance to the tune of his spontaneous plans. Whenever the six-week off-season arrived, I was will-ing and able to holiday with him. When he was ill or injured, I was his dutiful carer. When there were foot-ball events, team-mates' parties, or obligatory press events at which he wanted me on his arm, I was there, hanging off it. When he had to go to press conferences, make public appearances, take part in television shows or radio interviews, and he wanted me to accompany him, I was by his side.

I became his wife, housekeeper, secretary, escort, carer and primary emotional support. My life was not my own. My life was to be led during the in-between hours, when he wasn't home or when there wasn't a WAG demand to fulfil.

Aside from the emotional consequences, one of the main issues of being at my partner's disposal and not having an independent life or career was . . . money. I didn't earn my own and I didn't have any savings.

A WAG's daily routine is totally dependent on her budget. I know only a handful of WAGs who have control of the family's money, a.k.a. their partner's bank account. Generally, unless the footballer has no idea or has had no advice about how to manage his finances, he holds the purse strings. The few WAGs I know who are in charge of their partners' finances are more like personal assistants to their footballers; they do everything from seeing the accountant to organizing the mortgage repayments with the bank manager. They give their footballers 'pocket money' and make the final decisions regarding holidays and cars. These WAGs have unlimited access to the joint account and they spend it at their own leisure; a lot goes on their wardrobe.

I am not one such WAG, although my man has assigned me some roles in his business life. One of these was 'chief post-opener'. I was underpaid and undervalued for the task! I was so sick of my man not opening his letters and watching them pile up higher and higher on the desk in the study that he decided it would be better for my blood pressure if I addressed the problem. He's on top of our finances in every other respect: he speaks regularly to his bank manager, he's hands on with his tax returns, he set up all of our utility bills direct debits and arranged our mortgage, but he can't be arsed with opening letters that look 'boring'. He'll open the ones that look like cheques or share updates, but the rest can collect dust, as far as he's concerned.

So my job was to open the post. I had to read it, alert him to anything that was urgent, file anything that could be put to one side, or leave it in a special 'needs to be dealt with' box. That meant he'd have minimal amounts of paperwork to do in his spare time. He assured me that my secretarial duty was an essential contribution to the household finances and was part of our 'team work'. I realized he was humouring me, but I took on the role nevertheless. I also assumed his banking responsibilities, which wasn't such a bad job, given there was generally a Starbucks near to his bank.

When my husband made me his 'post secretary', he also set up my personal bank account. He sat me down at the kitchen table and asked me outright how much I considered enough to live off each month. Until that pressured conversation, I detested speaking about money at any time. I hadn't really had the need for a 'housekeeping' fund. My partner used to give me a wad of notes every now and again if he knew I wanted a new dress for a night out, or if I was meeting a friend for lunch. I would always wait for him to finish training before going to the supermarket as he would always pay.

However, he wanted to give me more freedom, and said that he recognized that, since his life impinged on mine, it was 'only right' that he do it. I didn't object. I felt I had made a huge sacrifice for him in uprooting myself so for him to donate a few quid into a bank account for me every month seemed a fair-ish trade-off.

In response to his 'How much?', I relished the opportunity to take the piss. I tried my luck with a preliminary offer of ten thousand pounds a month, to which he instantly burst into laughter and told me to piss off. In reality I could comfortably live off five hundred a month for what I needed. I played the proverbial ball back into his court: I wore my most sincere and humble expression and asked him to arrive at a figure that he deemed fair.

That was exactly what he did. My first WAG deal: on the first of every month, the sum of £2,500 was automatically transferred from his bank account into mine. From that moment onwards, I was officially a kept woman.

When I told my best friend about the deal I immediately regretted it; it felt wrong and unfair for me to gush about it when she busted a gut for a meagre seven pounds an hour at an estate agent's.

In the early days of being a WAG, my daily routine consisted of making my man's breakfast, completing a few household chores, then heading to the gym where I would stay until he rang to tell me that he was on his way home from training. We would meet up for lunch at one of our favourite restaurants, then head home for rampant sex. Alternatively, we would arrive home for me to carry on pottering about the house and he would play on his Xbox.

If my husband was ever given a rare day off we would spend every minute of it together . . . usually in bed.

We could afford to be totally selfish; we did what we wanted to do. We ate out practically every night, we saw all of the latest films at the cinema, we partied at the weekends, and whenever the opportunity presented itself, we spontaneously took road trips. Also, to add to our luxurious lifestyle, we had a cleaner twice a week. It was a big house, too big for us, and to be honest I hated cleaning it. My man could more than afford home-help so I completely supported the idea. I was damned if I was going to waste my days in my Union Jack Marigolds! I was more interested in burning off calories in the gym.

Exercise has been a consistent theme in my life, and since I became a WAG, the gym became a place of solitude. It may be ironic to think that a noisy gym full of sweaty people panting and posing could be considered peaceful, but it's a form of escapism for me. Wherever I've lived I've joined the nearest chain gym. I don't like the small cliquey ones, where everyone knows everyone else and people socialize together. I like the big branded gyms where most people are anonymous to each other.

I've never signed up to the exercise classes that gyms offer, and I've never bothered with a personal trainer. I've always tended to turn up at the gym already dressed for action, then run a few miles on the treadmill, row a few thousand kilometres on the rower and use the weight machines to give myself an even body tone workout. I don't enjoy public swimming for fitness, given all the hassles that are involved with getting changed, and I'm not one to laze around in the gym's spa facilities, given that we've always had hot tubs or sauna rooms at home.

However, my daily gym habits began to change when I started making friends with WAGs at the club, and socializing with them on my own. I quickly bonded with a foreign WAG, whose English was phenomenal; she was normal, down-to-earth and totally refreshing compared to the other WAGs. She wasn't particularly stunning to look at, but she always made the most of herself, and her personality made her immensely beautiful.

She introduced me to many of the secret, or not-so-secret, beauty tricks of the WAG trade. She wore the most luscious hair extensions, which made her thin, limp blonde hair look like a healthy and voluptuous mane; her false locks looked real and were A-list celebrity standard. I was so impressed with her fake barnet that I booked into the salon that Foreign WAG used and soon found myself sitting in the same salon chair for five hours while someone else's hair was glued to my head.

The hair extensions were not cheap: they cost approximately £1,000 and I had to perform a lot of sexual favours in order that my man agreed to me having them. They caused me a lot of sleepless nights: the nodules of glue that were attached to the roots of my hair made it feel like I was sleeping on a miniature ball pit. I ditched the idea of hair extensions after that experience: not only were they uncomfortable, I couldn't be arsed with the high maintenance. They have to be taken out and replaced far more regularly than I could be bothered with, and when they developed a mind of their own and wouldn't lie in a natural order, they looked tacky and false.

My foreign WAG friend had a wash and blow-dry twice a week at a salon to keep hers looking great, but since I went to the gym every day and needed to wash the sweat out of my hair at least once a day, hair extensions were no good for me.

Foreign WAG had also tried and tested what seemed like every single beauty procedure known to woman. She got me hooked on oxygen facials. An oxygen facial is carried out with the assistance of a machine that removes the impurities from the air and pumps out pure oxygen. The therapist cleanses the skin, then adds a concoction of anti-ageing and hydrating serums that the machine pushes deep into the dermal layer.

I used to have them regularly, and I believed each one was worth the eighty pounds I paid for it. The before and after results were unbelievable. I thought I looked like I'd had a facelift there and then! Unfortunately, the miraculous skin tightening only lasted for twenty-four hours, but even so, the facials served a great purpose. If ever there was a paparazzi-fuelled night out, I would have an oxygen facial in the afternoon and look five years younger for the photographers' snaps in the evening. The facials were highly addictive!

Given my great custom, I got quite friendly with the staff at the beauty salon. I was notorious for falling asleep during the procedure as it was just so damn relaxing. In the treatment room, music played discreetly in the background, sweet-smelling aroma-therapy candles burned by the bedside and the lights were dimmed. It was heavenly, and very soporific. On one appointment I fell into such a deep sleep that when the beautician left, after waking me up, I fell fast asleep again and the staff forgot I was there. They left me on the treatment bed asleep for two and a half hours! In that time I also got a parking fine, which made it the longest and most expensive facial I've ever had.

Foreign WAG also encouraged me to say goodbye to nail varnish and instead to have acrylic nails. They were forty-five pounds for a set and I had to have them filled in or replaced every two weeks. Acrylic nails felt more glamorous than simple varnish and I liked them because they made my large hands look rather feminine! They were an expensive luxury, but I enjoyed the pampering that went with their application: the hand massages and the idle chat with the therapist made for a relaxing part of a day.

A less relaxing treatment that Foreign Wag encouraged me to try was colonic irrigation. She professed that 'colonics' were the reason for her flat stomach and clear skin, and that they generally worked to give the body a much-needed clear-out. I was soon on her colonic therapist's bed with my pants off and arse cheeks clenched tightly in fear. A clear plastic pipe was shoved up my anal passage, then freezing cold water was pumped along it into me! When I next looked at the pipe, it was no longer clear: bits of shit, bubbles and sweetcorn floated along it! I felt so uncomfortable, ashamed and embarrassed that I don't remember breathing for the entire forty minutes of the procedure. I didn't even dare to cough in case the tube shot out of my arse and covered the therapist in a shower of my shit! The worst part was when she removed the tube – it felt like an internal organ was being pulled out of my arse! I'm sure some people greatly enjoy colonics, but I found the whole thing hideous.

There were some benefits from the procedure. The therapist concluded that I was wheat intolerant, hence the excessive bubbles in the tube, and the next morning the scales told me I had lost a whole pound! No pain, no gain, I guess. My poor arsehole has never been the same, though, so, as with the hair extensions, once was enough.

My beauty regime had become quite expensive, but I didn't make any noise about it. However, when we returned from our honeymoon, my new husband sat me down once again at the kitchen table and declared that he'd like to revise our monthly money plan. He very tenderly told me that he thought I deserved a bigger housekeeping allowance because he loved me so much, and not only were we married, but I deserved it for putting up with him for so many years. He said that I could consider the money my own, and that I could therefore do what I wanted with it.

Consequently WAG Deal Number Two was put in place and my new husband began to donate £5,000 into my bank account on the first day of each month. I felt very lucky, especially given my awareness of how much a person would have to earn per year in order to pocket such a monthly sum after tax. It was a phenomenal amount of money to receive for being his happy slave. To put things into perspective, his wages were well into £30,000 a week by now, so £5,000 a month was like pocket change to him.

The first month it arrived I remember thinking, holy shit, how in the hell will I ever manage to spend that? and I couldn't help but check my bank account whenever I saw a cashpoint on the street. It seemed quite incredible that my available funds had so many zeroes, and as the months passed, the amount continued to rise.

My husband still paid for practically everything we needed to live on, but in my free time I did a damn good job of trying to spend what I was given.

My days became more expensive and extravagant. I stopped shopping at the low-budget supermarket and perused the food halls of the 'posh' high-street brands. Our food bill doubled, but I could afford it and I enjoyed the experience so much more because I convinced myself that the food was better quality, and the aisles were certainly less busy.

I also joined an expensive gym, which only stinking-rich people went to. A few WAGs I knew were members and they'd always raved to me about how good it was, and the anonymity was worth it: the super-famous WAGs didn't get hassled there and even their menfolk occasionally went along because none of the other members were interested in their fame.

This leisure club was immensely grand – even the building looked like a stately home. There was a champagne bar, a cinema workout room where you could watch a film while cycling, an outrageously ornate tiled swimming pool, which was, of course, always perfectly warm, and a restaurant that verged on Michelin-star quality. The coffee-shop served only the most exclusive coffee beans and even the towels were a treat: they were emblazoned with the club's crest, always fluffy and pristine white, better than the newest guest towels in my home.

It was a deluxe place to exercise. When I completed my exercise routines, I did so in the company of sophisticated middle-aged ladies who gracefully jogged on treadmills, dripped with diamonds and smelled of Chanel. The place was full of WAGs, injured footballers or those on their days off, and women whose husbands owned multi-million-pound companies.

As well as my daily outings to the leisure club, my weekdays were peppered with WAG lunches. We would go to a new café or restaurant each time, regardless of the prices, sit and chat for hours, often with a glass of wine in hand, gossiping, speculating and sometimes bitching. I cannot profess always to see the best in people.

As the funds in my bank account grew, I began to shop a lot more and developed a taste for designer wares. The label bags in my kitchen 'bag cupboard' increased in number. I socialized with experienced WAGs who had been in the 'shopping game' for years, and since WAGs are known for their shopping, I adopted the approach of 'If you can't beat 'em, join 'em.'

I conformed to public opinion. The WAG group and I did very little to reject or avoid the paparazzi's attentions when we hit the shops. Even when we knew it was a WAG set-up, we moaned superficially about the intrusion on our private shopping time, but I'm sure most of us secretly revelled in the limelight. In our defence, to a WAG the temptation to spend is almost too great to avoid.

The fact was that the WAGs I socialized with were all kitted out in the latest trends, and their focus was simply on how they looked. My first shopping trip with such a WAG was an eye-opener. The girl could shop. We headed straight to Selfridges, as that was where almost everything she owned came from, and each member of staff greeted her by her name. It was unbelievable. She usually used the personal shopper facility to get her new outfits. She would be escorted into a small room where she'd sit on a comfortable sofa and sip champagne while she was shown garments by a petite and trendy girl. On this occasion, I refused that experience as I wanted to be hands on with my fashion choices. I have always had my own style and I didn't like the idea of someone telling me what to wear; to have a personal shopper seemed like laziness and I theorized that it would take all the fun out of shopping.

However, we did call upon the help of a shopping assistant. He was a super-hot gay guy who was on hand to guide us through the store and collect any item that caught our fancy. His head was well and truly rooted up our arses from the moment we met him. Compliment after compliment flowed out of his mouth, no doubt in an effort to guarantee himself some commission. My WAG friend and I walked around Selfridges like kids in a sweet shop. Wide-eyed, we admired the beautiful pieces of Dolce & Gabbana's new line, the sparkly Gina shoes, the new and vibrant Juicy tracksuits and many more designer thrills. We pointed out countless items to our shopping assistant.

We spent an age trying on our selections and eventually reached some decisions. When we got to the sales counter, it was clear that my friend was on a much better deal, or housekeeping budget, than I was. Her husband wasn't the club's highest earner, I knew that much, but she must have had some serious wedge in her personal bank account to be able to blow £3,500 on our midweek shopping trip!

WAGs are usually very discreet when it comes to discussing money, but often their actions give the game away. I had been perusing the rails with a budget in the back of my mind, but money seemed no object to her. I ended up spending roughly £250 on a pair of jeans, which was a huge purchase for me and I felt terribly guilty. I was blissfully unaware of the price tag until I had committed to the transaction. I wasn't used to spending vast amounts on clothes. I had been given designer items as presents by my man but that was different as it was his choice. I remember going home in fear of telling him what I'd bought, but when I did, he just said, 'They're smart. I like them, babe,' and that was it. My guilt evaporated in an instant.

When my husband transferred clubs and we had to relocate, I had to say goodbye to my fantastic

Colombian cleaner and I was totally gutted. Jokingly, I asked her to move with us but she didn't understand me and I couldn't really have made such a request for just two days of work a week. After we had moved, I searched online for a replacement: my husband had decided that that was the best avenue for finding reputable local help. I liked the sound of one woman's profile so I called her and invited her for a trial. It went well: she was thorough, reasonably quick at cleaning the rented house we were staying in and friendly, so we hired her.

I became fascinated by our new cleaner – she was far too well dressed, given the grime that accompanied her job. She turned up for work in a pencil skirt, blouse and stilettos. I have no idea how she cleaned the house in stilettos, but she did, and if I was at home, I'd marvel at her practised techniques. She looked like some sort of Stepford Wife, yet she got the job done efficiently and didn't drag it out so as to get more money.

I thought it even more questionable when I noticed that she had a really nice gold Cartier watch and a black Chloé handbag. After she had cleaned for us a few times, I decided to enquire tentatively into her private life to try to investigate how she had such luxury items yet worked as a cleaner. It turned out she was recently divorced and her ex-husband was very wealthy. She welled up when she told me how he had screwed her over with the divorce settlement. I remember thinking, That's the bag and watch accounted for.

However, as the saying goes, 'Assumption makes an ass out of you and me.' One cleaning day, my husband came home from training, took off his Rolex watch and wedding ring, as he always did, and placed them on the kitchen counter in their usual spot. About an hour later he went back to put his watch and ring on as he had a meeting to attend with his agent, only to find them missing. The items were worth a combined total of around £60,000, and they were both of emotional significance. Sensing his panic, I went to ask the cleaner if she had seen them. She immediately said she hadn't and asked whether he'd left them at work without realizing. I returned to the kitchen to tell him the cleaner's response. It was unlikely but not impossible that he had stepped out of his routine and left them in the changing room.

'I know for a fact that I put them there, just like I always do,' he said – he was nearly having a coronary.

We looked at each other, then turned to look at the cleaner's Chloé handbag, suspicion etched on our faces. My husband had never trusted our cleaner and had told me not to give her a key for at least the first few months of her employment. I thought she was fine, a little overdressed perhaps, but I figured that if she wanted to risk breaking an ankle in her heels while reaching to clean behind the toilet, then it was her risk to take. After a brief debate about who was going to search the cleaner's private property, my husband walked over to her handbag and opened it. I waited by the kitchen door – my heart was pounding at the thought of her returning and seeing what we were doing. Time was limited since she only had another five minutes before she left.

After just a few seconds' rummaging, he produced his ring and watch, as if he were a magician pulling a rabbit from a hat. 'Ta-da!' he said, as he raised the items into the air. His face turned red with anger. 'The bloody thieving bitch, how dare she?'

I was shocked; totally dumbfounded. Then we heard her stilettos clip-clopping down our wooden stairs.

As she approached the kitchen door, the sunny smile she always wore dropped into a look of horror. She realized she'd been busted. My husband wrenched his clenched fist up to her face, then unfurled his hand under her nose to reveal his watch and ring. 'You hadn't seen my ring? Hadn't seen my watch? Well, look what I found in your bag!' he seethed. 'Can you explain this?'

Her face wore her guilt. She stared at him, then grabbed her bag, said goodbye to me, and strutted out of the house. She didn't even apologize. We looked at each other, mouths open wide in disbelief. We had let her leave our house without calling the police. When the penny dropped, that she was probably a seasoned thief, I ran to my jewellery box and checked everything was there. Thankfully, it was, although one of my designer handbags was missing. To be honest, I wouldn't have been able to tell if much more had gone: I had far too many items to remember.

I called the police, and we made a statement about the incident. I reported my £1,500 handbag as stolen, but it was all to no avail. I had no details for her, apart from her phone number, which became void within moments of her leaving our house, and she had removed her online trader's profile. I couldn't help but wonder whose Cartier watch she wore and which heartbroken girl was pining for her stolen Chloé bag.

From that moment we decided that the risks of giving a stranger a key to our house and free rein within it were too great. I assumed responsibility for all of the cleaning. My days took a more domesticated turn.

They became even more domesticated when I became a parent . . .

Chapter Eight

The media relish a photograph of a pregnant WAG and there are two types of picture: 'WAG looks amazing with her tiny bump' and 'Pregnancy taking its toll as WAG looks fat and tired' caption. Any photographs of me just before first-time parenthood arrived would've fitted into the second category.

A few features editors from glossy magazines did approach me for some cheesy pregnancy photographs: 'We'd just want some images of the two of you around the pool, in the garden or next to the fireplace looking wistfully at each other . . .' but I graciously declined, despite their financial offerings. In fact, I made more effort than usual to hide from the paparazzi during my first pregnancy. Not only because I looked like shit throughout it but also because I didn't want to tempt fate. I didn't want to tell the world that I was pregnant, then later have to release a statement to say that I wasn't.

I adore children and had always wanted to have a family, but just as I thought my dream was becoming a reality, it turned into a nightmare.

I'd been with my husband for five years and we had just moved house in response to a high-profile and big-money transfer, but it had taken us even further away from my family and friends. I missed them more than I thought I could. My husband's need to further his career had again trumped my need for emotional security.

I used to telephone my mother and cry to her about how isolated and alone I felt. I split my time between the gym, infrequent modelling jobs, working a few irregular hours for a local charity and suffering the obligatory WAG outings. In general, my days were quite dull. Traipsing around shops and mornings in Starbucks can become extremely tedious, especially if not done with best friends. I spent every day killing time until my husband arrived home from training. I couldn't find any meaningful thread to my existence aside from being a 'supportive wife'.

I had never dreamed that my life would appear so amazing on the outside yet feel so sad on the inside. To add to my despair, the baby boom had started among my friends and relatives back home. People I loved were falling pregnant and having babies as if it were a new fashion. It seemed like I received a phone call every other week that began with 'Guess what?' When I began to feign excitement with a sarcastic 'Wow – you're pregnant! What a surprise!' I was forced to look within myself and question why I was becoming bitter. I began to consider the possibility that I was jealous. That maybe the apparent hole in my life was baby-shaped, and that I was hitting the season of broodiness.

It was heightened because, as well as being full of expensive perfume, Jimmy Choos and pencilled-in eyebrows, the Players' Lounge is always full of kids. At my husband's club there was even a professional crèche, with qualified nurses to look after the kids if the WAGs wanted to go and watch the game in the stands or relax and gossip.

The crèche was situated through a separate sound-proof door off the main lounge, in a room that was rammed full of toys. Noise rarely escaped the room, but whenever I'd peer through its port-hole window, the kids appeared to be having a whale of a time. As the weeks at the new club rolled by, I began to feel an unfamiliar urge to look at my own offspring in that room.

There were only three WAGs there without children. At most home games, we would usually gravitate to each other to chat about various non-child-related things: diets, clothes and other WAGs, I'm ashamed to admit. We had been forced into our own clique because the Mummy WAGs naturally gelled together, especially if they had children of a similar age. Also, while not all of the Mummy WAGs' conversations revolved around their kids, lots of them did, and us childless WAGs just couldn't relate to them.

In the Players' Lounge I eavesdropped on many an impassioned discussion about Andy from CBeebies, the trauma of potty-training and the pain of sleepless nights, but it all sounded so boring. The Mummy WAGs clearly had much more in common with each other than they did with us. They went to play centres for their coffee mornings and to the zoo on sunny afternoons. Our venues for WAG catch-ups spanned coffee houses, boozy bars and the occasional casino. Needless to say, I didn't feel upset at being marginalized by the Mummy WAGs: the idea of spending time with a WAG and her two-year-old did not appeal to me, not at all.

Some children in the Players' Lounge were enough to put anyone off parenthood. Sometimes a phenomenon would occur that became known as the Mexican wave of crying: when a baby at one end of the room started to bawl, in a domino effect they would all start, until the Lounge sounded like a place where souls were tortured.

There was one Mummy WAG in particular whom I felt extremely sorry for: Nervous Wreck WAG. Every time I saw her she looked emotionally broken and her kids' behaviour stank of 'spoilt brat'. They didn't listen to her, the nurses in the crèche or anybody else. They would spit, shout, smash things, hit other kids and repeat the rudest words they knew as loudly as possible.

I once found Nervous Wreck WAG in the Ladies' 'bawling her eyes out; she'd worked herself into a state about how the other WAGs thought her a bad mother for having such unruly kids. I reassured her that it wasn't the case, but at the time most WAGs did think that. What I really wanted to tell her was 'Man the fuck up and get a grip of your little shits,' but, like the placid idiot I can be, I hugged her and told her, 'All kids act like yours . . .' I should've added, '. . . if they're possessed by demons from the underworld.'

Her tiny terrors did little to silence the voice inside me. The biological pull towards motherhood was growing. The Mexican wave of crying was bothering me less and less, the time I spent cooing over the children in the crèche grew, and each new-born baby I held, product of the baby boom back home, brought a more intense sense of maternal longing.

When I began to consider it seriously – the risks involved in pregnancy, the sacrifices parents have to make for children – alarm bells began to ring. I am not good in situations that are out of my control, and I started to worry about how I would react to the guaranteed weight gain that pregnancy brings.

Some of the Mummy WAGs helped quell such fears: not only did they stay glamorous throughout their pregnancy, many looked young enough to be the older sister to their children. One in particular, MILF WAG, as my husband used to refer to her ('A Mum I'd Like to Fuck?' I don't think so!), the wife of a very high-profile player, was the epitome of what I would define as 'the perfect mother'.

Her four pregnancies had all been a breeze and she had remained beautiful and relaxed throughout them. The births were textbook, without drugs or dramas, and after each one, she lost all of her excess baby weight within weeks, apparently without invasive treatments or starvation. She and her children were always immaculately dressed and impeccably behaved. She was stunning, elegant, good-humoured and yet so darn motherly! If I hadn't seen her with my own eyes, I wouldn't have believed she existed. I could barely believe that MILF WAG had four children, yet still looked like she had when she was a model in her early twenties. What added to my disbelief was that MILF WAG used to wear white, a lot. Her kids were mud-players and chocolate-munchers, but not once did she have a stain on her. It seemed like some sort of witchcraft.

I wanted to be just like her. Watching MILF WAG with her children on match-day Saturdays eased my pre-parenting fears and inspired me. She helped me believe that I could be a parent, that having children did not have to leave me fat, ugly and stressed . . . if only I could borrow her spell book.

I remember the night I said to my man that I felt ready to start a family, to really try for a baby. I was determined to tell him, 'I'm ready,' before the day was out, but I felt extremely anxious about it. If he confirmed that he felt ready too, which I presumed he would, we would have to prepare physically and emotionally for the biggest life change we were ever likely to experience. Alternatively, in the unlikelihood that he would tell me he was not actually ready and that he felt the time was not right, my hopes and dreams would again have to be put on hold, and I knew I'd be more than disappointed.

I told him in bed, not because being in bed was romantic or because it's the one place where I can often manipulate him into my way of thinking, but because I had chickened out of telling him on numerous occasions throughout the day. It was an eleventh-hour confession.

He had just turned off the bedside lamp, pulled the covers up to our necks and snuggled up behind me, wrapping his arms around my waist. I was biting my lip and squeezing my eyes tightly shut as my brain was screaming at me, SAY IT! Just as our bedroom fell into silence, I spun around in his arms and looked at his face in the moonlight. I'm clearly biased, but my husband, as I've already said, is an extremely good-looking man, and he's even more handsome when he's sleeping or just on the brink of it. As I gazed at him, I felt the love I had for him surge through me and felt even more ready to have his children.

'I want to have a baby,' I whispered.

It was a cliché, but it was what fell out of my mouth in that moment. His eyes sprang open and he stared at me, a smile forming on his lips. 'Are you serious?' he croaked. I nodded. He put his hands on the sides of my face, gazed deeply into my eyes and whispered, 'Then let's have a baby.' Then he kissed me. It truly was a Disney moment. What followed that night was less fairy-tale and more top shelf, but needless to say we agreed, and indeed started, to try for a baby.

The next day we were so excited about our decision that we could barely have a conversation outside it. We pinpointed which room in the house could be the nursery, mused over what our baby might look like and even started debating names.

It's fair to say that in the first month of trying for a baby we gave it everything we had. It was a fun month, probably one of the most enjoyable of my husband's life! We have intense sexual chemistry but it took on a new form in that period. We were having sex anywhere and everywhere in the belief that any of those moments could be the one when we conceived. I'm unsure of how romantic an 'on top of the dining-table' conception story would have been, but it took on a sort of romanticism in our eyes!

In those weeks my husband treated me like a princess. He showered me with gifts and affection because he claimed to be 'so excited' about our decision, but I knew better: it was really because he had sex on tap. He didn't realize it, but that was the real reason for the more buoyant spring in his step and his new generosity: he was getting laid even more than usual.

The spring in his step lessened when, six weeks after I'd taken my final contraceptive pill, my period arrived. We were a little disappointed, but we rationalized that we'd been ignorant to assume we would conceive so quickly. When my periods continued to arrive, disappointment gave way to worry. As more months rolled by, we began to think something was wrong with us.

I started to use an online app that told me the most fertile dates in my cycle, and when those days arrived, I demanded that we have sex morning, afternoon and night. Sex became formulaic and a bit of a chore. Its purpose was no longer for love and enjoyment but solely to make a baby. My husband, though, was in his element. He loved being in sexual demand and couldn't understand for one moment why I didn't seem enthused whenever my phone app buzzed to signify a fertile day.

As well as employing an app for a little conception assistance, we tried every sex position in the *Kama Sutra* in an attempt to encourage his sperm to get to my eggs. In one hilarious effort we were having sex while I was literally upside down in the hope that gravity would pull his little swimmers towards my ovaries.

I also began to check our temperatures and monitor how hot or cold our bedroom was in order to provide the optimum baby-making conditions. I would even check that my husband's testicles weren't too hot or cold for action, not that I could support my testing with any real scientific evidence.

We ate special foods such as chickpeas, pumpkin seeds and spinach, and we cut down on alcohol and caffeine (the former was difficult for him, the latter was difficult for me), all in the hope of it helping us make a baby.

Consequently, as the weeks rolled by, the romance in our sex life died. The mission took over and I became easily angered, agitated and teary. I would completely overreact if we couldn't have sex on a fertile day or if my husband went out for drinks with his friends. Tempers ran high as my patience began to run out.

Eventually, my man became frustrated too. Footballers like to win: they are competitive and do not take well to things not going their way. He took it

143

personally that I wasn't falling pregnant, and began to feel he had failed me in some way. Ironically, I felt I was failing him. It was difficult to understand why conception was not happening, given that we were young, fit and healthy, and having sex at every opportunity.

When twelve months had passed and we had still no baby joy, I decided that we should seek medical advice. My husband didn't agree: he certainly didn't want to talk to a doctor about it. According to him, the problem was mine, and it was less physical and more psychological. He believed that if I relaxed and stopped obsessing about it, Nature would take its course.

I managed to convince him that either way, whether he perceived the problem as mental or physical, we needed a professional diagnosis. It turned out the correct thing to do. We attended an appointment with our GP, who enquired as to the frequency and duration of my periods, then concluded that I wasn't ovulating regularly. She prescribed some hormone-based pills to stimulate my ovaries into a more regular rhythm. I walked away from the clinic immensely relieved that we had an answer as to why we had not conceived, and felt reinvigorated.

I had to take the first dose of the medication on the first day of my next period, which was due to arrive two days after our consultation, on a Thursday. The Thursday came and went, as did Friday, Saturday and Sunday. We were used to false hope, so we didn't get excited when a week had passed and my period was still a no-show. However, when it was twelve days late, I noticed that my breasts felt extremely tender to the touch, and that they were decorated with blue veins. I didn't give these symptoms too much attention, for I was much more concerned with wishing my period to arrive so I could begin the medication.

When it was a full two weeks overdue, I decided to take a pregnancy test. We were due to go out that evening for a few drinks with friends so I wanted to err on the side of caution before allowing myself a rare hedonistic night. I would take a pregnancy test before any night out, even if I was halfway through my menstrual cycle, because I was so paranoid about getting wasted and potentially endangering the pregnancy.

A few hours before we were due to meet our friends, as per my routine, I took a Clear Blue pregnancy test from the collection I had accumulated, went into my en-suite bathroom, peed on the test end of the stick, and left it on top of the toilet seat to review later. Then I went to get dressed and apply my makeup; I had become a pro at testing and tasking. After I'd applied enough mascara to render my eyelashes immobile, I remembered the test. I felt neither excitement nor expectation at the prospective result as I was so used to seeing the single blue line in the test window to indicate 'not pregnant'.

Casually I picked up the stick, glanced at the screen and tossed it into the bin. It was an automatic reaction, but my brain probably allowed it because it was in shock at what my eyes had seen. I snatched the test out of the bin. To my utter shock there was a blue cross. I was pregnant! I couldn't believe my eyes and was momentarily rendered rigid and speechless.

Then the magnitude of the situation began to dawn on me. 'I'm pregnant,' I said to myself. 'I'm finally pregnant!' Then I screamed, 'There's a cross, a bloody cross! Arrrrgggh! Shit! Bugger! Oh, my goodness! I can't believe it! There's a bloody cross!'

My husband had bounded upstairs and appeared at the door while I was still mid-screech. 'What's wrong?' he asked, with genuine concern.

I spun around and, grinning like a Cheshire cat with the test still in my hand, I spluttered, 'I'm pregnant! I'm fucking pregnant!'

He threw his arms around me and I burst into tears. We were so happy, we were ecstatic. We stood holding each other for a while, him kissing my head and repeating, 'I'm going to be a daddy,' and me now dumbfounded with shock. I couldn't believe that just a few days earlier I had been in a doctor's surgery and prescribed medication, yet I had conceived naturally. It felt unbelievable, truly magical.

I rang my parents first and told them the news. They were both over the moon; my mother cried and my father did his best to not allow his voice to crack with emotion. My husband then told his parents to an equally heartfelt reaction. The third recipient of our news was my best friend, and while she was immensely excited for us, she joked that she was losing her going-out buddy. I knew it masked genuine sadness for it was the season of the baby boom and she didn't have a baby, or any plans to have one.

I must have been just six weeks' pregnant when I found out, so we decided not to share our happy news with anyone else until I'd had my twelve-week scan. However, I'm not known for my patience. I couldn't wait to tell people! As soon as I saw someone I knew I blurted it out. Everyone was, of course, thrilled for us, which added to our excitement. While I was pregnant, barely a day passed by without us discussing baby names, pushchairs, nursery designs and what the baby might look like.

Sadly those conversations ceased just before my ninth week of pregnancy. One morning in week eight I woke up feeling a bit under the weather. I had light cramping stomach pains, a fever and generally felt rough. I thought that maybe I had a touch of the flu that was going around so I stayed in bed until my bladder forced me out of it. It was when I went to go to the toilet that my life felt as if it had shattered into a thousand tiny pieces. I was bleeding, and not just a bit: a lot.

I began to cry. I felt helpless; there was nothing I could do.

The feeling of helplessness swiftly turned into mania as I began incessantly screaming my husband's name. He had been sleeping but after only a few of my blood-curdling, high-pitched shrieks he arrived at the bathroom door, dishevelled, perplexed and half-asleep. The sight that greeted him, of me crouching over the toilet, blood staining our floor and tears staining my cheeks, woke him immediately. He quickly deciphered that I was miscarrying.

I couldn't move for my body heaving up and down with the weight of my sobs. I was utterly devastated, rendered immobile by shock and grief. My husband helped me into the shower, then cleaned up the mess on the floor. It must have been awful for him to have to take charge of that situation.

The day of the miscarriage and the weeks that followed were quite honestly the worst times of my life. I mourned for the baby that might have been, for the parents we could have been, and despaired at what the future might hold. I was scared that perhaps I would never be able to have a baby, not just because of my body's rejection of the pregnancy, but because at that point I couldn't imagine facing the potential for such loss ever again.

Sharing our sad news with those we knew was equally difficult. Everyone reacted with kindness, compassion and offers of support. I received many bouquets of flowers, sympathy cards, phone calls and texts, and even a few home visits from the WAGs at the club. There was a real outpouring of love – so many people genuinely cared about us.

However, as much as I really appreciated the support from our loved ones, it didn't make me feel any better inside. It didn't take the emptiness, disappointment or grief away. It didn't stop me feeling a deep, gut-wrenching sadness whenever I saw a baby or a pregnant woman.

Chapter Nine

*A*t was only when I began to read online and talk to others that I realized how common miscarriages are. I learned the astonishing fact that one in four pregnancies fail. I took some comfort in this, as I had honestly blamed myself for losing the baby. I was convinced that I must have done something wrong. I questioned whether I had eaten the wrong foods, been too stressed, and had even started wondering if it had happened because I'd had my hair dyed the week before I miscarried. It took me a long time to realize that Nature can take circumstances out of our hands, and that sometimes, things just aren't meant to be . . .

I'd stopped going to the gym when I found out I was pregnant, so when the dark clouds of post-miscarriage depression began to disperse, I renewed my membership and returned to the treadmill. I also hauled myself out to some WAG coffee mornings and focused on project-managing some fundraising events for the charity I was associated with. Additionally, I took it upon myself to participate in a *lot* of shopping – for medicinal purposes, of course.

With such concerted efforts to stop feeling sorry for myself and copious amounts of support from my man, slowly life returned to normal – apart from our sex life, that is. If libidos have rankings out of ten, then mine had dropped from an 8.5 to a frosty 0. I felt as if my lady bits were damaged goods in some way, and at the back of my mind I feared getting pregnant again.

However, time played its healing role and after a few months of drought in the bedroom, the rainy season arrived and my libido started to rise. As you can imagine, my husband was most relieved. Sex was so much better as we weren't consciously trying to conceive, just enjoying each other again. And happily, five months after I had miscarried, I discovered I was pregnant again.

My husband was in the games room when I found out. We've always had a games room in every house we've ever lived in, with a pool table, juke box, bar, large leather gaming chairs and – the *pièce de résistance* for my husband – an eighty-four-inch plasma TV with various games consoles attached to it. This was his domain: a ridiculous luxury as it only served his needs when he was in man-child mode. Now it serves a real purpose for our children.

That day my husband was acting like a child and playing some pathetic war game on his Xbox. His eyes were locked on the screen and he was jumping up and down in his chair, like he had some sort of debilitating disorder, while shouting into his headset microphone to a team-mate in the USA. He was and is an absolute nightmare when he plays his Xbox; it hypnotizes him and he can't register anything outside the screen.

I grabbed a roll of sticky tape, boldly walked in front of the television, completely blocking my husband's view, and stuck the pregnancy test to the centre of the screen. At first, he angrily waved me out of the way, but when I stepped out of his line of vision the expression on his face was priceless.

'Really?' he questioned.

He ripped off the headset and threw the controller down, raced towards me, picked me up and spun around until we were both dizzy.

During my first pregnancy MILF WAG had told me about a private doctor who had delivered all four of her children and the offspring of many other WAGs, including some famous names. Apparently he was expensive, no shock there, but according to MILF WAG it was money well spent since his reputation was second to none, the care he gave was top quality and he was discreet. He was something of a guarded secret in WAGdom, MILF WAG told me: his details were only passed on to a WAG if she was considered 'worthy' of such a genius physician. It seemed that MILF WAG didn't consider me riff-raff!

At first, the doctor's secretary rebuffed my requests for an appointment with curtly spoken one-liners such as 'His patient list is full' and 'He couldn't possibly see anyone at such short notice.' So I did something I detested doing then and still detest now: I name-dropped. First I mentioned that the doctor had been recommended to me by my 'good friend' MILF WAG. Upon hearing this, the secretary's tone became much warmer, if not a little flustered. She then tentatively asked for my full name, which I gave her. I have to confess, I emphasized my surname a little more than I usually would.

After a substantial pause and a little comedic throat-clearing, the secretary told me in a kindly voice that she would call me back ASAP. Ten minutes later, my phone rang and I was booked in to see Super Doc the next day at three o'clock.

When Super Doc confidently strolled into the room at the clinic, blood rushed into my cheeks and I could barely look him in the eye when he thrust his hand out to be shaken. He was drop-dead gorgeous. I wished I'd been warned: I'd have dressed in a much more outrageous outfit! He was in his late thirties, easily over six feet tall, tanned, and through the cut of his Versace suit, I could tell that he had a hot body. It gripped and sculpted him in all the right places. His face was chiselled yet kind, with a strong jaw, full lips, a straight, lightly freckled nose and piercing blue eyes. I made notes. He even smelled divine. I melted. No wonder the WAGs keep him a closely guarded secret, I thought.

My husband rolled his eyes. He could tell I fancied Super Doc. It was quite obvious because my face had turned bright red and I was batting my eyelashes like a camel in a sandstorm. He took it all in good part, though, as he usually does when he knows I find someone attractive, which is often, given the circles we move in.

Super Doc decided to scan me there and then to establish how many weeks pregnant I was. He warned us that it might be too early to see anything significant but that there was also the option of having an internal scan, which would offer more clarity. That was probably the moment at which my husband began to wonder about how much the treatment was going to cost. We have been stung many a time for overpriced goods and services. However, the chance of having a scan at this stage was priceless in my book, if only for peace of mind. I didn't like the sound of the internal one, though.

I lay down on the treatment bed next to the Sonograph machine. The doctor then proceeded to squirt warm gel over my stomach and move the probe over it, pushing it gently into my skin and circumnavigating the entirety of my lower abdomen. I felt immensely anxious at what he would find in my womb, still unconvinced that this pregnancy was real – yet even through my nerves I could still appreciate Super Doc's sexiness!

While he had warned us that there might be nothing to see, there on the screen was a teeny baby. I could just about identify its head, torso and limbs. When I focused closer on the screen I could see something flickering in the chest area. It was the baby's heart beating. My husband and I looked at each other with tears in our eyes and smiles on our lips. We were just so happy. Super Doc seemed quite pleased too, and after a few more moments of general 'foetal checks', he confirmed that I was well and truly pregnant, eleven weeks. I was absolutely elated.

At the next home game, I couldn't help but tell each and every WAG my good news. They were delighted for us, including the two other childless WAGs, and I was instantly welcomed into the Mummy WAGs group. They swooped in and fired questions at me.

'Did your mother have stretch-marks?'

'What pushchair will you buy?'

'Will you book a caesarean?'

They were intrusive, but their interest flattered me and, for that moment at least, I felt proud to be one of them.

It transpired that Super Doc had delivered most of their babies. I wondered whether some of the Mummy WAGs' second and third births had been a means to get in front of the doc with their legs open again! There was certainly agreement that just the sight of Super Doc eased a difficult pregnancy. I couldn't help but cast a thought to Super Doc's wife. I wondered if she felt any jealousy at her husband's clientele, whether their over-dinner conversations went anywhere along the lines of 'Which WAG's vagina have you been looking up today, then?'

Thankfully, the weeks of my pregnancy passed smoothly, and once I arrived at week twenty my stomach started to expand and harden. I had been desperate to have a 'bump' to show off, to draw people's attention, so initially I welcomed it. Until I began to bloat. I rapidly piled on the pounds and soon outgrew every article of clothing I owned. At twenty-six weeks my wardrobe was literally the entire collection of Manchester's flagship Topshop store's maternity range. My nose morphed into someone else's and my ankles turned into 'cankles': there was no discernible difference between my calf and the bone that held my foot in place. Put simply, I got fat. I ate for two, craving doughnuts and steak, and generally slobbed out because I was so scared that doing too much would jeopardize the pregnancy. However, for the first time in my life I didn't care about my weight or what I looked like.

I knew many WAGS who'd put themselves under great pressure not to gain excess weight in pregnancy. Some had personal trainers for the full forty weeks, some became yoga addicts, and some still went to the gym as normal and lifted heavy weights or ran miles on the treadmill, all in the hope of regaining their pre-pregnancy figure as soon as their baby was born. Such torture worked for some WAGs. I knew some who actually put on their size-six jeans on the day after giving birth.

There was no hope of that for me. In total I put on a whopping four and a half stone, and while I knew that once the baby had arrived I would be back into obsessive weight-loss, I allowed myself to relax until that moment came. The baby's safety was my priority.

I avoided all WAG outings and high-profile events. Even though I was proud to be pregnant, I didn't want to give the paps the satisfaction of a Fat WAG picture. Also, the 'what if things go wrong' question never left my mind. Consequently, I turned down all the media approaches made to us for our photographs. I didn't want my pregnancy to become a commodity and, to be honest, I absolutely hate those ridiculous pictures of pregnant celebrities. Most images are staged and touched up in an effort to sell a range of overpriced maternity clothes by a designer who is in bed with the magazine owners.

Three days before my baby was due, my waters broke. I had just hauled myself into bed, after a nice long bath, and as I was wiggling around in a vain attempt to get comfortable, I felt a warm sensation between my legs. I remember feeling surprised and lying dead-still, questioning if I had accidentally let go of my bladder, but when I squeezed the relevant muscles to stop the flow, it didn't stop. In fact, it began to feel like liquid gushing out of me. I lay there saturating the bed sheets, frozen in confusion, before the reality of the situation sank into my consciousness: I was going into labour.

My adrenalin surged and my heart began to pound. Then my husband appeared at the bedside, having just brushed his teeth. I stared at him open-mouthed. He returned my look with a quizzical one of his own before pulling back the covers to reveal my sodden nightgown and the spreading damp beneath me. Quite unromantically he said, 'Have you pissed yourself?' I shook my head slowly from side to side yet kept my eyes fixed on his face to watch the realization creep over him.

'Er . . . have we g-got to go to the hospital?' he stuttered.

I slowly nodded.

Then the first intense contraction came. It felt like all

the muscles in my womb were being stimulated by some sort of paralysing electrical current. It forced me to curl up into a ball and moan in pain but only lasted for a few seconds. There wasn't too much time for recovery: no sooner had I uncurled my heavy pregnant body and my husband helped me to stand up than another contraction arrived, slightly more intense than the first.

Despite the contractions becoming more frequent and agonizing, I managed to get dressed, with my husband's help, then into the car and to the hospital without any other fuss. I didn't manage to get hold of Super Doc, though. In between waves of pain and bouts of panic at my husband's erratic driving, I frantically rang his secretary, who consequently paged him, but to no avail. We were extremely anxious at not being able to get hold of him: he had kept us cool, calm and collected throughout the pregnancy and we were relying on him to do the same through the birth.

When we arrived at the hospital, the contractions were so strong that my husband and a nurse had to help me out of the car and transport me to the labour ward by wheelchair. In true pain-ridden woman-in-labour style, I rather loudly informed my husband that I didn't 'give a fuck who delivered this baby'. I just wanted it out . . . and safely.

That was my final lucid recollection of the events to follow: everything else passed in a blur of agony, until the moment of giving birth. I vaguely recall asking for pain relief and being refused because I was 'too far gone', then thinking that I couldn't possibly cope any longer, that the pain might actually kill me, it was so intense.

As soon as that point arrived, my body took over and began to do the work for me. I instinctively began pushing at the same time as the midwife told me to, and I could feel that each contraction was finally resulting in the baby moving down the birth canal, although it felt less like a baby and more like a bowling ball trying to make its way out of my bowels. I gritted my teeth and used every last bit of strength I had to push away the pain of each contraction.

During that stage I remember opening my eyes only once and seeing my husband standing at my side with a rather distressed expression on his face. My leg was rested against his thigh and he was looking from my face to my private parts as if they were playing a tennis match with each other, his eyes wide with concern.

After what seemed like only few pushes, which I later learned to have been an hour's worth, I felt the baby's head crowning. That moment was horrific on the pain scale: it felt like someone had taken a red-hot knife to my lady bits and sliced them in two. I think that was the moment when I screamed, '*Fuuuuuuck!*'

Then the next and final push came and our baby arrived, crying on its first breath of air.

Before any weighing or washing, my baby was placed in my arms, against my chest, and I fell, there and then, into a deeper love than I had ever known existed. The surges of pain I had felt were replaced with rushes of endorphins. As I gazed into the beautiful, perfect, scrunched-up face of our baby, my brain temporarily erased my body's aches of labour. My husband cried and cut the umbilical cord as I softly kissed my baby's face. We almost forgot to check the sex since we were so lost in the moment of our off-spring's safe arrival! It was quite literally the happiest moment of my, of our, life. Finally, our family felt complete.

My husband and I spent the first two days after the birth doting on our child. We spent hours staring at the tiny face before us, trying to identify if our child had my nose or his eyes, trying to imagine what the little person would look like, or be like, when grown. We were helplessly infatuated with our wonderful little creation and both admitted to feeling that life could not get any better.

On the third day the baby blues arrived, along with my milk. I woke up in the early hours of the morning to find that my breasts had swelled to the size of small honeydew melons. They ached with a sore heaviness and the skin was stretched so tightly across them that it felt like it might tear. I had two giant, painful zits on my chest that desperately needed to be popped.

I quietly eased myself out of bed, shuffled into our en-suite bathroom, leaned over the sink and tried to milk myself! In an attempt to start the flow I squeezed my breasts and pulled at my nipples until they hurt more than I could bear. No milk came. I then filled the sink almost to the brim with warm water and dunked in my tender red mammary glands, to some light relief but still no milk. All the built-up emotions and exhaustion of the last few days came spewing out of me: I cried like a baby, then my baby cried like a baby, and then my husband woke up. His amusement at finding me with my boobs in the sink was not well received!

Chapter Ten

The realities of parenthood had arrived. To make matters worse, my husband transferred to a different club in the first few weeks of our baby's life, and the commute took almost two hours. With his rigorous training and match schedule, he was rarely at home. And when he wanted to spend time with us I would often be catching up on sleep or chores, and was beginning to feel resentful that he wasn't helping me more. I was doing everything for our baby. Sometimes a week would pass without my husband even changing a nappy.

I also assumed the baby night-shift, which left me immensely sleep deprived. The physical demands on a footballer are great, and sleep is a valuable commodity; the gaffer would not accept tiredness as an excuse for poor performance, therefore *I* was on baby-duty 24/7. I found the lack of sleep extremely tough, especially as on average our baby slept for only two hours straight at any time.

As for babysitters, the only person I trusted, aside from my husband, was my mother, but she lived hundreds of miles away. When we did plan a rare night out, and book in my parents either at their house or ours, I would either be called back early because our bambino wouldn't settle or I would be too tired to stay out for more than a couple of hours. Our social life and time together as a couple became almost non-existent.

I acknowledge that most parents experience the same difficulties we had in those early days of parenthood, and I recognize that it is quite normal for the woman to assume the majority of the childcare role. I don't feel sorry for myself because of it, and I don't seek sympathy. I have empathy with all first-time mothers and the sacrifices they have to make. I could have made my life much easier. It wasn't as though we couldn't afford extra help in the form of a nanny or au pair. Many of my WAG friends paid for childcare, and quite a few had live-in help.

A WAG I know hired a night nanny, who was employed to be on duty every night of the week to do the baby's night-feeds and wake-ups while the WAG slept peacefully in her bed. The nanny was very experienced, in her late fifties, and had worked in assisting babies' sleep routines her whole life: a real-life 'baby whisperer'. As soon as her work was done, she moved on to her next family, just like Mary Poppins left Jane and Michael when the wind changed. Her service came at a great price, of course, a whopping £1,000 a week in fact.

Many WAGs hired Filipinas via an agency in London, paid them roughly £1,000 a month to live with them and do whatever was needed to make their lives easier. One WAG I know, after the birth of her first child, employed one woman to cook, another to clean, another to look after her child and a man to be her driver-cum-gardener. While I thought she was relinquishing her parental duties a little too easily, she was at least kind to the people she employed. That could not be said of all the WAGs I knew.

Once I went to a WAG's house for a coffee morning and was appalled at the manner in which she spoke to her young Filipina nanny. She was derogatory, rude, patronizing and aggressive to the woman, who was no more than twenty-two, simply because she didn't understand a few instructions. There was an obvious language and cultural barrier between the two, but the WAG couldn't see anything beyond the hired-help's inability to follow 'simple instructions'. It was quite upsetting to witness, and I attempted to reprimand her for her terrible behaviour but it got me nowhere. Well, it got me home a little earlier than expected and there was one less Christmas card to send.

Although the burdens of motherhood could have been significantly lessened if I'd had someone to help with childcare, the concept did not, and does not, sit well with me. I didn't put my babies into nursery and I didn't have a nanny. I wanted to be their primary carer, and since I didn't work, I felt it was my obligation as a mother to raise them with my own hands.

Bloody-minded, I refused all paid childcare assistance and struggled on. The monotonous and tiring routines involved in caring for a young baby were difficult. I began to get depressed and started to comfort-eat. Once again I felt desperately lonely and longed to live nearer to my loved ones. I began to resent my husband for the way his life had remained the same.

Our baby was perfectly content but I wasn't. I was a wreck. I would cry every day and cause arguments with my husband at every opportunity. I needed support but I couldn't have turned to the WAGs as they were neither trustworthy nor empathetic. If I had shown them the cracks in my mental state, news would have spread like wildfire that I couldn't cope with being a mum. I didn't want to worry my mother or best friends, and I didn't want to confess to my health visitor for fear that word would leak to the media. I even lied on the post-natal depression test, which is given to all new mothers, so forfeited any clinical help.

My husband couldn't comprehend what I was going through either. As far as he was concerned, I was living in an amazing house, driving around in a car that most people would dream of owning and had the beautiful baby we had so desperately wanted. On paper my life looked perfect. But I felt broken and alone, and I began to believe that I was an awful parent.

When our baby reached four months old, I read a book on depression and recognized my feelings in the symptoms. I realized I needed to take action to sort myself out. I had never felt so low before, and it didn't seem as if the negativity would subside on its own. I reckoned that my body was another source of my blues: I was still heavier than I had ever been. The time had arrived to lose weight and get fit.

After I had plucked up the courage to confide to my husband the extent to how down I was feeling, he played a major role in helping me to see things positively. It's quite unbelievable how mentally strong my husband is. Perhaps it's the years of sports psychology he's been exposed to. Whatever it is, he doesn't let anything bring him down, not even illness. A huge part of his preparation for a game involves mental rehearsal and visualization, where he imagines himself in positive situations on the pitch and believes they can happen. He helped me employ these techniques in my life; we spent hours talking through how I wanted life to be, and thus how to visualize it actually happening. With his help, I began to see the new me and I resolved I was going to 'man the hell up'.

It may be controversial to admit, but the first thing I did was to stop breast-feeding. To be honest, I hated it. I'd found it painful and could barely keep up with our baby's milk demands; it was making me physically and emotionally exhausted. I was nervous to make the switch to bottle-feeding, but on the first night of the change it seemed as if a magic wand had been waved over my baby: I got five hours of solid sleep.

I then began to leave the baby with my husband most days after his football training sessions in order to go to the gym. It may seem crazy that before then I hadn't regularly left the baby in the charge of its father but that in itself was a manifestation of the control and anxiety issues I had developed. Each time I returned from the gym he reported a better experience of father-hood. Then I found it easier to be on my own. I worried less and our baby became more settled without me.

As my weight dropped, my sleep increased and our baby spent more time with my husband, my mood improved. I resumed calorie counting and weighing myself, but to me, that only proved I was getting back to normal. If I could ever be referred to as normal, that is.

Slowly but surely I began to realize that my dream of being a mother like MILF WAG was not achievable: what she showed on the surface was probably not how she felt or acted underneath. I rationalized that parent-hood is tough and, regardless of how it looks to others, or how many people you can hire to do things for you, there's no escaping the physical, mental and emotional toll a new baby brings. I decided I would be the best parent I could, and that would be good enough. I loved my baby and my husband more than words could describe, and I was starting to like myself again. That was enough to build on, and this baby would not be our only child.

I'm very thankful that there are no official pictures on the Internet of the pregnant me. However, my husband and I did allow a certain broadsheet newspaper to publish pictures of our new-born baby. We released them retrospectively as part of my contribution to an article that attempted to dispel the rumour that wealthy and/or famous women are 'too posh to push'. I'm shocked at how many WAGs and other women choose to have Caesareans for personal not medical reasons.

One WAG I know had a general anaesthetic so that she wouldn't witness anything to do with the birth of her child: she was put to sleep pregnant and woke up with her baby in a cot beside her bed. She claimed that a natural birth would traumatize her, not that she'd been through one before, and that she didn't want to risk her 'perfectly pretty and tight vagina' being mutilated by a baby's head.

I'm unsure whether my vagina looks like it's designer or faulty goods, but I know one thing for sure: I'd put my baby's well-being over what any part of me looked like. The photographs I have of my lard-ass pregnant self prove that . . . irrefutably.

To say that my days drastically changed with the arrival of my children is the understatement of the century. However, I did get a new deal. WAG Deal Number Three consisted of £7,000 being put into my bank account on the first day of every month. It seemed an enormous amount, but I didn't refuse it. He wouldn't have allowed me to anyway. My man was on more money than he'd ever earned before.

He figured that I would have to spend a lot on the children, with regard to their clothes, nappies, toys and food, so he wanted to give me a 'top-up', as he put it. In fact, I hardly touched the money. It all built up in my bank account. I wasn't purposely saving it: I simply didn't have the opportunity to spend it. I was no longer a member of the opulent leisure club as we had moved away from it, and instead of spending hours in the gym, I spent all the hours of the day with our children . . . and cleaning.

My days became centred on my kids; my husband came second and I came last . . . after our dogs. I didn't have time for any primping and preening, and some days I barely had the chance to shower. My hair was always greasy, my nails were chipped and often I didn't get out of my pyjamas until well into the afternoon. The only time I had the opportunity to visit a beauty salon was when I went home to visit my family and friends and my mum gave me some me-time. I timed it so that I went home every six weeks in order to visit the hairdresser and get my roots done.

Once parenthood arrived I very rarely met my WAG friends in swanky restaurants. Lunch out became a generic shrink-wrapped panini from the local soft-play centre; a reward for having scrambled through the plastic shitty-nappy-smelling tunnels after our beloved offspring. When I took my kids out to be entertained, if I wasn't in a play centre I was sitting with my legs crossed singing nursery rhymes and shaking a tambourine at a baby group.

Shopping in Selfridges was off the cards, for now at least, so when I became a parent I also became an online shopper. I always wondered whether the kids I saw in shops who sat calmly in their buggies while their mothers looked through an entire rail of clothing had been drugged. Or whether the mother had kept them up all night just to ensure that they'd be too exhausted to perform the usual shop tantrum.

No matter how tired my kids were, if I were to put either of them into anything that restrained them, they would lash out and have a tantrum. Even if I'd got them to sleep, then carried them into a buggy and strapped them in, at the 'click' sound of the seatbelt they'd wake up and scream. They hated to be restrained in a pushchair and any attempts I made at taking them shopping always ended up with me giving up and storming out of the shop in desperation to get home. No amount of toys, lollipops, doughnuts or ice creams could bribe them to be quiet and still so that Mummy could spend some money.

Net-a-porter became my new best friend. I got just as much pleasure from the arrival of their black shiny boxes as I did walking out of Selfridges swinging a little yellow bag.

Another luxury that ended when the children arrived was dining out. They were so close in age that if one of them decided to throw food, they all would, or if one of them decided to scream and wail or become impatient, the others would follow suit. Going to a restaurant became far more hassle than it was worth.

I became our household's galley-slave. I made a nourishing dinner every day and always ensured we ate fresh fruit and vegetables. I perfected many of my mum's dishes and spent big chunks of my time cooking for my family. I loved the sense of fulfilment I got from watching my kids sit and eat my creations, hoovering up the vegetables shaped as dinosaurs on their plates.

I wouldn't miss my children's precious moments for the world. I was once offered the opportunity to present a television series that had to be recorded in another country far away. It was billed for a prime-time slot, paid extremely well, and the exposure from it would have been great for my career. The producers required me to spend three to five weeks there. Many of my loved ones were encouraging me to accept the opportunity, but at the time, my eldest child was only six months old, so I turned it down. In all honesty, I can't imagine being away from my children for more than three days, let alone three weeks. My husband has questioned me on what I'll do if and when my eldest child decides to go away to university. He's insinuated that I won't be able to cope. I will. I'll move the family to whichever university my child wants to go to. We're used to relocating . . .

I will literally do anything for my children if it means aiding their happiness and well-being. I admit that our children are spoiled. They have the best of the best. They've never wanted for anything. They have no idea what it's like to dream about owning something, or any experience of saving their pocket money to buy something. If they want it, they get it. I cannot resist buying them things I know they would like. Their wardrobes are bursting with clothes and their bedrooms are teeming with toys. They have always lived in large homes with cinemas, gyms and swimming pools.

We lavish our children with luxuries not because we are weak parents or because we want to buy their affections. We do it because we love them. Quite simply, my husband and I have both adopted the stance that if we can provide what they want, then we will. We donate money to charity, pay huge bills every month and make sure our parents live comfortably, so we feel justified in spending money on our children. But our children do not act like spoiled brats. I hope they never will.

I have never feared my children becoming materialistic because I had a similar upbringing to them, and I am not. What I do fear is the paparazzi and the media. My husband and I try to protect our children as best we can from the press intrusion on our lives. When we socialize as a family we keep a low profile and we tend not to accept invitations to family film premières or glitzy charity events. We do not dine with our children in celebrity hang-outs and we don't generally accept offers from famous friends to spend time with them in public places: we feel such behaviour would almost be asking for press attention.

We do allow our children to view positive exposure in the media, such as my husband playing football or appearing on *A Question of Sport*, or me being interviewed about the charity I represent: we believe that our children should be aware that we are in the public eye. It's a huge part of our life. However, we want them to see the positives of our footballer and WAG stereotype. They will see the negatives later, when they grow up and Google our names, but hopefully by then they will be old and wise enough to know the facts from the fiction.

Chapter Eleven

The press holds a double-edged sword for WAGs. The elaborate spreads in glossy magazines raise media profiles and feed egos – and sometimes families – while the footballer scandals on the front pages of tabloids feed gossip hounds and divorce lawyers. The paparazzi are the lifeblood and poison of the celebrity world. They have torn many WAGdom relationships apart.

My own marital bliss nearly died a death because of a well-placed pap, a carefully engineered photograph and the decision of a Sunday newspaper to go to print. That particular autumn Sunday was glorious. As I woke to the sun beaming through the gap between our heavy velvet curtains and to my husband's warm sleeping body wrapped around mine, I would never have guessed what devastation lay ahead. Ironically, I vividly remember lying in bed for a little longer that morning, revelling in the peace and thinking about how lucky I was to have such a life.

We lived in a large mansion in an exclusive area up north. The house was a listed building, with three floors, situated at the end of a long, winding driveway.

It had an exquisite stone exterior that was made all the more beautiful by a tangle of ivy and wisteria. Our lawns were manicured, we had an orchard of fruit trees, a tennis court and a hot tub that was permanently bubbling on the garden terrace. The kitchen was enormous, fitted out with all the latest mod-cons and an Italian marble dining-table that could seat eighteen.

Our home boasted six bedrooms, spread over two floors, and each room of the house was glamorously decorated on the advice of an 'interior designer to the stars'. Most of them were complete with a huge widescreen television. We had a cinema room, a games room with neon bar, a 'posh lounge' and a 'slobs' lounge', and my husband and I each had our own dressing-room. In case you were wondering, he has more clothes than I do.

Also, to some of my school-friends' amusement, we did have large blown-up canvas pictures of the two of us in loving embraces displayed on walls around the house. That's just standard decor for a footballer and a WAG's home.

While I'm not shallow and do not rate possessions over people, I am a home bird and I loved that house. I loved my husband more, though. I had loved and trusted him since I was eighteen. We were a young and healthy married couple, with no real worries.

Life felt sweet on that Sunday morning. Also, I felt unusually physically good, too. My husband and I had opted for a romantic meal the night before, instead of the usual Saturday night piss-up, and we'd gone to bed early. So I was clear-headed and relaxed. I began to make a mental list of how I would ensure that the day was a productive one. Then, as I do every morning, I instinctively reached for my phone. I registered that it was seven forty-five and that I had a text from my best friend.

It's funny how so many seemingly unimportant details can be recalled from when tragedy strikes. I can't tell you the exact minute I woke up today but the details of that day are etched in my mind for ever.

The text read: 'Are you OK? Have you seen the paper? Call me . . . please . . . I'm worried about you.'

My heart sank. Then adrenalin surged through me. Instantly I knew what that text meant. Let's face it: it wouldn't have taken a genius to guess.

As my partner remained peacefully sleeping in our marital bed, I jumped up, threw on some clothes, then dashed out of the house and along our winding driveway. I forgot my shoes but, as it turned out, that mistake was fortuitous.

When I reached the electric gates to our property, I heard a low chattering of voices. I stopped, pressed my head against the thick wood and listened. They were male. I bent down, lowered myself onto my hands and knees and peered through the two-centimetre gap between the gate and the Tarmac. I saw shoes shuffling, lots of shoes . . .

The paps were already on the story, whatever it was, and they were waiting to pounce, like vultures circling a dying wildebeest. However, due to my barefooted sprint, they hadn't heard me coming. Result.

Holding my breath, I turned on my heels and ran back up the driveway, to the secret exit used only in such emergencies. It was actually an informal pathway through the bracken, thorns and bushes that separated our property from next door. Our neighbours were fantastic: they were a retired couple in their seventies who had, on a few occasions, witnessed my husband and me darting through their gardens to avoid being papped outside our gates. They would always wave us on our way with that wistful those-crazy-kids look on their faces, as if we were playing hide-and-seek.

I didn't even consider whether they would mind me trespassing on that Sunday morning so I navigated through the undergrowth and sprinted through the neighbouring landscaped rear gardens to the suburban back road in the direction of the local corner shop. The presence of the paps had not put me off my mission: I needed to know immediately if my gut instinct was right. Unfortunately, as soon as the newspaper stand came into view, my suspicions were confirmed. I snatched up the well-known Sunday tabloid and darted to the counter.

As I paid the shopkeeper, I was shaking so much that my teeth were chattering and tears were already pricking my eyes. The shopkeeper probably thought I was another victim of a heavy Saturday night out, given my smudged mascara, and I croaked, 'Thank you.' I made a note to self: 'Thank God you avoided the paps, you look a bloody state. Same back route home.'

As soon as I left the shop, I took a deep breath and

looked at the front page; at the large, bold headline and the picture of my husband in his football kit. I read the few words boxed off underneath: 'Married Premiership footballer in steamy romp with ugly, desperate nineteen-year-old whore . . .' OK, it didn't quite say that, but that's the edited version I choose to remember.

As my legs walked me home on autopilot (via the back route), I turned to the double-page spread that detailed how my husband had allegedly cheated on me. The pictures were horrendous, disgusting, vile . . . but a total cliché.

My husband could be seen seated on a leather bench in a nightclub, wearing the Armani shirt I'd given him the previous Christmas and looking beyond wasted. His hair was dishevelled – a sure sign of inebriation: his hair is never otherwise out of place – he was glowing with sweat and, on a table in front of him, sat an enormous champagne bucket flanked by a high stack of empty glasses tipping to one side like the Leaning Tower of Pissedness. There was no shock about that sight. That was the picture almost every Saturday night.

The shock came in the form of his apparent drinking companion. A girl was draped over him, to his right, if I remember. She had long, dark hair, her face was caked in make-up, her large boobs were falling out of her tiny black halter-neck top and her slutty white-hot-pants-clad legs were angled over my man's thighs.

She looked cheap and nasty – a right tart, as my mother would say. The expression on her face added insult to injury. She looked drunk yet smug, in a way that suggested the cat had got the cream. I felt so angry. If she had bumped into me at that moment, I don't know what I would've done. However, at that point, I already had an idea of what I wanted to do to my husband. Regardless of what the truth was, I am a great believer in the saying that 'There's no smoke without fire.' And in my mind, his arse was toast.

I had arrived home before I had even got to read the story. Having avoided the waiting paps twice now, I shut the front door behind me. I tiptoed through the hall and into the kitchen, closing all the curtains en route. I was as quiet as a mouse as I didn't want to wake my husband: I wanted to read the paper in my own time and get my head around the allegations. In my mind, I was praying over and over, Please, God, let this story be made up. Please, please, please . . .

I spread the paper on our kitchen table, where my husband and I shared every home-cooked meal together, and began to read the words that could've ended those shared dinners and all that I knew as my life. My tears dropped on to the pages, smudging the ink and making the paper soggy. The girl claimed that my husband had approached her in a nightclub and invited her into the VIP area with him and his team-mates, where he'd spent the night flirting excessively and supplying her with endless amounts of champagne.

She said he had kissed her 'passionately' in the club, in full view of everyone, then taken her back to his hotel room, in which they'd had sex three times. She went into all sorts of details: how he undressed her, the sex positions, the grunts and moans he made. I began to gag. She was quoted as saying that she had left my husband at six in the morning after they'd met and that she didn't realize who he was until later on that day when she saw him in a match report in a newspaper.

'Bullshit!' I said.

I knew, at least, that that line was a total and utter lie. Not just because of what I assumed her intentions were but because, when my husband is drunk, he cannot help but tell the world what he does for a living. He's not necessarily boastful but he is beyond proud to be a footballer. She definitely knew who he was.

When I had finished reading, questions began racing through my mind. What had he done with this bitch? Why is this happening to me? What the hell are my parents going to say? Each question brought its own piercing migraine-like pain. And then the vomit I'd been holding down for so long made an appearance. I ran to the kitchen sink and threw up, sobbing between retches.

I stared into my vomit, splashed my face with cold water and my attitude changed. I felt purged of my upset and renewed with a different emotion. I was overwhelmed with anger. How dare he do this to me? I thought. Time to confront the bastard.

My adrenalin surged once more as I ran, paper in hand, up the stairs to our bedroom. I kicked the bedroom door open so it noisily smashed into the wall, cracking the plaster, and my husband's head instantly shot up from the pillow. For added drama, I picked up my dressing-table chair and hurled it at his head. It missed – lucky for him, unlucky for our bedside lamp.

'What the fuck? What the fuck?' were the only words he could manage as I climbed onto the bed, like a woman possessed, to begin, with all my might, whacking him with the newspaper. The sobbing returned as I screamed, 'You fucking bastard!' over and over again.

He jumped out of bed, away from my newspaper battering, with a look on his face of complete confusion. I could see him quickly registering the mental equation: furious wife + newspaper weapon = someone's sold a story on me. I almost heard his brain click when he realized the reality of the situation.

'What does it say? I've done nothing wrong,' he kept saying. I threw the paper at him and looked at him with the most scornful expression I could manage. At that moment, I had an urge to pack my bags and go back to my parents' house, to the comforts of my uncomplicated childhood, to leave him and his protests for ever. In that fleeting moment, it felt like running away would solve everything.

However, my second thought was to stay. I convinced myself that I would be able to tell if he was guilty simply by watching his reactions as he read the story. He slumped onto the bed and began to read. As his eyes scanned the words, his brow furrowed and his face contorted between expressions of pain, anger, dismay and bewilderment.

When he stopped reading, he looked up at me and I began to cry again. The realization had dawned on me that millions of people read that Sunday tabloid; the humiliating thought of everyone reading the story over their morning coffee, laughing and tutting about another footballer cheating – my man cheating – was gut-wrenching.

My husband was initially speechless. He continued to stare at me and shook his head, perhaps in embarrassment, disbelief or devastation. Or a mixture of them all. It was obvious that he was just as shocked as I was. When he spoke, it was to deny the story: 'I didn't do it! I swear to you! I didn't do it!'

Then he became angry. Seething. I stood and watched the same emotions that I had felt unfurl in him. He was livid. 'Some bitch I've never met has hurt my family, my reputation, my wife,' he shouted. I believe his reaction was an honest one. I did not for one minute think he was acting. There certainly was not the time or privacy to script a response. Also, he's always been a rubbish liar. Then I ordered him to talk. He told me the events of that night in as much detail as he could recall. I asked question after question. He cried, I cried.

After what felt like hours, I told him to stay out of my way while I cooled down and took in everything he had said. I was unusually calm, like the eye of a storm. I went back to the kitchen table and pored over all of the information I now had. It was then that I started to see the cracks in the story. Yes, my partner had been in the specified nightclub that evening, but he had come home to me that night. There was no hotel stay. Also, there could have been no six a.m. goodbye – he had arrived home before three since we have an agreement that neither of us can arrive home later than three if one of us has work to do the next day.

There was no other photographic evidence, either. Surely, I reasoned, if they had spent the night together in full view of everyone, and there was a sneaky pap in the building, there would have been more photos. More photos mean more money for whoever's selling the story.

Then, after my own rationalizing of the events, I made a few telephone calls to his team-mates. I'd already had a barrage of texts from his friends, saying things such as 'It's all bollocks' or 'We were with him that night and it's not true' arrive on my mobile before I'd even confronted my husband. So I called the relevant parties and tried my best with all the reverse psychology or double-bluffing tactics I could think of. But all their stories added up. They all fitted perfectly with my husband's, not the tart's, account of the evening.

So I concluded, while there's no smoke without fire, the fire in this instance was my husband's idiotic, drunken behaviour. I believe he got totally wasted on booze, went into show-off mode in the club, got a few girls into the VIP section to feed the boys' egos and was, unfortunately, snapped in a premeditated pose by someone wanting to cash in. The girl probably exchanged details with the lurking pap, who then gave her an insight into the pay-offs for an explosive kiss-and-tell and, hey presto, a money-making story was born.

I felt – and still feel – sure that my interpretation of the facts was correct, or at least somewhere near to the truth. However, it didn't make up for the fact that my husband had acted like a complete and utter twat. To get absolutely shit-faced drunk, so much so that he had no recollection of a strange woman draping herself over him for photographs, makes a footballer more than vulnerable. It puts their families and careers on the line, too. The press, the paps, the kiss-and-tell-hopefuls: they just want to make a fast buck, and a drunk footballer is a prime target. Pay day all-round.

For the remainder of that awful Sunday, I was like a tornado ripping through our house. I shouted and cried, smashed things and slammed doors until I was too exhausted to go over it again. The curtains remained closed all day. Some of the paps had taken to climbing up our gate in the hope of getting that elusive broken-marriage picture. We called the police but, as it turned out, there's not much they can do to stop people standing on a pavement.

My husband and I went to bed that evening two different people. He had realized the sad realities of being a public figure and I had changed from his trusting wife to a wife with doubt. No matter what anyone says, when you are faced with a cheating scandal in your relationship, it damages the trust you have for your partner, even if just a tiny bit.

It damages the trust others have for them, too. I

think, in some ways, they remain a suspect for ever. Of all the people I spoke to on the day the scandal hit, no matter how many times someone said to me, 'It'll be tomorrow's fish and chip paper', I knew the story would never be forgotten and that someone, somewhere, would think I was a fool for believing him or that he was a lying, cheating rat. He hated this prospect, too.

Although, let's face it, it's never as bad for the man at the centre of a scandal, especially a footballer: it was nothing too out of the ordinary for his working environment. In the aftermath of the story breaking, he was certainly far from being outcast at the training ground. Most of the other footballers were really sympathetic towards him, as many of them had been there that fateful night as witnesses, and some had been through such an experience themselves. The trouble is, not all of their experiences were fabricated ones.

For the record, if I had seen any incriminating pictures of my husband which could have backed up the girl's story, I would have been gone in a flash. Our marriage would have been over, without a doubt. In that instance, I would have had solid evidence, and I know I wouldn't have been able to get over that sort of devastation. Also, I'm no mug. I don't suffer fools and I don't allow anyone, husband included, to take the piss out of me.

My husband and I thought about suing the paper that first printed the scandal – its sister papers followed suit over the following few days so a reduced version of the original article appeared in at least three other tabloids – to get some sort of satisfaction. And to set the truth free would have been nice, to say the least. We toyed with the idea for a while and had a meeting with my husband's agent. But the question we kept coming back to was: is it really worth it?

It would have cost a small fortune in legal fees, not to mention the time and energy we'd undoubtedly have had to expend, and, really, for what? For the newspaper to apologize via a tiny statement on a page deep inside the paper that barely anyone would read? For a compensation fee that would probably only just cover the legal bills? We decided that the most positive thing we could do was to put the whole episode behind us and allow the dust to settle. Ultimately, anyone we cared about knew the story stank and, sure enough, the next week there would be a new kiss-and-tell for the gossip hounds to sniff around. Our 'story' would soon be forgotten.

But I have never forgotten the pain it caused me.

Kiss-and-tells have happened for years. I remain stunned that footballers haven't wised up to such women, given the obvious visual stereotype of such creatures. If footballers want to cheat on their partners, just for the sex thrill, then surely a prostitute would be a better option. At least they would pay the women up front and save themselves the humiliation of being sold to the papers. Then again, there was that Wayne Rooney scandal . . .

My husband has since been much more wary when under the influence. He tells me that when he's in a nightclub or a bar, he gives girls with fake boobs, cheap hair extensions and heavy make-up a 'proper wide berth'.

However, as much as the press and paps can be our nemesis, they often catch out the real cheating bastards. I've lost count of how many times I've counselled a fellow WAG on a kiss-and-tell story that I've known to be true because my husband has confirmed it.

A few years ago, a high-profile kiss-and-tell was pinned on the wrong footballer. It allegedly happened while he was on an end-of-season piss-up with his team-mates in Puerto Banús.

Puerto Banús is a luxury marina near Marbella in southern Spain. It's rammed with expensive designer shops, swanky bars and restaurants, most of which sit on a strip facing the docked yachts. The area is a magnet for the rich and famous, and a prime location for supercar spotting. It is therefore an excellent place for the paparazzi to lurk and a no-brainer destination for being papped, should one desire such attention. That is probably why many of the *TOWIE* cast and other not-so-inconspicuous celebs, the Z-listers, go there: for extra exposure.

Spain is a beautiful country – we have a holiday home there – and there are many towns, cities, beaches and marinas to visit that offer the Spanish sun, fabulous shopping and good food. Those celebrities who return again and again to Banús mostly go there to spot and be spotted. It baffles me why some footballers go there at the end of the season because generally, after a long campaign, they just want to 'get on it' and have a blow-out party week with the lads. So, surely, that would be best done in a place where they can keep a low profile. I suppose it just highlights that not all footballers really do hate the attention of the press.

This particular story claimed that the footballer had pulled a twenty-something brunette poolside in Banús, then taken her up to his room for 'mid-afternoon wild sex'. The article revealed that, when the deed was done, the girl realized her conquest had a girlfriend in the UK and thus decided to sell the story to an English tabloid. The girl claimed that her kiss-and-tell was not for the money (ha!) but as revenge and as a 'rude awakening' to the somewhat unsuspecting WAG. However, the 'cheated-on' WAG was not rudely awoken and remained unsuspecting because the story named and shamed the wrong footballer.

The most shocking thing was that the poor guy whose name was wrongly splashed all over the papers that week didn't challenge the mistake. He remained loyal to his team-mate (I cannot comprehend this sort of male solidarity) who had actually done the cheating and took the grief from his furious wife. That's got to be going well beyond 'take one for the team'.

His wife spent many an hour offloading to me about the whole incident but my husband had told me the real story and sworn me to secrecy, so I had to remain tight-lipped. I felt terrible for not being able to tell her the truth to put her mind at ease, especially as I had been through such an incident myself. I felt guilty too.

I had to listen to the player's wife's confused questions while knowing that her husband hadn't actually done it. We WAGs cannot help but be traitors; knowledge is power but, in these situations, it is a cross to bear.

My husband told me that the falsely accused footballer had decided to take the flak because admitting who the real cheater was would only upset the apple-cart on the pitch, open a huge can of worms for his mate, and it seemed to make more sense to deny the claims to his wife, who would ultimately 'get over it' (his words). In his mind, he was innocent, so he could afford to swear on his kids' lives to his wife to prove so. However, his wife would never fully get over it. It would be a stain on their marriage inflicted by the press and another calculating kiss-and-tell girl.

The actual cheater is a notorious philanderer who is well known behind the scenes for his illicit liaisons. He's been caught a few times by his wife but never – well, not so far – by the paps. His wife is a very nice woman, quite plain as far as WAGs are concerned, but very easy to talk to and extremely kind-hearted.

He was quite the big cheese in the world of football and he knew it. He would have eaten himself on crackers if he could have. It was quite obvious that part of his reason for cheating on his wife was that he thought he could 'do better' than her but he didn't want to end the marriage because they were childhood sweethearts and she doted on him. She was like part of the furniture to him – or maybe the mat he could wipe his feet on – whereas he was the centre of her world.

I was with his wife, then girlfriend – or let's call her

In Denial WAG – on one of the occasions when she caught her partner cheating. We were part of a large group of WAGs enjoying an evening meal in a Manchester restaurant. It was a swish venue with a buzzing atmosphere, big windows, low lighting and delicious food.

Our party was dressed up to the nines, obviously, and we were having a great night, until In Denial WAG's phone rang. It was her boyfriend's number and, since he was away on international duty, she was desperate to take his call. She scurried outside the restaurant to talk to him, all smiles and clip-clopping heels.

Between mouthfuls of a divine fish dish that tasted as if it had actually been made in heaven, I glanced over to the window to look at In Denial WAG and watched her demeanour change from schoolgirl-in-love to murderous vixen. Soon, other diners in the restaurant turned to stare as she began screaming like a banshee into her mobile phone.

The call did not last long. She stormed back into the restaurant, observed by a now not-so-buzzing clientele, and slammed herself into her bench seat next to me. 'Fucking bastard is cheating on me right now!' she seethed. 'Fucking wanker, fucking bastard!' I quietened her down by reminding her that other people were watching and possibly taking notes. She then told us other WAGs what had just happened.

The call she had taken from her boyfriend was not intentional. His phone had accidentally, and rather fatefully, called her number. She listened to her partner's voice begging a girl to go back to his room and have sex with him. She said she listened for as long as she could, then began shouting to try to get his attention until the line went dead. Perhaps he heard her shouts and cancelled the call or perhaps whatever had triggered his mobile to call her then triggered it to hang up. Yet fate had given her a window into what her man was up to.

In Denial WAG couldn't quite regain her party spirit after that incident so the evening was short-lived. Sadly, her relationship was not. Her man called her the next day. He acted innocently and, at first, denied that the call had ever taken place, asserting that paranoia had led her to make up such a story. After she had reminded him that she could prove the call via her mobile phone's call history, his memory magically returned and he proceeded to blame what she had heard the previous night on another person, a single team-mate trying to pull 'some dog'. It seems that loyalty is not in every footballer's code of conduct.

He insinuated that, since she had been drinking before she took the call, she had not identified the voice correctly and simply jumped to the wrong conclusion. Essentially, 'It wasn't me, guv' was his excuse. Somewhat unbelievably, she bought it, so she is In Denial WAG to all of us.

Chapter Twelve

Some footballers and WAGs, of course, use the papers for their own benefit. I find it quite comical that the WAGs who leak this-is-where-we'll-be information to the paparazzi arrogantly believe that none of the other WAGs in the group realize what they've done. It's always obvious who the tip-off source is, not least from their appearance on the day. The photographs will always give her away. Without a doubt, the conspirator WAG will be the one in the chat mag's pictures pouting and looking absolutely gorgeous while the other WAGs will be totally oblivious, minding their own business. Or once, in my case, wiping my nose on my sleeve!

In addition to the 'looking fabulous' pictures that WAGs and footballers receive as a reward for keeping the press onside, the other bonus is in story trading: to stop a scandal being published, they leak another equally juicy one. WAGs and footballers stitch up someone else, sometimes their friends or team-mates, to save their own arses.

Other footballers employ clever PRs, who revel in a revelation and do the story trading and damage limitation for them. Sadly, it comes back to the notion that, if you have a lot of money, you can buy your own truth. Or, at least, stop the truth being spoken.

Even when some footballers get exposed by the press for their philandering ways, it doesn't seem to do them too much long-term damage. Appalling though it is for the injured party at the time, the WAGs can sometimes end up benefiting from it career wise too. The John Terry and Wayne Rooney scandals are perhaps the best points of reference for this. The papers disclosed that Terry was having an affair with Wayne Bridge's girlfriend. And sex stories about Rooney were sold by a prostitute – the second exposé of its kind for him – detailing his illicit liaisons with her while his wife was pregnant.

Terry and Rooney no doubt received professional PR advice about how to deal with the public backlash and their responses took a similar path. The boys seemed to eat humble pie, 'stuck by' their families and carried on as if life was normal. Well, that's what the press presented. While the public hasn't forgotten what they did, it hasn't exactly affected their employment prospects or marital status.

The WAGs, Toni Terry and Coleen Rooney, the injured parties, received public sympathy and their every move, post-revelations, was closely followed by the paps. For Coleen, her dignified silence and apparently forgiving nature has done wonders for her public profile. I admired her for how she handled the second scandal to rock her marriage, especially as she was such a young wife and mother.

I first met Coleen when she had just finished school. She seemed so youthful and innocent, timid and sweet. She was just a normal Scouse girl-next-door, with no concern for fashion, tans or hair extensions. Yet from the moment she was pictured in her school uniform, she was papped left, right and centre.

Over the years of being trailed by photographers and commented on in magazines, she was almost forced by the press and public to conform and mould herself into a more WAG-like character. However, I believe she moulded herself in a way that kept her true to herself and to her humble roots. She is still as lovely and charming as she has ever been. She's not a WAG who seeks the spotlight – she had no choice in it from the start: it was shone on her.

I've watched Coleen grow and blossom into a very attractive and extremely successful businesswoman in her own right. She has cleverly capitalized on her public platform by becoming a positive role model for young girls and women. While I'm not sure I whole-heartedly agree with her decision to remain married to Wayne – it'd be difficult to forgive a partner if they slept with anyone else, let alone two prostitutes – in terms of self-respect, as far as I'm concerned, she wins hands down over Toni Terry.

I definitely lost some respect for Toni, given how she reacted to her man's inability to keep it in his trousers. She took him back immediately, albeit after a nice trip to Dubai to patch up their marriage during which she was pictured in one of the tiniest bikinis known to womankind.

If my husband cheated on me, and cheated with one of our friends' girlfriends, I wouldn't set foot on a plane with him. In fact, my foot would probably have had to be surgically removed from his face. The photographs of the Terrys were so contrived. In my opinion, Toni wanted to show the world that her marriage was not over and the paps helped her do it. The fact she got to show off her hot body along the way must've been a good bit of compensation.

The paps can stroke a woman's ego, but they can also smash it to smithereens. Since we are now in the age of the digital camera, if we perceive ourselves to look ugly in a photograph, we can order the photographer to delete it. Or press that little picture of a dustbin and delete it ourselves. *Pff*, it's gone, for ever.

Facebook pages, Instagram accounts, all social net working outlets are bursting with photographs of us at our best. This is because we edit them. Generally, we veto the ugly ones and OK the pretty ones. But those pictures that you want to hit delete on, the ones where you have your eyes half open, look stoned, pissed or in mid-seizure, where that horrid crop of spots, scars or wrinkles take centre stage, where you look twice the size you actually are, or where your legs look like orange peel: they are the ones the paps want to capture and keep. Those bad boys bring home much more bacon for the photographer.

The press seem to want to stitch up WAGs to line their own pockets. They love to catch a WAG with her boob hanging out, drunk and falling out of a taxi. Or, even better, a WAG looking like shit when her footballing partner's love affair has been exposed.

I've had some hideous pictures taken of me in my time as a WAG. I've been photographed red-faced and sweating, taking the kids to school in an overcoat with my pyjamas underneath, drunk as a skunk, with no make-up on and looking green after a messy night clubbing, on beaches with my boobs out, in cars mid-argument with my husband. And while taking a pee.

The latter refers to an incident in an exclusive nightclub in London. I was out with my husband and our close friends to celebrate a birthday. We were all aware that there were paps hanging around in the club. In fact, we knew one of them. You can get to know some paps because often it's the same faces taking your picture. I've learned the first names of a few and, usually, I'm polite to them.

Our group in the VIP section was being guarded by a bouncer and we were all being very careful not to let our guard drop too much so as to give a pap 'the picture'. Flashes were going off left, right and centre but we were having innocent fun, not too merry and, generally, there was no controversy to capture.

Towards the end of the evening, I went on my own to the unisex loos. The only aspect of this that was unusual was that I went alone as, most of the time, I, like many other girls, prefer to go in a pack. After I had locked the cubicle door, edged up my super-tight fuchsia-pink bandage dress, yanked down my tiny thong, slumped onto the toilet and let my bladder go, a camera lens appeared under the cubicle wall. I was on the toilet with my thong around my ankles, dress pulled up to my stomach, having a pee and someone was trying to take a picture of me!

Instinctively, I kicked the camera lens and it was swiftly pulled back to the other side of the cubicle by the callous snapper. He or she didn't get a chance to take a picture. Even if they had, I'd probably smashed the lens. I have no idea who the culprit was. I shouted from my peeing position, 'Stop them!' but, unfortunately, in my tipsy state, I couldn't get dressed and out of the cubicle quick enough to see who had done it.

Being in the public eye is not a bed of roses. In fact, it can be rather thorny, which I realized from the very first time I was papped. I remember it clearly. I got a call from a friend, who excitedly told me that my picture was in the paper alongside an article headlined 'Footballer's New Girlfriend'. Me! In the paper! I thought. My stomach performed somersaults at the idea of seeing my face in a national newspaper. I was excited, nervous . . . and worried. Vanity is a terrible thing.

As soon as I'd been alerted to my new fame, I drove like a bat out of hell to a nearby shop, rushed to the specified tabloid and ripped it open. I frantically scanned each page. Then I found it. There I was, staring back at myself. My picture was next to an article about Tony Blair. It felt surreal. I was in a newspaper, next to the then prime minister, for doing absolutely nothing. Well, just for having a boyfriend, but not for anything extraordinary that I had done.

The article was small and boring, star-player-meets-his-star-girl type of stuff. On the other hand, I felt that my picture was large and terrible. I had been photographed in the stands watching my then new boyfriend play a match. It clearly looked like I was enjoying the game. My teeth didn't want to stay in my mouth – I had such a big, open smile on view. Oh, my teeth! Those big tombstones and pink gums jutted out like I was a horse eating an apple, like a camel about to spit. It was the pre-whitening era, too, so they were not perfectly white gnashers, either . . . slightly dis-coloured, if I'm honest.

My nose looked distorted, probably because my teeth were trying to dominate my face, and my hair was lank and as dry as straw. I had no make-up on bar a light coat of mascara – I NEVER leave the house without mascara, BTW – and I also felt I looked chubby because I was wearing a huge duffel coat and scarf. After all, it was a cold winter's day and I was outdoors at a football match.

The most frustrating thing about my first pap-snap is that the picture still crops up in the papers. I want to scream when I see it. That's the problem with the press. Once a photograph or an article is published, once it's online, once it's out there, it's very difficult, almost impossible, to delete. So, after that first picture had been published, I thought very carefully about what to wear to a game or, indeed, when leaving the house. To have to give special thought always to how you look is draining. I don't know how Victoria Beckham does it, although large sunglasses do hide a multitude of sins.

What I don't understand is why most WAGs wear such high heels. Why, oh why, do they wear sky-scraper stilettos to walk their children to school or go to a match? The number of women I have seen almost topple down the steep steps in the stands of a football ground because of their ill-advised footwear! While watching them painfully totter up to their seats, I've always wanted to call out, 'A photographer won't get your feet in the picture, love. Trust me.'

No amount of money or cosmetic procedures, though, can mask what the camera can capture. The camera, after all, never lies. Those bad photos of WAGs? They're all real. The cellulite, spots, scars and wrinkles, they're real too. The point is that most people don't have to see their flaws blown up and exaggerated in the national or international media.

Yet I have had some fun avoiding photographers. While out jogging one morning with no make-up on, sweating like a pig in old sweatpants and an ancient top, I noticed a pap hiding in a bush halfway along the alleyway I was about to enter. Instead of taking another route and thus feeling defeated in some way, I took control.

I turned around and jogged back until I had arrived at the alley's midway point where I heard the frantic rustlings and scrambling of the photographer trying to get out of the bushes. I then pirouetted, in a rather dainty and dramatic fashion, and sprinted off along the alley leaving the not-so-cunning pap to eat my proverbial dust and, more importantly, with no picture of me.

It was a dog that helped my husband and me dodge another paparazzo. We were shopping in Richmond, London, one busy Saturday in December. We were minding our own business and on a mission to buy Christmas presents for our family. Suddenly, a photographer bounded in front of us and thrust his lens into our faces while clicking ferociously. This kind of pap behaviour is not only hugely embarrassing for us 'normal' people who do not welcome such attention but it's also very annoying since your personal space is totally invaded.

Such scenarios are incredibly intrusive and uncomfortable and often quite scary. However, on this occasion, the only visible fear was in the photographer's eyes as he tripped over a dog lead and fell to his backside, smashing his camera to smithereens. Members of the public laughed at the sprawling mess of that pap on the ground, scrabbling around in an attempt to salvage his totalled camera. If I'm honest, we were cracking up too.

It's not just sex scandals that get leaked to the press. Footballers fighting make for sensational headlines too, and my husband can testify to that. In the year before our wedding he and I were enjoying a Saturday night out in a popular nightclub near to his team's ground. We were part of a large group of footballers and WAGs celebrating our 3–1 win over a rival club, a win that put us in prime place on the league table. Needless to say, we were in the VIP area with the champagne and vodka in full flow; the girls were sexily dancing to the R&B tunes that were blasting out of the DJ booth and the boys were downing their drinks at a rate of knots.

It seems that with every high there will be a low to follow. When the DJ announced that the players were in the club celebrating, this stirred dissent in a small group of local lads. They were in their late teens to early twenties and fans of the losing away team. They manoeuvred themselves in front of the VIP booths and stood in aggressive and threatening poses – legs astride, arms crossed, scowling – while swigging from bottles of beer.

Since I love a good dance – in all truth I can be considered crazy on the dance-floor – I shook my booty a little too close to the barrier between us and the menacing group. I cannot remember if I did this on purpose – perhaps I did as a stupid attempt to make them laugh or to antagonize them, as young girls occasionally and ignorantly do – but I was naive and unprepared for the men's reactions.

Mid-shake to the Pussycat Dolls' 'Don't Cha', one of them yanked up my skirt and wrenched my hair back, then venomously shouted 'SLUT!' into my ear. I felt totally violated and completely shocked, but before I could regain my composure, my husband and some of his team-mates had jumped up from their seats, hurdled the VIP barriers and pushed the gang backwards. A huge fight ensued. I lost count of how many other revellers joined in.

Some of the WAGs and other girls in the club were screaming and crying, a few were pitching in with punches and kicks, and others were trying to drag their partners away. I belonged to the first and last categories. I was in floods of tears, trying as best I could to drag my man out of the tangle. Unfortunately, there were three men on top of him in a bundle and I kept getting knocked backwards.

It felt like an eternity until the bouncers and other staff arrived and helped the non-fighting men pull the bruised and bloodied bodies apart from each other. Many people were kicked out of the club with immediate effect, including the fight initiators. Those who remained made the club looked like carnage. Men were walking around in ripped and bloodied shirts, dazed, drunk and angry, with bruises already forming on their faces, and girls had wet cheeks, mascara-smudged eyes and laddered tights, helping the men hobble around as if they were victims of a war.

I was no exception. I looked a state and felt worse. I was worried sick and felt extremely guilty. My man looked horrendous. His shirt was hanging off him, he was missing a shoe, his chest was red with punch marks, one of his eyes was already beginning to close, he had a swollen lip and blood was trickling from a small but deep cut over his eyebrow. In retrospect, it's a small miracle none of his facial bones were fractured.

The WAGs and footballers who had remained –

some had escaped when the fight broke out – were swiftly ushered out of a fire escape. Unfortunately, we were sent into the path of the awaiting mob of angry men who had started the fight – and the press. Bad news spreads like wildfire and a handful of photographers was already on the scene. Another scuffle broke out, but thankfully it was short-lived as the bouncers worked quickly to restrain the aggressors.

The cameras worked quickly to capture it all, and in the week that followed, the fight was splashed all over the press. There were different variations of the story depending on what paper you read, which photographs had been used and which eye-witnesses had been quoted: some said the footballers were the victims, some said they were the criminals. However, all of the articles pinpointed my husband and me as playing a central role in the events. Some reports claimed I had been drunkenly shouting abuse at the men before my partner threw the first punches; other reports implied he 'deserved a good kicking-in' for his 'arrogance'. It was hurtful and humiliating to read the exaggerated and false reports, and to think that the press could degrade us so badly without knowing us or having all of the facts.

We were encouraged by my husband's agent to do a set-the-story-straight interview, but we decided against it. We wanted to put it behind us and did not need – or think we would get – any public sympathy.

The stories of that night eventually died down, although the images remain on the Internet and in our memories. My husband still has a small scar above his eyebrow and I have a scar on my conscience, saying, 'Don'tcha shake your arse to angry young men who support your partner's rivals.'

Chapter Thirteen

orrying is my forte. I worry about almost everything. I'm quite convinced that worrying is a woman's prerogative, that there's something primeval about us ladies being the worriers much as men are the hunters. If we didn't worry about the health of our kids, our parents, our neighbours, our friends, the cleanliness of our cave, the proper cooking of the meat, then we'd all be dead a lot quicker. Worrying about *everything* is not for the menfolk, nor do they seem to understand it. At least, my husband doesn't. He thinks that because I cannot possibly know what it feels like to be pressured by forty thousand fans and an angry manager I don't know what worry is!

I imagine there may be many more people who cannot understand what a WAG could possibly have to worry about. I realize that I am lucky in many ways. I have money, I live in a beautiful house, I have a wardrobe full of designer clothes, I have always owned new, top-of-the-range cars, I can travel to any destination I wish to explore, my kids are healthy and enjoy the perks of a private education, and my husband and I love each other. Sickening, right? I live a bloody great life by all accounts and I'm very grateful for it.

I also realize that my privileged lifestyle removes a lot of everyday worries that many people have. Aside from health concerns, real worries are not being able to pay the bills, not being able to find the deposit for a home, not being able to put food on the table for the family: the financial hardships that terrorize many a hard-working soul. Moreover, I feel a great sense of guilt for being financially stable without having had to graft for it. While I do what I can for charity and bring my children up with awareness of the world, it doesn't ever feel enough.

But my 'bloody great life' is not without worry. Wealth can bring many worries. It can make you a target, not least of anger and envy, but a target for crime. My husband has been physically attacked in nightclubs and I have been verbally abused on the street on the assumption that I have become 'unfairly' rich. We live grounded lives, but because of what we've experienced, I fear what will happen to my children in the future if they are seen as rich kids. Consequently, I worry hugely for the safety of my family.

Our home has been broken into once, and we have experienced two attempted burglaries. The former was at the end of the football season and we were on a long-awaited family holiday in Portugal. The novelty of being able to enjoy a family holiday has not worn off. Football dictates when we can take a break, but thankfully it doesn't control where we can go or how much we can enjoy it.

Our enjoyment of that vacation was short-lived. We had barely been in the Portuguese sun for two days before my husband received a phone call from his father to say that we had been burgled. We flew home that day to see what the damage was. The ground floor and our master bedroom looked as if they had been turned upside down. There had been no efforts made to clean up because the police needed to preserve the crime scene to take fingerprints and photographic evidence. The thieves had stolen most of our jewellery and expensive watches, some electronic gadgets and, worst of all, my laptop, which held thousands of photographs of our family and friends that I had not backed up.

According to our next-door neighbours, the house alarms began sounding at two a.m. in the early hours of the Tuesday that we were away. They had called the police but, by the time they had arrived, the perpetrators had scarpered. They hadn't smashed any windows or doors to get in so the alarms were not initially triggered. The house was over one hundred years old with many outside access points and, when planning our security system, we had overlooked the entrance to the disused coal cellar. It was barely visible from the back garden for its covering of thick shrubs and bushes. Apparently the criminals had broken in through it and forced their entrance into the main house via the internal trap-door that led up into the hallway.

The police deciphered from the trail of mess left in the house that the burglars had probably gone in aiming to steal our cars – a Lamborghini, Range Rover and Mercedes – but when they couldn't find our car keys, they had gone for the next obvious assets in the form of jewellery and expensive electronics.

The police said we had been targeted because of my husband's wealth and fame. We were told that there had been a spate of burglaries and attempted burglaries in the area and that a significant proportion of the victims, or potential victims, were footballers and their families. That knowledge struck fear into my heart. We then assumed that the criminals had watched our home, perhaps even watched us and our children, and waited for an opportune moment. It made sense. It would have been too much of a coincidence for the burglars to get lucky and strike while we were on holiday.

I felt my spine chill at the thought that the people who had looted our home had been stalking my family. I felt afraid that they were still at large. I wondered if we would be targets to anyone else, whether we would be mugged on the street, whether my children were at risk of kidnap. Hundreds of different hypothetical and devastating scenarios echoed around my mind. The police did their best to reassure us that the gang would most likely be caught or, at least, not return to our home. However, their words did nothing to quell my worries.

After that burglary I no longer felt like my home was my sanctuary. The thieves had taken many of my treasured possessions, including a diamond ring given to me by my husband after we'd been together for a year and an antique St Christopher necklace I'd inherited from my beloved nan, but, even worse, they had stolen my feeling of security. I could move on from losing 'stuff'. I reasoned that our possessions could be replaced because even if they symbolized people or special moments, the memories themselves could not be snatched away. But my peace of mind had been taken, never to be returned.

Shortly after our return from Portugal, my husband went to great lengths to install a new security system that included CCTV inside and outside the house. It was a high-spec set-up. However, despite its manu-facturer's promises and five-star reviews it failed to ease my fears of another burglary. And eighteen months later we suffered an attempted break-in and it wasn't the security systems or alarms that discovered the crime. It was my father.

It happened on an England international weekend that my husband wasn't involved in, when he was using his rare few days off to spend time with friends in London. On the Friday afternoon he departed and my parents arrived to give me a hand with the kids and to generally have some down-time together. We were living three hundred miles away from my family at the time so my being home alone with toddlers was as good an excuse as any for my parents to visit.

In the early hours of Sunday morning I was woken by a muffled banging noise. I had actually heard it in my sleep, but my subconscious probably presumed that it was my husband arriving home late, as he so often does after a Saturday night on the town. I got out of bed and heard my father shouting, or rather roaring, before I opened my bedroom door. He was running up the stairs and then stormed into my three-year-old's bedroom, which was next to mine.

I burst out of my room and ran after my father into my child's room, to be greeted by a horrendous sight. The outer glass of the reinforced double-glazed windows was smashed and the top of a ladder could be seen resting against the windowsill, inches above my dazed and confused child's head. My father didn't pause to digest the scene. He ran out of the room, shouting, as if he were trying to scare off a wild animal, and turned on all the lights in the house. I cradled my child in my arms, ran back into my bedroom and called the police.

At this point, my father was bravely, or stupidly, brandishing a golf club and tearing around the flood-lit back garden, shouting, 'Come on, let's fucking have ya!' Whether it was the threat of my father or the flight-rather-than-fight reaction in the criminals, it seemed they had bolted into the darkness, leaving only their ladder as evidence.

The police response was fast. They arrived on the scene within five minutes, and the rest of the night was a blur of officers searching the perimeters, witness statements being taken, tea being made and me trying to convince my children that it was not time to get up.

Once again, the police told us that there had been a spate of burglaries of footballers' homes in the area, but that all of the break-ins had occurred at times when the homeowners had been out or away. They asserted that the perpetrators would not be back because they had most probably been scared off by the noise my father made – well done, Dad – and the blue flashing lights.

Needless to say, none of us went back to sleep. I was in shock. I couldn't believe people had tried to break into our home, in the middle of the night, when we were sleeping. Questions raced through my mind the next day. What if my father hadn't woken up? What if I had been alone with the children? What were they intending to do if they got in? To this day the potential answers to those questions make me shudder.

Once my husband got back, the children and I left with my parents to go to their house. I was too scared to sleep another night in our home and my parents would not have let me even if I had wanted to. We didn't return home until my husband assured me that the security systems had been revised and revamped. A security man patrolled the grounds around our property and the road on which we lived. Panic buttons had been installed in all of the main rooms in the house. Additional CCTV cameras scanned every inch of the exterior.

Despite my husband's conviction that the house was now on a par with Fort Knox, I never felt safe there again. I desperately wanted to move, and when we learned that our next-door neighbours had been broken into by four men armed with machetes, as shown by their CCTV footage, my husband could no longer challenge my fears. This was one house move that I welcomed. No money in the world can purchase the feeling of peace and security.

My other main worry concerns my obsessive compulsive disorder, the condition that blights my life.

My worries, or obsessive thoughts, always occur at times of stress. They usually start with an unprompted belief that something bad, generally disease or death, will befall someone I love. Next, the anxiety arrives, and I rerun the negative thought over and over in my mind until I'm completely obsessed with it and believe it will happen, like it's some sort of prophecy. Then my brain tricks me into thinking I can do something to stop it coming true. It bribes me into developing a compulsion, a repetitive behaviour, to avert the disaster.

For example, when my grandma was ill, I worried obsessively that she would die in her sleep on a specific Saturday in May. For some unknown reason my brain then told me that, to avoid this happening, every time I turned on a light I had to flick the switch five times. And so, until my grandma had recovered and that Saturday in May had passed, I became a compulsive light-switch flicker. I was saving her life every time I turned on a light! If only she knew.

I have struggled with OCD since I was a young girl. I have tried to deny it and tried to hide it. It has produced endless worry in me and my loved ones and at times it has driven me to despair. I cannot recall the number of occasions I have broken down to my parents about it.

I cannot remember when my brain first decided to induce me into performing odd behaviour to save people's lives. Neither can I recall why it is so imperative that I walk in and out of a door three times before I can properly enter it. I just know that sometimes, when life gets a little crazy, I have to do some crazy things to make me feel a little better. Defeating craziness with craziness! I never have been one for logic.

Fortunately, as I have become older and a little wiser I have managed to get some sort of grip on my OCD; I've read self-help books and anonymously joined online sufferers' sites to talk with others about the condition. All my efforts have played a part in helping me beat it into the background of my life. I can now talk myself out of most obsessional thoughts. Ironically I have to think obsessively positively in order not to think obsessively negatively!

For instance, my husband and I attended a high-profile charity event held in a swanky hotel in central London. It was a dinner, dance and auction, the house band was a world-famous group and the list of attendees read like a *Who's Who* of the twenty-first-century sport and entertainment industries. We were at a table with Sting and a host of other automatically recognizable faces. I felt agitated in the lead-up to the event, but hadn't quite anticipated how star-studded it would be.

I walked up the red carpet with fake confidence and greeted the barrage of shouting paparazzi with smiles, but when I was at the dinner table, my anxiety peaked.

211

I felt like an outsider and I believed that my neighbours judged me in the same way. The OCD turned up my negative thoughts louder and louder in my mind: They think you're a footballer's accessory. Why do you deserve to be here? You're going to say something that confirms you're just a dumb WAG.

At almost the point when I thought I would have a panic attack, with the stress of trying to play normal and beat down my paranoid thoughts, an infamous girl band member burped loudly at the table. She followed it up by saying, 'Fucking shit champagne,' and proceeded to pour the remainder of her drink onto her companion's dinner plate. Everyone at the table was stunned. It was surreal, but it lifted my tension. I knew that, even if my OCD broke through, I'd not do anything as bad as she'd done! The table's attention would definitely not be on the weird WAG.

The OCD always rears its ugly head around food, exercise and stepping on the scales. I'm quite aware that worrying about my weight feeds straight into the negative stereotype of an air-head self-obsessed WAG but, sadly, the truth is that how much I weigh has become a real and obsessional worry to me.

I realize that it is a ridiculous thing to worry or even think about. We live in a world of poverty, war, and great inequality and here I am worrying obsessively about how much I weigh! The frustrating thing is that before I met my husband, before I became a WAG, I didn't care how much I weighed. I was always a little body-conscious in my teenage years – show me a teenage girl who isn't – but not obsessively so.

I used to judge my weight gain or loss by how I felt in my clothes. If my size-ten jeans were feeling a little tight or my love handles were hanging over the sides a little more than usual, I would think it time to exercise a little more and eat more fruit. That was the extent I would go to in order to lose weight. Quite honestly, when I was younger I could lose about three pounds simply by going to the toilet for a number two!

The way I now lose weight is neither natural nor healthy, and where I was once unfazed by the reading on the bathroom scales, I'm now obsessed with it. I am not anorexic or bulimic, but what I do know is that the need to control my weight controls my life and it makes me really, really unhappy.

I can clearly remember when my obsessive thoughts about my weight began, because they followed, strangely enough, the receipt of a house-warming gift. It was on the first day in our second home together. That morning, while my man was at football training, I sat on my own on the shiny, laminated wooden floor of our downstairs hallway among our heavy, sealed cardboard boxes. The house felt imposing and hostile. It was a huge, wooden chalet-style building, of bespoke design, with six bedrooms. It was too big for just the two of us and the wooden interior did nothing to add comfort. Each room begged to be filled.

When the doorbell rang, I opened the door to see the smiling face of one of my boyfriend's team-mates, a well-known footballer who was not in training due to an injury. He was single, a huge flirt and fit, super-fit, in fact, and not just in the healthy sense of the word.

He knew it too, and he was well known for it, so the vision of him on my doorstep was enough to make me feel a little better. Eye candy and positive attention should never be underrated for their medicinal purposes.

I invited him in, gave him the obligatory house tour, found some mugs and a kettle and made us a cup of tea in the new kitchen. It was then that he produced his house-warming gift, the gift that unbeknown to me would change my every waking day. Oddly, he urged me to unwrap it in front of him, at that moment, despite my protests of 'Can't it wait till he's home from training?'

I'm not the greatest actor when it comes to receiving a crap or pointless present. However, Fit Footballer Friend urged me, 'It's more for you anyway,' so, under his watchful and sexy gaze, I tentatively untied the neat red bow and peeled back the elegant silver paper. I tried to conceal my shock when I laid eyes on what the pretty wrapping revealed. He had given us bathroom scales! It seemed like a bizarre present for a single bloke to give as a housewarming gesture. I could have understood a pack of beers, a bottle of bubbly, a knife-set, even a candle, but a single man giving bathroom scales seemed very strange . . . to my mind at least.

In typical footballer fashion, the scales were top-of-the-range, digital and chrome, complete with body-fat analysis systems and other programming delights. It was the coolest piece of weighing technology I had ever seen, that was for sure, not that I had ever considered the diversity of bathroom scales.

The probable reality was that the gift had not been sought out by the Adonis sitting in my kitchen and was more likely a purchase made by his mother or some other female on his behalf, but my OCD piped up from its dark depths, 'He thinks you're fat. That's why he bought you scales. That's why he's made you open it. It's a message. He thinks you need to lose weight.'

As I have already admitted, rational thinking is not my forte in stressful situations and the OCD usually makes an ungraceful entrance – it's obsessively consistent. The next thought that shot through my mind was: I need to lose weight.

And so it began.

The scales became a character in my life. I even named them: Sydney the scales. As soon as Fit Footballer Friend left on that fateful day I jumped on to Sydney, and his bright blue digital display told me that I weighed nine stones and four pounds. I didn't feel happy with that; the little voice in my head told me that I needed to 'weigh less or else'. I then consulted the Internet to check the minimum healthy weight I should be, and found that, according to height and weight BMI ratios, I was just within the guidelines for what is OK. In fact, I was just above the underweight category.

However, I decided I had to shed two pounds. I knew for sure that I didn't look remotely underweight and I had no desire to lose huge amounts, or put any more on. So nine stones and two pounds was my goal, and once reached, there I should stay.

Since the day Sydney was given to me, I have not stopped thinking about him and I am ashamed to say that I remain unhealthily obsessed with him. Every day, I compulsively weigh myself an extraordinary number of times, too many to keep track of. Sydney became and remains the first thing I think about in the morning and the last thing I think about before I shut my eyes to go to sleep at night.

If Sydney's display reads above nine stones and two pounds, even by a fraction of a pound, then my day is ruined. My mood automatically turns sour and I begin twenty-four hours of self-denial and punishment to ensure that Sydney shows me the magic number the next morning.

Matters are not helped by the fact that WAGs talk a lot, and I mean a lot, about losing weight, gaining weight, personal trainers and diets. They will chat about anything weight-related, and usually be doing all that they can to lose weight or to stay stick-thin. The point is that most WAGs feel pressure to be skinny. The media constantly reinforces a Victoria Beckham-based stereotype of what a WAG should look like, and the Players' Lounge has become an extremely competitive environment. No one wants to be the Fat WAG. I definitely know that I don't want to be her! No WAG wants their man's head to be turned by a slimmer woman, and no WAG wants to embarrass their man by letting themselves go. Sporty, fit men generally demand the same body type of their women, so the pressure is on.

My attempts to shed a few pounds in one day have

included going to the gym four separate times in twelve hours, sitting in our home sauna until my blood nearly boiled, and even initiating rampant sex with my man, the latter only considered as a last resort if the gym is closed, the weather is poor and the sauna is broken.

Exercise is a prominent feature in my life, but while once I used to exercise for fitness, now I do it purely for weight loss. I will work out for hours on end until I think I've sweated enough for Sydney to show me the magic.

I've followed hilarious exercise DVDs, broken a lamp with my child's Wii remote during my Wii Fit obsession, tried many different gyms, have given both Laughing Yoga and tap-dancing a go, endured pre- or post-workout hot body wraps and electronic muscle stimulators, and participated in team sports, from netball to rowing.

Some WAGs I know take their exercise obsession further than I do. One of them, Fitness Freak WAG, has a personal trainer who comes to her house five times a week, sets her food plans and gives her supplements to take. She carries around so many vitamins and minerals in her YSL handbag that she rattles when she walks. Fitness Freak WAG lives in her own personal boot camp, and what her personal trainer puts her through begins at five thirty a.m. and sounds like hell. A pre-dawn jog followed by two hundred press-ups followed by a raw egg and juice, followed by . . . You get the picture.

Fitness Freak WAG is a permanent source of gossip

in WAGdom because the WAGs are either jealous, in awe, appalled or worried at how much weight she continues to lose and how ripped her body is becoming. Whatever their reactions, there aren't many WAGs who haven't asked Fitness Freak WAG for her personal trainer's number. I have, not that I used it, especially when I found out that her PT costs roughly £1,000 a month.

It's scary to watch how some WAGs become exercise-obsessed in response to the pressure to be thin. One WAG in particular, Skin and Bones WAG, exercised for four hours a day, every day, in the two months leading up to her wedding. She ate like a bird, too, and consequently lost so much weight that she looked malnourished for the big event. Her dress swamped her minuscule figure and she looked so frail that she appeared almost plastic; her bones and joints were clearly visible through her tightly stretched skin and one could have been forgiven for thinking that she might literally have snapped if the groom hugged her too hard. It was dainty hand-shake congratulations all round on her wedding day.

I had some empathy for Skin and Bones WAG because my OCD is especially prominent before a high-profile event, especially one that will play host to a ton of celebrities. In the days beforehand, in the belief that the paparazzi will be lurking in every corner, that tabloids or chat magazines will be desperate to get their hands on any Fat WAG pictures from the event, I up the ante. I'll often survive on water and crackers and over-exercise just to ensure

I'm bordering on the emaciated look. Awful, isn't it?

I do not appear painfully thin or fragile, even though nine stone two is supposedly an underweight BMI category. I look slim and healthy. Thank God my unhealthy mind is not on show.

I have also put myself on every new fad diet ever spoken about on breakfast television or promoted in some emotive and persuasive viral Internet campaign. I'm one of those gullible idiots who will believe any marketing campaign if it tells me what I want to hear, namely, Immediate Weight Loss.

I've tried a no-carbohydrates diet, which made me feel dizzy and gave me bad breath and constipation. I've tried a meal-replacement diet, which gave me insomnia and nausea, as well as immensely boring food options. I've tried Slim Fast Shakes, Slimming World and WeightWatchers, although the latter two did not have me as a member. Had I tried to officially join either organization, they would probably have laughed me out of the door when I showed up for a weigh-in and instructed me to go and eat a big meal, pronto.

My husband detests my dieting obsession, not necessarily for my goal of staying slim but for the time and money I waste on the diets and the flatulence that low-calorie consumption so often brings! When I once put myself on a strict 1,000 calories per day meal plan, consisting entirely of steamed fish and vegetables, my bottom-burps were so potent that I was seriously concerned my gas could be a fire hazard!

I've tried so many breakfast cereal diets that my

husband once suggested that I should invest in shares in the company and I've purchased so many weight-loss concoctions from Chinese herbalists that I could have paid for a few return fares to Beijing. I've also drunk so much Chinese slimming tea that I'm quite surprised now to have solid stools.

I've tried almost all the over- and under-the-counter vitamins, minerals, lotions and potions that claim to help people lose weight. I've tried them legally and illegally. Once, I tried a course of new prescription-only weight-loss tablets that in the UK would be prescribed only to morbidly overweight people but were readily available on the Internet. They worked to restrict the body's absorption of fat from foods. Not only was ordering medications from an unknown online source an extremely irresponsible, irrational and downright stupid thing to do, but the tablets gave me severe diarrhoea and stomach cramps, and I was leaking fat from my arsehole to the extent that I had to wear panty liners to soak it up!

Needless to say, I don't stick to one diet or technique for too long because no method of fast weight loss is without consequence, especially if you don't *really* need to lose weight.

As our world revolves around football, this also makes me feel almost totally out of control, and therefore almost constantly anxious. The matches themselves bring me great anxiety, which inevitably influences my OCD. I think I feel the pre-game nerves just as much as my husband does, especially before derbies or big televised matches.

One such match was an England World Cup qualifier. My husband was in the squad and I had gone to my parents' house, along with other family members and friends, to watch the game.

The build-up had been the most nerve-racking I have ever experienced – my husband had been a bundle of nerves. He's usually sickeningly positive before a match, foolishly optimistic in some people's books, but unusually before this particular match, he was in a state. He hadn't slept well in the week leading up to it, he was agitated, snappy and he couldn't sit still. He was torturing himself with worry before he had even stepped on the pitch, questioning his own abilities and the dynamics of the team, fearing a slip-up that would cost the game and bring him untold shame and self-loathing.

He relished playing for his country, it was a dream come true for him and every England cap meant the earth, but the pressure he put himself under before that England game was immense. He faked positivity to everyone else, of course, but behind closed doors his private negative mind-set was very apparent and rubbed off on me. I started that week offering words of encouragement, positivity and hope, but underneath, I was worrying too.

By the end of that week he'd succeeded in convincing me that the forthcoming match would end in national and personal misery. I saw him being sent off, scoring an own goal, or getting badly injured. I was visualizing these scenarios right up to the point of watching the pre-match commentary with my loved ones. I was totally disengaged from the excited buzz around me because my OCD demon had returned.

It told me that if I was able to touch my husband's framed and signed England football shirt that was hanging on the wall in my parents' study every five minutes, on the dot, then he would play well and there would be no negative dramas in the game. So as soon as the match began I set the stopwatch on my phone to vibrate after five minutes and on the buzz I left the room, touched the picture, and reset the stopwatch for another five minutes. This pattern continued until half-time, then restarted with the second half and continued to the final whistle. I literally left the room and touched the picture nineteen times during that game. I thanked God out loud that there was no extra-time and no penalties. England qualified for the World Cup . . . and I actually believed that my temporary compulsion had had something to do with it.

My behaviour throughout the match must have appeared totally ridiculous. The other people in the room couldn't understand what I was doing but I successfully fobbed them off with the generic 'It's the nerves' excuse. After all, it *was* my nerves. I couldn't help but conform to my crazy thoughts as I honestly believed that if I didn't, my husband would disappoint the whole country and himself. I am still reminded of that day whenever I look at the framed shirt: my fingerprints remain in a smeared cluster around the left breast area.

Finally, and I'm sure most WAGs will agree, having

222

a footballer as a husband is a major source of worry in itself. I worry that he may crack under all the pressure he is put under and I worry that I will crack under the pressure he puts me under! Then there's the obvious elephant-in-the-room worry – the cheating.

The kiss-and-tell story that cited my husband as the 'love rat' broke my heart; I'm not a machine, it hurt like hell to read it. Even though I believed it was a load of fabricated crap, my trust for him went from ninety-nine per cent to ninety per cent and has remained there. Like other WAGs, I sit and worry to the point of neurosis about what he is up to when he is out with his mates on a Saturday night.

A friend of mine, Paranoid WAG, checks her husband's phone at every opportunity she can, examines his clothing after a night out for lipstick stains, perfume aromas, phone numbers and probably uses a laser light over his pants! She is constantly on his case, and grills him about every inch of his whereabouts. She even challenges her friends on her husband's nocturnal movements. I have received a few 3 a.m. calls from her enquiring as to the locations of our husbands. When I once replied to her the truth that mine was asleep, drunkenly snoring next to me, Paranoid WAG turned into Angry WAG and screeched, 'Where the fuck is he? I'm gonna kill him!' before hanging up. Whoops.

I am not by any means as bad as her, but I do fear being the last to know that my husband is a cheating bastard! I would be mortified if other people knew something about him, therefore about the intimate workings of my life, that I didn't. The thought of reading another sex-scandal headline with his name in it, without any warning, completely freaks me out.

Therefore I have turned into a snoop. I am now a phone-checker, and as far as I'm concerned, if he leaves his Facebook account open on our home computer, it's fair game for me to look at his private messages too. I do it secretively, though, for I know he would be livid with me if he caught me in the act. I have to do it: perusing his recent call activity or a quick scroll through his messages just serves to ease my mind. If I see that he's been communicating with a girl I don't know, I investigate as quickly as I can, whether it be reading the message in full or looking her up online. So far, nothing I've found has been incriminating, although I still wonder if he's outwitted me by inputting girls' phone numbers under male names, since there are so many names in his phone of people I've never heard of. That's my ten per cent lack of trust talking. He hates it that I don't trust him one hundred per cent, but I think I'd be an absolute fool if I did.

All WAGs worry about their partners cheating, believe me, and any WAG who says she trusts her partner one hundred per cent is a liar.

Many WAGs have good reason for their doubt. I've known a number of WAGs whose relationships have broken down because of their footballer cheating on them. One poor WAG, Destroyed WAG, discovered before her first wedding anniversary that her husband had been having an affair with a stripper. None of their friends or family saw it coming because her husband seemed a loving and devoted spouse, and together they behaved like a loved-up pair of newly-weds. The revelation of his cheating sent a huge wake-up call to the other WAGs. It told us that if he could cheat, the person you would least expect to be a philanderer, then any man could and it could happen to you.

I just pray that many of my worries and my OCD will ease off once I get a little bit more control over my own life; once my husband hangs up his football boots and the pressure is off him, once my days as a WAG are over.

Chapter Fourteen

A'm not sycophantic. I don't enjoy name-dropping, and I don't use my husband's fame to get me places . . . well, not all the time anyway.

I detest people who brag about who they know, where they've been and what they have. Swimming in the shallow end of the pool of life is not where I'm at. However, there is no escaping that my life as a WAG has given me a window into a world that some people can only dream about. At times, WAGdom is a living nightmare, but the dream-like aspects certainly provide a silver lining to the dark clouds that can hover, and there's no denying that sometimes things that glitter can bring a little short-term happiness.

Sadly, there are some WAGs who place most of their happiness in the 'things' that WAGdom can offer; they see it as the route to fulfilment, that their valuable 'stuff' makes them valuable. Such women can only converse about their financial assets, where they've been or where they're going on holiday, and which celebrities are in their phonebook. It's as if that's all they've got.

My WAG friend was recently out to dinner with a Billy Big Balls-type WAG and their footballer partners. Apparently the whole dinner conversation revolved around listening to Boastful WAG bragging about her new car, her forthcoming holiday to Barbados, her next cosmetic surgery procedure and her 'bezzie' Coleen Rooney (it's common knowledge that they are mere acquaintances).

After dessert, Boastful WAG threw her leg up onto the seat beside her and took her shoe off. She then strategically placed the shoe on the table with the inner sole facing my WAG friend: the Jimmy Choo label was virtually thrust under her nose. Boastful WAG then rubbed her bare foot and said, 'These Jimmy Choos just aren't as comfortable as my Pradas or my Louboutins.' My friend got the message. Although perhaps not the shoe-show message Boastful WAG was trying to convey. The message my friend received, loud and clear, was . . . twat.

My first car was a brand-new blue Ford Fiesta and I named her Emily. My parents purchased her for me as a gift when I passed my driving test. I was shocked and grateful to receive the car and used the money I earned in my part-time job to pay for the insurance and tax. My father said later that he'd bought it for me because he was worried about me and wanted to ensure that I had a good, safe, reliable car.

My man has bought me a few cars. For my twenty-first birthday he arranged a spa experience for my best friend and me, followed by a huge party in the evening. As I went to leave the house in the morning, he threw me a set of keys and said, 'You' best take your birthday present. It's in the garage.'

When I pressed the buzzer to open the garage door, I couldn't believe my eyes. There, in front of me, was a brand-new, shining silver convertible Mercedes with an enormous red bow wrapped over the bonnet, and my initials on the number-plate. When my brain registered what my eyes witnessed, I burst into tears. I couldn't believe that my man had bought me a car! I ran back into the house, thanked him profusely and hugged him so tightly that I must've almost broken one of his ribs. I kissed him nearly a hundred times and said, 'Thank you', between each peck. I had never felt so spoiled in my whole life.

I did feel sad to see Emily One go but Emily Two was so damn sexy that it was impossible to remain upset for long. I quickly moved on from my mourning.

My footballer gets bored with cars very quickly; he only keeps them for a year to eighteen months. I've never had much input in choosing the elite vehicles that we have owned over the years. Ultimately, he has the final say since he is, after all, the one who buys them. Consequently, I have driven many different expensive cars. I've had three BMW X5s, two Mercedes GLs, an Audi Q7, a Range Rover Sport and a Range Rover Vogue. My husband has had Porsches, BMWs, a Mercedes, a Ferrari, a Lamborghini, a Bentley and a Rolls-Royce Phantom, all of which I have been insured to drive. It's quite incredible how many heads turned to look at me when I drove the Ferrari. It was an absolute pulling machine!

My husband has also presented me with an obscene amount of jewellery and watches. I'm the type of person who loses jewellery. I have a jewellery box full of random single earrings and hardly any pairs at all, so I get very nervous about wearing the beautiful diamond earrings that he bought me for Christmas one year. In fact, instead of enjoying regularly wearing my exorbitant bling, I only ever wear such pieces on special occasions. They are otherwise kept in a safe . . . safe!

However, I do share my husband's passion for watches. Between us, we have an extensive collection that is worth hundreds of thousands of pounds. I quite often catch my man getting them all out of the safe and looking at them with utter admiration. I am very lucky to have two Rolexes, a gold Cartier, a Chopard, a Patek Philippe and one very sparkly bling Franck Muller watch, all given to me over the years as birthday presents. My husband has a total of twelve watches; he wears them all with great pride and care, and co-ordinates them with each and every outfit. He also relishes the fact that he can pass his watches down to our children as part of their inheritance.

Akin to my husband's passion for his watches, I often go through my wardrobes to admire my beautiful designer garments hanging in all their glory. My wardrobe is full of clothes that I could only have dreamed about owning when I was younger. I have at least six pairs of Louboutins, four Hervé Léger dresses and a hefty collection of designer handbags.

I love, love, love clothes, and appreciate everything

that goes into making the wonderful pieces I own. Possessing exclusive and bespoke creations and wearing them gives me an incredible feeling. That's another reason why I respect and admire Victoria Beckham: she looks like a work of art whenever she is photographed. Her style is so chic and sleek, and she's always immaculately turned out.

I take great care of my dresses, hanging them all in individual plastic covers. The majority of my exclusive wares have been given to me by my husband, but roughly four years ago I made the biggest purchase I have ever made on a dress for a footballer's wedding we were going to.

It was a gorgeous spring day. I was shopping with a couple of WAGs and we were in high spirits, having quaffed a few glasses of champagne over lunch in a lovely little Italian restaurant. I needed something to wear for the approaching weekend, but I had no idea what I was looking for. On our travels around the city, we went to an expensive boutique in the centre because one of the WAGs in our group knew the owner and could get a ten per cent discount on purchases.

The shop oozed affluence. It stocked all the latest ranges from Chloé to Hervé Léger to Armani – you name it, it was there on the rails. As soon as I walked in, I saw *the* dress on a mannequin. It was an Emilio Pucci wrap dress, with blues and greens and black pattern detail. I immediately envisaged the perfect pair of strappy Gina shoes and matching handbag, which I already had in my wardrobe and would match it perfectly.

I instantly fell in love with it and decided I had to try it on. The shop assistant gently and cautiously undressed the mannequin and left me alone with the dress in the changing room. It was so beautiful and fitted like a glove. When I came out to show the others, they all went, 'Wow, you have to have it.' In my mind it was sold.

The dress didn't have a price tag on it, but I knew it was going to be expensive. I didn't quite anticipate just how expensive; I nearly keeled over at the till when the lady said, 'With your ten per cent discount, that comes to £2,800.' I couldn't believe it! I was then in a quandary. I felt I couldn't say, 'Actually I don't like it after all,' and what I really wanted to say was 'Are you shitting me?' To save my embarrassment in front of the other WAGs, I handed over my credit card and left the boutique with the most expensive bag of shopping I have ever purchased.

While I knew I could afford the dress, I was uneasy about the prospect of breaking the price tag news to my husband. I didn't usually spend money frivolously, and had never before spent that much money on one item. I felt worried about telling him because I hadn't checked with him first; not that I had to, but morally I felt that such a big spend would warrant at least a quick call to my man for his opinion.

When I told him, he looked at me in surprise. He wasn't used to me being so extravagant. 'Did you have enough in your account?' he asked.

'Yes, of course,' I replied.

'Oh, good,' he said. 'If you hadn't, I could've transferred some more to you.'

I was a little shocked at his reaction. Not only was he fine about me making such a transaction, but he was prepared to give me yet more money to pay for it too. I actually felt dismayed at how lavish my life had become. I was so much more fortunate than others I knew, and I didn't have to work for my lifestyle. It had been handed to me on a plate. I sensed the unfairness in the world, yet equally, I felt bloody lucky.

The houses I've lived in have been dream homes by most people's standards. One looked like the Barbie Dream House I had as a child; it even had huge white pillars that flanked the front door. At the tender age of just twenty-one I lived in my boyfriend's five-bedroom house with a gym and a swimming pool. It was worth well over a million pounds. We then moved to a house that we sold for £1.5 million; it was huge, too big for us. Some of the rooms we used only at Christmas when we had family to stay.

The house had six bedrooms, an enormous open-plan kitchen and seating area, and a gorgeous sunken lounge. We had his and hers dressing rooms, which we put in ourselves. I even had a wardrobe for my hand-bags, an ornate hook in place for each one. I had a shoe wardrobe with metal frames that could be pulled out to display my whole collection. My husband had a tie wardrobe for his hundreds of ties. Even the rented houses we have lived in have been gorgeous; one cost £7,000 a month. It's no wonder I have never been short of friends and family coming to stay everywhere we have lived in the country. They've often said that when they visit it's like being in a five-star hotel. I make swans out of towels and put them on their beds for when they arrive.

I've been amazed at some of the people I've met during my time as a WAG. I met a super-celebrity after I'd gone to watch my husband play for England. I was with my parents and my parents-in-law. We all watched the game together and revelled in the atmosphere of the Players' Lounge, which was full of WAGs, their families and friends. The atmosphere was electric during the match – there was raucous cheering, then collective 'oooohs'. At tense moments – the important corners, the near-to-goal free-kicks – you could have heard a pin drop in the room.

My man had played extremely well; he more than deserved the England cap he received for it. I felt so proud of him. After the match, the noise of us all chatting and laughing filled the air, and the room was warm with nervous energy. Photographs of famous footballers adorned the walls, an immaculate red carpet decked the floor and the chairs and tables were of a sleek, modern design. The bar was stocked with every variety of drink possible and the staff were dressed in crisp suits.

We sat down at a large, circular polished table to wait for my man to arrive from the changing rooms. I was totally exhausted. It had been a very emotional day. My nerves felt shot, my adrenalin must have reached new levels throughout the match and I had a sore throat from all the shouting I had done.

I could barely keep my eyes off the door because I was so excited to see my man, to give him a big cuddle and a congratulatory kiss. As usual, he took ages to arrive. One by one the likes of Gary Neville, Michael Owen, Paul Scholes and Rio Ferdinand entered the room. Before they even reached their families they were swamped by people shaking their hands and asking for autographs.

Suddenly, the crowd that had gathered near the door began to divide, as the Red Sea did for Moses. I couldn't see who had entered, but I kept trying to stick my neck out to see what the commotion was all about. Then, as if someone had pressed mute and a spotlight had been switched on, the most famous, and gorgeous, England footballer of all time walked through the throngs. It was only bloody David Beckham!

He headed straight towards me. I didn't know where to look. He looked so good in his England suit and shiny shoes. As he approached me I felt hotter and hotter and my cheeks, no doubt, became redder and redder. He was smiling, and it seemed as if he was coming to talk to me. Me? Surely not! Then, as he came within touching distance and just before I could mouth 'hello', as if he was an old friend, he brushed past my chair and knocked my coat off the back of it.

He stopped, picked it up, and said, 'Oh, sorry about that,' and I responded with a rather eloquent 'Err, err, err, yeah!' and giggled like a nervous teenager. He rendered me a stuttering mess. As he joined the group of men he had come in to see, who were positioned immediately behind me, I sat back and breathed in the most beautiful scent I have ever smelled. His aftershave was as gorgeous as he was. That man has the most amazing aura. He can literally silence a room with his presence.

A little later, once I had cooled down and returned to a more appropriate shade of fake tan, my man walked in. He moved quickly through the crowds that gathered around him for his autograph and arrived at our table. I literally jumped into his arms. My mouth went into overdrive with praise for him, and our parents rose from their seats to hug and kiss him in recognition of how well he had played.

We decided it would be best if our parents left together through the main entrance and that we took the back way to his car. There were hundreds of fans patiently waiting for the players to leave the ground. We walked down the back staircases, chaperoned by a security guard, then waited for a moment before the door was opened. There were a few other players waiting too; we had formed a small group. I didn't know whose shoulder brushed against mine, or who was behind me, but I looked down to my right and saw the most beautiful pair of black pointy stilettos.

Instinctively I looked to see who owned such stunning footwear and came face to face with Victoria Beckham! She was stunning, looking as perfect as she does in her images; her glossy, tousled hair rested immaculately about her shoulders. She also smelled phenomenally good. She gave me a quick smile, then once the doors opened she darted off to the blacked out car that had pulled up for her.

I was a massive Spice Girls fan when I was younger and have always loved Victoria Beckham's style and image. As for David Beckham, what girl in their right mind would not quiver in his presence? The guy put on a skirt and rocked it. They are the king and queen of the football world and I am well and truly star-struck every time I see them.

When I was engaged, my footballer surprised me with front-row tickets to see Elton John in concert in London. I was immensely excited as I am a huge fan and adore all of his songs. The concert was awesome, magical. We danced to 'Saturday, Saturday' and I cried to 'Candle In The Wind' as it reminded me of the wonderful Princess Diana. I was gutted when he sang his last song, thanked the audience and left the stage.

My fiancé suggested that we hang around for a bit, and that was fine by me. I couldn't be bothered to be pushed and shoved by the crowds hurrying to leave the theatre. It seemed the whole front row had the same plan in mind, and no one attempted to leave the theatre. After a while, I turned around and saw that the place was empty. I told my husband that we should leave, but he requested that we stay 'just a little bit longer'.

Moments later, a steward approached our row and asked everyone to follow him. Then, the penny dropped. We were going to meet Elton John! I was gob-smacked. 'Are we meeting Elton?' I whispered to my fiancé.

'Yep, we sure are! Surprise!' He smiled back.

I started shaking. I couldn't believe I was going to

meet such a legend in person. As we followed the steward out of the side door and up onto the stage, there sat Elton, at his very shiny white grand piano. It was a surreal moment. He stood up and greeted each one of us, shaking all of our sweaty hands. He was much shorter than I'd thought, but just as camp and outrageous as I imagined him to be. He had true star quality. I couldn't tell you what he said to me, it's all a little hazy; I couldn't believe I was standing next to the man himself. I had never felt so in awe.

I met Lionel Richie after one of his concerts, and what a bloody nice guy he is. He was an absolute gentleman to talk to, friendly, enquiring and, by all accounts, normal. However, I wasn't able to say much to him: I could barely string two words together, given how humbled I felt to be in his presence.

I have also met Prince Charles at a Prince's Trust event and seen his over so dashing son Prince Harry on a night out in London, in an elite, members-only club. From what I saw of him, he behaved particularly well, contrary to his hedonistic reputation.

I have met practically the entire cast of *Coronation Street* and partied in the same top-end venues with the cast of *Made in Chelsea* and *The Only Way Is Essex*; I'm a big fan of the latter. I have also met Tess and Vernon Kay, who are a lovely couple, Rihanna, Usher, Claudia Schiffer and Caprice. I've been so close to the boys from Westlife that I could smell their deodorant. I've rubbed shoulders with famous Formula 1 drivers, although I can't for the life of me remember which ones they were, and that's not to mention the vast

array of world-famous footballers and sportsmen I
have met, or in some cases am privileged to call
friends.

Chapter Fifteen

*M*eeting celebrities is a fun perk in the dream-like aspect of WAGdom, but I appreciate the dream holidays more than anything. As a child we always went abroad. I was taken skiing every year from the age of five, and I visited many parts of America and Europe with my family. I was used to going on nice holidays, staying in expensive hotels and travelling Premium Economy.

The first holiday my footballer took me on was to St Tropez in the South of France. I hadn't been there before, but I'd heard that it was full of rich people, multi-million-pound yachts and Ferraris. When we got to the airport, we checked in with the airline and headed to the departures lounge. Unbeknown to me, my boyfriend had managed to get us into one of the VIP lounges to wait for our flight. I had never had such treatment before. I was used to aimlessly walking around the duty-free shops and obsessively staring at the departures board for the gate to be named when I was early for a flight.

A lady in a sharp suit sat at a desk at the entrance to the lounge, checked us in and gave us each a glass of champagne. The room was tastefully decorated. There were beautiful displays of orchids in large black vases positioned around the room. Huge comfortable sofas skirted the walls, and on one side of the room there was an enormous floor-to-ceiling window that looked directly out onto the runway. There were showers, changing rooms and immaculate toilets with individual towels to dry your hands on; there wasn't a paper towel or hand-drier in sight.

When we had found a place to sit, another woman approached us and asked if we would like anything to eat or drink. The choice of food was extensive. I opted for Eggs Benedict and my boyfriend had smoked salmon and scrambled eggs. As I sipped my champagne I couldn't help but think how lucky I was to have such special treatment. My boyfriend was totally used to it. After an hour or so, the receptionist reappeared and informed us that our flight had been called. We didn't even have to check the board.

When we arrived in France, we grabbed our bags off the carousel and headed to the exit. I had assumed we would be boarding a transfer coach or joining the taxi queue to get to our hotel. That idea was quashed when my man ushered me to a black limousine that had pulled into the pick-up area. He had pre-booked our luxury travel. His thoughtfulness made me feel very special, and our transport made me feel like a film star.

The hotel was magnificent. It was pristine, and of sleek modern decor, with five-star service. We ate out in top restaurants where I tried oysters and caviar for the first time. We shopped in the outrageously overpriced boutiques that St Tropez has to offer and we had the most wonderful time soaking up the sun on the beach.

From that first experience of a first-class holiday with my footballer, the standards have never dropped. Whenever we go away together we do so in style. We book into the airport's VIP lounge before every flight. We have been to the most amazing places and seen the most amazing sights.

Being a WAG has enabled me not only to become well travelled, but cultured too. I am actually now fluent in twenty-three languages . . . if only! I'm not even bilingual, but my Spanish phrasebook gets a lot of use . . .

As soon as the football fixtures are released for the forthcoming season I immediately put the date of the last game into my diary. On that day, the minute my husband leaves the stadium, he is a free man for a whole six weeks. Football is a footballer's life, not just their job, so when the holiday season hits, it's the only time of the year that they are within no one's jurisdiction but their own.

The off-season is another reason why it's difficult for a WAG to get a steady, full-time job: few employers would let a member of their staff bugger off for six weeks of every year to go on holiday with their partner. Equally, there aren't many footballers who would be happy to hang around the house in their holiday season until their wife or girlfriend can get a week or two off work.

I certainly wouldn't be happy without my man in

the holiday season, given it's the only time of the year that I feel like I have a real husband, and my kids remember that they do actually have a father.

So, the lifestyle I gained upon becoming a WAG has included many foreign holidays during that six-week off-season. I could give Judith Chalmers a run for her money with the places I've been to. We both decided that to go to the same place every year would be boring. My husband and I like to experience new things, and we made a pact that we'd explore as much of the world as we could while we were still young enough to do it, and while we have enough money to afford it.

We made a list of all the places we would like to visit before we die, and we've already ticked off quite a few. The one I cannot wait for is a skiing holiday to Val d'Isère. The trip will only be possible once my husband has retired as unfortunately his football insurance would not cover such a high-risk sport. He is itching to see the Great Wall of China and to drive Route 66 in a Winnebago. He also wrote 'a space shuttle to the moon' on the list, which at the time was a joke, but in this era it seems a viable future opportunity. It would be his dream to go up into space; he takes a great interest in astronomy and I often catch him teaching our children about the star configurations and the planets.

In recent years we've been to Barbados, the Bahamas, Jamaica, Bermuda, the Maldives, Orlando, Miami, Marbella, St Tropez, Nice, Dubai, New York, Las Vegas, Rome, Venice, Sardinia, Paris, Tenerife,

Ibiza and Greece. When I look at the places I've been to, I feel extremely lucky. I doubt I would have visited half of these places at my age if it wasn't for my husband's employment. I am more grateful to him for the travel experiences his profession has afforded us than any of the material things he has provided for me.

I was also fortunate enough to be one of the WAGs who were invited to accompany the England squad on an international trip. The England manager at the time saw WAGs as an important support network for the players, unlike the perception of current football managers. The break was seen as a chance for everyone to bond and to get some real team spirit flowing. The gaffer had chartered a British Airways plane specifically for the England players and their WAGs to fly to a beautiful part of the Mediterranean.

I was nervous prior to the trip. In preparation, I'd panic bought eight different bikinis and sarongs and spent a fortune on primping and preening myself. I feared the undoubtable presence of the media and was concerned about how the dynamics of the WAG group would work.

When we arrived at the airport terminal we were met by airport staff and the paparazzi. I adopted my dark-sunglasses-and-head-down position to avoid the camera flashes, and the airport staff escorted us swiftly and directly to the first-class lounge. It wasn't difficult to identify our group of fellow travellers: the WAGs were always dolled up to the max. The majority wore stilettos and all of them had a designer handbag as their hand-luggage. The footballers looked more relaxed, but their well-honed physiques and sharp dress sense ensured that they stood out from the others in the lounge.

Everyone seemed excited, and nervous in anticipation of where we were going. We were introduced to each other and made football-related small-talk about who we knew and where we lived until it was time for us to walk onto the Tarmac and up the steps to the plane. I was so nervous that I had the shakes; when I was handed a glass of champagne by the smiley BA air stewardess on the way into the cabin it was a great feat not to spill it over myself.

The seats in first class were amazing, like big leather armchairs. My seat faced towards the cockpit and my footballer's seat faced towards mine so that we could easily look at each other. Each couple had their own interconnecting 'love seat', as we nicknamed them, and I couldn't help but constantly look around to see what everyone was up to. I wondered if anyone would dare to make any Mile High Club membership attempts.

The flight was short and smooth and the WAGs did a lot of champagne-drinking throughout it. Our glasses were constantly being filled, while our men in their England kit sipped orange juice and water, being the true professionals they were. Hardly anyone left their seats to socialize during the flight. After we had landed we were again escorted through the airport terminal, flanked by yet more camera flashes, and into individual chauffeur-driven cars.

We were all impressed with the resort we arrived at.

It was huge, and the architecture of the buildings was hacienda-style. It had every type of sports facility imaginable, and was complete with a nightclub and a casino. The hotel suites were large and modern; we had a high-tech Jacuzzi bath in ours and the coastal views from our terrace were breathtaking.

Even before we had unpacked, the lads were made aware of their strict training schedule. The majority of hours in their days had been accounted for; some days they had to train well into the evening. The WAGs had no pre-prepared itinerary so we all quickly concluded that the only thing to do was to sunbathe by the pool. Tough times.

I knew a couple of the England WAGs prior to the trip. One was foreign and her temper scared the hell out of me. She was hilariously funny, warm and empathetic to those who were in her good books, but if anyone crossed her, even if they unwittingly did so, she let them know it – and loudly. Fiery WAG was fluent in English and she swore like a trooper bilingually; she was very petite and smoked like a chimney, which marred her beauty a little.

The other WAG I knew was very tall, slim and beautiful. She was the type that no one would want to sunbathe next to since her goddess-like figure was enough to make even the most narcissistic WAG feel a little self-conscious. Tall WAG was well educated, and I had previously connected with her on many levels since she'd had a similar upbringing to mine and we therefore shared a lot of the same views. The only reason I knew who the other WAGs were was because

I recognized them from the pages of glossy magazines or from my various Players' Lounge experiences at away matches.

The WAGs formed cliques relatively quickly. The foreign WAGs, young WAGs, older WAGs, southern WAGs and northern WAGs bonded in like-for-like groups. There were also a few WAGs who made it clear that they hadn't come along to make friends.

I was one of the youngest WAGs on the trip and bonded with those nearest my age. We weren't married to our partners and most of us weren't even engaged at that point. We naturally created a routine to our days whereby every morning we would meet at the sunbeds around the pool, then chat for hours. We mostly spoke about the other WAGs, and they probably talked about us. We read magazines, swam, dozed, discussed fashion and, of course, we couldn't avoid the subject of football.

It was refreshing to learn that we were all in the same boat. Most of us had followed our partners to live away from our families and all of us were new to experiencing the shit that came with being a WAG. Meeting those WAGs was the first time I felt I wasn't alone in WAGdom. My friends at home didn't really understand what the hard times were like. They just saw I was living in a huge house, driving around in a brand new 4x4 and had decided that I was 'living the dream'. They had no idea of the pressures and strains I was under, but the WAGs did.

I knew from the start that one WAG wasn't going to be my cup of tea. Her conversation was infantile, she was bitchy, and ultimately came across as ignorant and arrogant. Her accent got on my nerves too. Her boyfriend was also an idiot: he was her in male form. Their combined IQ scores may have just exceeded a gnat's. When she made relationship comparisons it was as if she believed that they had one up on everyone else because theirs was established and secure and ours were, apparently, temporary and without any foundations. Physically, they didn't look well matched as a couple; she wasn't as blessed in the looks department as the other WAGs were.

I had silently predicted that it would be just a matter of time before he cheated on her, given how shallow he was and the female attention that footballers command. What I didn't expect was for the dumb WAG to remain with her man after not one but a handful of kiss-and-tell stories printed in the newspapers over the subsequent years, despite appearing in public as if they have the perfect relationship.

Thankfully, her presence on that first England away trip did not spoil the experience for me. The food we were served was exquisite, the relaxation we had in the daytime was greatly appreciated and the evening dinners with our partners in our WAG cliques were hugely entertaining. All of the players got on well together and conversation flowed around the dinner table; it was surreal to think that the seemingly normal guys I was spending time with were actually England footballers. Then again, I found it difficult to make that association with my own partner: people are people, regardless of their job.

Sadly, the invitation to England away trips isn't always extended to WAGs, these days. The negative stereotype of WAGs as a detrimental distraction has put a stop to it. And to think of all the WAGs who were looking forward to sunning themselves in Brazil . . .

As well as going on dream holidays, being a WAG has also enabled me to fulfil some smaller bucket list-type dreams. For example, from a young age I had always wanted to have tea at the Ritz. My parents took me to London every year to see the Christmas lights and we always walked past it. I remember that I used to think what an absolutely amazing building it was. I was mesmerized by the Ritz sign that glowed brightly in the London sky, and I remember feeling curious about the well-dressed ladies and gentlemen who went in and came out of the front doors. I used to think that the Ritz was where the Queen had her afternoon cup of tea! I also read that Marilyn Monroe had stayed there when she was in the UK. I dreamed of experiencing it for myself.

After I gave birth to our first child I was in need of a break. My parents had agreed to babysit for a weekend when there was an international game that my husband wasn't involved in so he could take me away somewhere. I decided on London, because I didn't want to go too far away from my baby. Plus I love everything about the city: the culture, the nightlife, the shopping, the hectic hustle and bustle.

We travelled early on the Saturday morning and checked into the Dorchester Hotel on Park Lane. It's a dream place to stay. It oozes grandeur, wealth and history. The rooms are beautiful and the service is fantastic. I adore staying there. In the afternoon, after we'd spent hours in Harrods and Harvey Nicks in Knightsbridge, my husband hailed us a cab.

When the taxi driver asked where we wanted to go, my husband said, 'The Ritz, please.'

I looked at him in shock. 'What? Why are we going there?' I asked.

'I've booked us in for afternoon tea. It's what you have always wanted to do, right?' he replied, with a smile.

I was overwhelmed. Once again my husband had totally surprised me with a heartfelt gesture . . . and made one of my dreams come true.

When we arrived at the Ritz, a man dressed in the traditional black tails and top hat opened the taxi door for us and greeted us with an eloquent 'Good afternoon, Madam and Sir.' I instantly felt like a VIP! We then walked into the outstanding building. I admired the beautiful chandeliers, which twinkled from the ceiling, and the decadent gold detailing on the walls, enhanced by the opulent marble. It was so damn stylish. I felt like we had stepped back in time and travelled to the 1950s. The afternoon tea was incredible. The finger sandwiches and cakes were served on a gorgeous three-tier silver cake-stand and it was all delicious. The tea tasted dreamy; in fact, the tea I drank in the Ritz was the best tea I have ever had.

Another memorable 'dream come true' was when my husband and I dined on the Orient Express. Unforgettable. As we travelled through the English countryside on the stylish and historic train, we sipped champagne and ate the most exquisite food. It really was a remarkable experience and very romantic.

We also had VIP Grand Prix tickets at Silverstone one year and got to meet racing legends such as Damon Hill and Michael Schumacher. I'm not a fan of Formula 1: the noise of the cars racing around the track is almost deafening. But it was a fantastic experience. I particularly loved the three-course lunch we had as part of the hospitality package. I also got to watch the Monaco Grand Prix from my husband's friend's apartment. His multi-million-pound penthouse had views over part of the track and it was truly magical to view the cars whizzing round the streets below.

On the sporting theme, I've had the privilege to sit at Centre Court for a few Wimbledon finals. I was there when Andy Murray beat Novak Djokovic in 2013, when Roger Federer beat Murray in 2012, and when Serena Williams beat her sister Venus in 2009. The contact number my husband has to get these tickets is the best on his phone, in my opinion. The tickets are not cheap – he has to pay a few thousand pounds for each one – but I think it's money well spent. A final at Wimbledon is a priceless experience. The pressure the tennis players are under is tangible from the seats. It's intense and immensely entertaining. I have always loved watching Wimbledon, and in keeping with tradition, I always eat an abundance of strawberries and cream during the weeks it's on.

Another highlight of my life as a WAG is walking down the red carpet at various film premières. My favourite was *Bridget Jones*. My husband didn't fancy it so I ended up asking three of my friends from home. When I arrived at their houses to collect them, they were so excited because, as a treat, I had booked a black limousine to take us to London and back. They had never been in one before so were quite over-whelmed. I also arranged for it to be stacked with bottles of champagne that we managed to drink on the way. Consequently we made a good few toilet stops.

We got to walk up the red carpet to the cinema in Leicester Square to hundreds of camera flashes. My friends were intimidated by the masses of press present. Nevertheless, we really enjoyed the film and we got to meet Renée Zellweger, which was a surprising bonus. To this day we still reminisce about that evening.

Finally, the dreamlike aspects of being a WAG have included partying in some of the most exclusive nightclubs in London, Miami, Las Vegas and New York, those that are strictly members or guest list only. I've rubbed shoulders at the bar or on the dance-floor with many famous people in such places. My husband has a contact who can get him into any venue he so desires. The contact's phone is switched on 24/7: if we leave one club and want spontaneously to go to another, the opportunity is always just one call away.

We always secure one of the best VIP tables in any

given establishment and it is guaranteed to be laden with champagne, vodka and mixers upon arrival. At one club in Las Vegas we were seated next to Paris Hilton's table. I couldn't help but stare at her all night. She really rated herself and I wasn't impressed by what I saw. She strutted around the club as if she were a goddess. She was so thin too; she looked like her limbs might snap if even the slightest pressure was put upon them.

The exclusive experiences I've had, the expensive possessions I own and the world-famous celebrities I've met have all produced a thrill in me. I'm very grateful and appreciative that I've had such opportunities and made some wonderful memories that other people can perhaps only dream of.

However, I am not 'living the dream'. My life is by no means constant entertainment and excitement. Show me a life that is. It makes me cringe to watch or read about the Z-listers who screech, 'I'm living the dream.' What is this dream? I'm still unsure.

I think it was Chantelle Houghton, the previously unknown girl who went on to win a series of *Celebrity Big Brother*, who propelled the phrase into existence. She thought she was 'living the dream' because she got fame and fortune overnight, catapulted from being a normal girl one day to being a public figure the next. I recently read an interview she gave to a glossy magazine and her life doesn't sound like a dream. Failed relationships, press intrusion, single parenthood and body-image issues seem to be some of the themes to her life as a celebrity.

Also, dreams can come true without money and fame. The most important dreams that have come true for me are falling in love, having a family and still having my health and sanity, albeit only just, as far as the last two are concerned . . .

Chapter Sixteen

*A*m a very impressionable person. I had a best friend through my school years who, while not officially diagnosed, clearly suffered from anorexia. The more time I spent with her, the less I ate. Her behaviour and attitude towards food rubbed off on me: food became my enemy, as it was hers. 'Food makes you fat' and 'Eating is cheating' were the mantras we adopted.

During this phase I worried my mother senseless. At school I would throw my packed lunch away so she would think I had eaten it, and at home I would scrape whole dinners into the bin whenever her back was turned. The best thing that ever happened to me was my best friend leaving my school as her father had relocated. When she departed, so did my dangerous non-eating patterns, and my mother's sanity returned.

It's inevitable that the person you reside with, the person you spend almost every waking hour with, the person you talk to most in your life, will influence you in some way or another. I live with a professional athlete who is not only the epitome of physical fitness and health but also in the public eye, so he has a very strict grooming regime. The knock-on effect of having someone like him around me for years is that I, too, have exhaustingly high-maintenance health, fitness, grooming and dieting habits. Some I am not proud of; others I would encourage.

I also live my life in the bubble of WAGdom where there is pressure to look not just good but perfect. In WAGdom there is one big competition to be the best: to have the best skin, to be the thinnest, the fittest, the hottest WAG. No one wants to be the ugly fat WAG. It's as if we WAGs are constantly trying to prove to each other that we deserve our WAG title, our foot-baller partner, our big house, our huge monthly housekeeping budget, and we prove it via manufac-turing and maintaining our appearance. We conform to the stereotypical image of beauty in attempts to fit in with each other. Consequently, I, along with the majority of the WAGs, have tried and tested every ridiculous fad diet, miraculous gym equipment, the latest wonder face cream, and gone to extreme measures of meddling with cosmetic surgery to try to compete.

It's not just the WAGs who strive to be the best groomed or the most flawless. The media pollutes minds with images that they encourage women to aspire to. Celebrities are depicted as looking immacu-late and body beautiful, and the odd normal pictures of celebrities letting it all hang out or without their make-up on are often slated by the press.

The only difference between WAGs and every other

normal girl on the street is that we can afford to do more in order to present the most perfect picture of ourselves. We can spend thousands of pounds on hair extensions and the most expensive anti-cellulite creams. We can pay for personal trainers to kick our butts into shape. We face the same body-image pressures as the next person, but for WAGs the pressure is amplified, given that our footballers are considered great catches and other women scramble for their attention, including the beautiful celebrities.

The media has stereotyped WAGs always to look glamorous; we wear designer garments, oversized sunglasses and carry labelled handbags as a rule, and if we step outside of that norm and leave the house looking different, it creates a negative sensation. WAGs who dress down and look normal are described as run-down, fat or ugly.

I would absolutely hate to be photographed with the roots of my hair on show, with no make-up on or flabby bits of skin hanging over my jeans. I think about how I look every time I leave the house. I feel great empathy for those celebrities pictured on an off-day: the human ego is delicate, and being publicly humiliated for looking your natural self hurts like hell.

It's ridiculous that the press concoct elaborate explanations as to why a WAG looks tired, is make-up-free or wearing a tracksuit: 'She's depressed' or 'Her relationship's on the rocks' are some of the generic fallacies. Their explanation is rarely that the WAG is simply a normal human being who doesn't want to have to leave the house looking like she's going to a nightclub *every* day. That story wouldn't sell newspapers.

I believe that looking good begins with being healthy. Quite frankly, good health is all that matters in life and without it you have nothing.

I'm fortunate enough to be healthy. I'm rarely ill or at the doctor's. I eat my five-a-day, drink at least two litres of water a day and take daily vitamins, including cod-liver oil and milk-thistle capsules. I have not and will never smoke. In my opinion, there is just nothing good about it and I simply cannot understand why people still do it when they know the hideous consequences it can have on the body. Additionally, it's an expensive habit, it stinks and, these days, it's highly inconvenient since smoking inside public places is banned.

My husband hates smoking more than I do. He even went as far as to threaten, 'If you ever smoke I will divorce you.' I had been arguing with him and had jokingly stated that I would perhaps have to start smoking to deal with the stress he brought me. He probably would divorce me if I started smoking. If he had a mental image of me sparking up a fag, I'm not sure he would ever be able to get an erection for me again.

Furthermore, I've never taken drugs. I am totally and utterly clueless on the subject. I am not a risk-taker and I feel that if you are prepared to take drugs, you are risking your life. I have never even tried a 'happy' cake. I know people who regularly smoke cannabis as if their joints were cigarettes, and those who have parties and serve marijuana brownies as party food. I have friends who regularly take cocaine, especially when socializing in bars and nightclubs.

However, apart from those three WAGs at my wedding, I have not heard any other rumours in WAGdom to indicate that there are WAGs who regularly take drugs. I'm sure there must be some, the odds of probability would suggest so, and perhaps my naivety blinds me a little, but I am convinced that WAGs, as a general rule, avoid illegal substances. Perhaps it's to stay healthy, or because they can get their false highs from a shopping trip. Whatever, it's a refreshing phenomenon.

I know a few WAGs who smoke. I also know a few footballers who smoke socially. They would curl up and die if they were photographed in a paper smoking and would surely shit themselves at the gaffer's re-action to such images the next day. Nevertheless it is their guilty pleasure, and most of us have one.

My guilty pleasure is alcohol. I'm ashamed to say that I'm a binge-drinker. I don't drink a glass of wine most evenings, like some WAGs do; I drink a whole vineyard on a night out instead! My preferred drink is vodka with soda water and lime cordial, simply because it is one of the lowest-calorie beverages, coming in at 63, as compared to a glass of white wine, which is roughly 250. On some big nights out my low-calorie vodka mixers may be chased with a few rounds of Jägerbomb and shots of tequila, but I pay for it the following day. I get deathly hangovers. I could be wiped out for days with the repercussions of a

Saturday night on the lash. I don't condone binge-drinking: it's reckless, irresponsible and dangerous, yet equally often copious amounts of fun!

My daily diet is well-balanced and healthy. The wholesome breakfast I make for my husband consists of coffee, brown toast, porridge or poached eggs: he needs the energy for the gruelling training session ahead of him. For me, breakfast consists of a coffee because I usually go to the gym in the morning and if I exercise on a full stomach I'm prone to getting cramps. After the gym, my mid-morning snack will consist of some sort of fruit. Lunch is a salad or soup or a jacket potato and my man will have the same, but a portion that is four times bigger than mine. I will perhaps have more fruit and a coffee in the afternoon to get me through to dinner, or a low-calorie cereal bar.

Freshly steamed vegetables are always a major part of our evening meal. We tend to eat four kinds of vegetables served with a chicken breast, or salmon or tuna steak with brown rice. We also have a steak once a week, but that's it for red meat. We very rarely have pudding, but we more than make up for that of an evening. When the kids are all tucked up in bed, we crack open some chocolate, stuff our faces with biscuits, or dive into the ice cream. We're terrible for craving sweet things. My husband always has a huge bowl of cereal before bed too, usually in a Pyrex dish filled to the brim. I desperately want to have the same, but there is a line I try not to cross: I try to limit myself to one naughty treat of an evening.

Generally, I try hard to stick to 1,500 calories a day. I

constantly calorie count and log each and every thing I put into my mouth in my diet and fitness app on my iPhone. I use the app more than my diary. It's made me aware of the shocking calorie content of some normal foods. Before, I was blissfully unaware of the calorie content of some food so I would happily eat anything that was put in front of me. A huge treat used to be a Big Mac Meal in McDonald's. I'm not stupid, I knew it was fattening, but I loved its taste! However, when restaurants and food brands began writing the calorie content of their offerings overtly on the menus or packaging, I began avoiding lots of dishes. If I go to Maccy D's now I'll have a Filet-O-Fish because it's one of the lowest-calorie items on the menu. Oh, how sad my life has become!

Although I maintain a well-balanced diet, I do limit the amount of pasta, white bread, and rice I eat. Not only are they all terribly calorific but they make me bloated. I once did the famous low-carbohydrate diet for about three weeks and, although I struggled to keep to it, as it turns out that pretty much everything has carbs in it, I actually lost ten pounds and my stomach had never been as flat as it was then. However, as soon as I finished the diet and started eating jacket potatoes and brown bread again, the pounds piled back on. Therefore, from my experiences, low-carb diets are great for quick weight loss if there's an occasion to slim for, but they're not a realistic diet to be on for ever.

The only diet I recommend is the gruelling detox diet I put myself through every January. It is when I eat 'clean'. I eat raw and organic greens and fruit, and drink copious amounts of water and herbal tea. I do not touch alcohol or caffeine for the whole month. It's just what I need after all the toxins I put into my body from drinking mulled wine and eating chocolate over Christmas. In the first few days of January I feel like shit. I have headaches, my skin breaks out with acne, and I'm constantly on the toilet due to my increased fluid and fibre consumption. However, with much perseverance these symptoms soon go and then I start to feel energetic and healthy, while my skin clears and glows.

When February arrives and the detox is over, I celebrate by ordering a huge takeaway pizza, then slowly slip back into my old ways of snacking in the evenings and binge-drinking at weekends. At least my liver thanks me for the January off-season.

I have only very recently concluded that fad diets do not work. Just because I read that Kim Kardashian has been on some stupidly unrealistic Hollywood diet, I shouldn't follow suit. It's not rocket science to appreciate that the hyped-up diets the press or PR companies circulate on social media are short-term and sheer hell to do. Since seeing the light, I am probably the healthiest I have ever been: my diet nowadays is more varied and includes a bit of everything.

There are a few diet tips that I do try to abide by and that I can recommend as reliable ways to lose weight. First, drinking a pint of water before a main meal definitely results in eating less of what's on the plate. Second, not eating after six in the evening results in a less-bloated feeling the next day. Third, I find that brushing my teeth at regular intervals during the day tricks my brain into not eating: a clean, toothpaste-tasting mouth doesn't want food in it. It works for me. Also, I find that exercising in the morning is a good way to start the day; it kicks off the metabolism and brings energy to the body. Exercise can be in any form: the gym, an exercise DVD – anything is better than nothing.

I have always exercised and generally been an active person. Currently, I go to the gym at least three times a week where I do roughly forty minutes of aerobic exercise on the treadmill, thirty minutes on the cross-trainer, twenty minutes of weights on the resistance machines, then two hundred sit-ups. Also, my husband has developed a few fitness programmes for me that have been very useful; professional footballers are probably just as knowledgeable as a personal trainer.

I am a bad candidate for any class that involves coordination so I avoid them; when I have ever tried them out, I've been the one who turns the wrong way or accidentally falls into the person next to me.

Once I got roped into a pole-dancing class as a WAG friend told me it was fantastic for body toning. She had her own pole installed in the corner of her bedroom to practise on. No wonder her footballer had a permanent smirk on his face. Pole-dancing was the hardest exercise I have ever tried. When I first tried to hoist my legs into the air, I literally couldn't get them off the ground without gripping the pole – I resembled a chimpanzee. When the instructor pushed my bum to get me to the top of the pole, I got a bout of vertigo and nearly passed out! The lifts and twists on the pole were immensely difficult even to attempt, let alone achieve.

After that experience, I gained a new respect for strippers, although I've not lifted my husband's ban on him going to strip clubs. Pole-dancers must be so damn strong and flexible. I ended up sitting out most of the session since I felt defeated by the demands of the instructor! I was in awe of my WAG friend's ability on the pole, although I did have a laugh when she stripped down to her thong just for the craic!

I think it's imperative that people try lots of types of exercise. When a person finds what they enjoy doing, that's when exercise will have the best result on the body: if it's enjoyable, you'll keep doing it.

I have never had a personal trainer unlike most of the WAGs I know. They spend thousands on them. Although, from what I see, they spend a lot of their personal training sessions chatting up their trainer and often end up having crushes on them. If I were a footballer, or any man for that matter, I wouldn't want a fit gym guy assisting my wife with a squat or helping them stretch in pseudo-sexual positions. I prefer to exercise alone. I plug in my iPod, listen to pumping house music and get on with it.

I am a big fan of Power Plates. I use them every time I am in the gym to warm up and cool down my muscles. A Power Plate is a machine that gives your muscles a high-speed workout by using vibrations to make muscles contract and relax. It produces a strange sensation in the body as body fat is literally shaken at a high intensity – it's like standing on a vibrating washing-machine. I was very embarrassed the first few times I used one in the gym; I was overtly conscious of the fact my bum was wobbling up and down like a mound of jelly. The results from using Power Plates are brilliant: I now have muscle definition that I would never have developed from just working out. There are claims that ten minutes on a Power Plate will have the same results as a sixty-minute aerobic workout! It's genius: all you have to do is stand still and shake!

Around the end of June I start playing tennis. I suspect it's the Wimbledon effect. I challenge my WAG friends to games in the mistaken belief that I'm as good as the Williams sisters! I even let out the odd dramatic grunt when I serve! Racquet sports are not my forte, but I enjoy them. Aside from netball, which I have played in teams since I went to school, sports involving bats or balls are not my thing. I once got knocked out playing rounders: a fellow pupil hit the ball hard into the air, I positioned myself to catch it with my hands held above my head but it slipped through my butter-fingers and my head took the full impact.

I am also not good at running, proper running that is. Jogging like Phoebe from *Friends* is my style: awkward and without control. I am too embarrassed to attempt it, these days. I have all the gear in my wardrobe – the hi-visibility clothing, the sweat band, the special trainers – but most of it still has the labels on. I could look the part of a marathon runner when leaving the house, but I don't want to scare drivers into thinking that I'm running while having a seizure. A couple of my WAG friends have run ten-kilometre races and some have even run the London Marathon. I think they're utterly crazy. I would rather stick pins in my piles than run for that long.

Once I've finished my exercise for the day, I take great pleasure in logging in my app the calories I've burned. I then watch delightedly as my daily bar chart of calorie consumption significantly decreases. It may sound pathetic and obsessive, but my weight-loss tactics prove that an effective way to lose weight, or maintain weight, is not to consume more calories than the daily recommendations. It's an obvious cause and effect: if a person eats more calories than they burn off, they will put on weight.

Anyone can lose weight and be the size they want to be if they just make a few life changes, be strong and persevere. Although I am never completely happy with my body – I'd like a rounder, firmer arse, a few inches off my thighs, more defined arms and defined abs – I am at my happiest when I am the weight I want to be. I believe it's very hard to be totally happy in life unless you are happy within yourself. My motto for exercise is 'You won't see a change unless you make one yourself.'

Chapter Seventeen

An aspect of my body that I was never happy with was my breasts. I wasn't blessed in the chest department: when puberty came, Nature forgot to work on my boobs. I struggled to fill an A-cup bra. They were pert little puppies, but seriously small. I yearned for big breasts and used to look at Pamela Anderson's rack on *Baywatch* with utter envy. I used stuffing in my bra, like the chicken-fillet-shaped sponges and gel pads for instant big-breast fakery.

I've had some hilarious times with those bad boys – in fact, they had names, Bobby and Barb. One drunken night out with my man and a few of our close friends, we were throwing some energetic shapes on the dance-floor in a club packed with football fans when Barb flew out of my bra and flopped straight on to the floor! Then, like something out of a comedy sketch, some poor guy who was dancing behind me slipped on Barb and collapsed with a resonating thud. We were all bent over in hysterics. Some people tried to help the poor guy up, but before they'd managed to get him to his feet, the bouncers waded in, picked him up by his armpits and frog-marched him out of the club, assuming he was too drunk!

The next thing I knew, a girl was holding Barb, asking girls, 'Is this your chicken fillet?' I never did see Barb again. I had a lop-sided boob for the rest of the evening and a guilty conscience regarding the guy who got chucked out. Bobby's boob-span ended that night too. When we got home, I decided drunkenly that it would be funny to cook him to see if he tasted remotely like chicken. I can report with confidence that he didn't. Poor Bobby was laid to rest in the bin. RIP Bobby.

On a serious note, my issues regarding my tiny breasts got worse as I got older. After I'd had my second child, they became hideous. The stretching and shrinking of my breast tissue in pregnancy had made my boobs look like what I can only describe as skanky old tea-bags. They were even smaller, and droopy. I lost my confidence in the bedroom; I would slap my husband's hand away if he ever went in for a good grope. If he wanted a shag, he had a choice: either my padded bra stayed on or the lights went off.

A lot of WAGs have lovely big boobs. One in particular had what I would consider as the dream rack: round and pert, not too big or too small. I wanted mine just like hers. One day I plucked up the courage and asked her if they were real. She replied, with total honesty, 'Are you serious? Of course they aren't! These puppies cost me nearly five grand!'

Her confession got me thinking that I, too, could have a boob job, although I'd never before thought I'd be able to go that far. I wondered if having nice tits might solve my chest and bedroom insecurities but I didn't think my husband would let me go under the knife.

Surprisingly, he practically marched me to the private hospital for a consultation! I'd always felt he was disappointed with my small tits. He used to rib me about them, thinking his jokes would get me over my insecurities. Men can be idiots! His banter included nicknames such as 'Small Tits' and 'Fried Egg Breasts'. I served a few mock insults back his way – 'Pencil Dick', 'Go take your face for a shit', 'You'll never be the man your mother is' – but mine were in jest. I felt his insults were rooted in truth.

His positive reaction to my wanting a boob job did nothing to refute my concerns. That alone made me even more convinced that I could go through the operation. After a few consultations with the private doctor who had been recommended to me by my WAG friend with the great fake tits, the day arrived for my surgery, which would take me from a 32A to a 32C. On the morning of the operation, I was shitting myself with fear.

At that time, my children were very young. My parents had therefore come up to our house to stay with us and to help my husband with them, so I knew they would be fine while I was out of action. However, even leaving my babies for twenty-four hours was upsetting.

As I waited in my private room at the hospital, I started to reconsider my decision. Fear amplified my initial worries about having the operation: I might not wake up after the general anaesthetic, or I'd wake up in the middle of the operation and be paralysed but feel the pain. I worried that something would go wrong and that I'd die on the operating table, leave my kids motherless, and all for the sake of my own vanity. The negative thoughts played in my mind on repeat, like a horror-movie scene stuck on replay. I kept thinking how selfish I was being, risking my life just to have bigger tits.

However, I resolved to go through with it. My husband was behind my decision and, as my WAG friend reminded me in the eleventh-hour phone call I made to her, 'No pain, no gain.' I wanted the change so I had to be brave. I wanted my new boobs badly: I just didn't want to die in the process.

Walking down to the anaesthetic room in my posh hospital gown was one of the scariest things I have ever had to do. I was a shaking, blubbering mess – the nurses must have thought I was an emotional wreck. I lay down on the hospital bed, the anaesthetist arrived, and the last thing I remember was talking to the nurse about her tan! After she told me she'd just got back from a Mediterranean cruise, hey presto! I woke up in a different room, feeling groggy.

After I opened my eyes I vomited a few times, which always happens when I've had a general anaesthetic, then tried to sit up. As I tried to contort my sluggish body into an upright position, a nurse appeared at my side and pushed me back down. I tried to force against her but she resisted my every move, saying, 'Please relax. You don't want to cause any bleeding.'

It was only then that I remembered why I was lying in a hospital bed. My boobs! I looked down and saw two big moulds on my chest. I couldn't see past or over them; it was bizarre. They were rock hard. I wanted to see my nipples, to check that they were in the right place, but it was impossible as they were strapped up tightly with bandages. I was told not to remove them until I was given the all-clear by my consultant. I felt ecstatic at the size of them, and was seriously relieved that the surgery was over.

After I'd been wheeled back to my posh hospital room, with pink curtains and nice serene country scenes on the wall, I couldn't stop looking at my two new friends. I was buzzing, and couldn't wait for my husband to see them too. 'Hello, Pinky, hello, Perky,' I said. Those remain their names today! Pinky and Perky are still as pert and buoyant as they were when I first had them done, and if you ask my husband who his best friends are, he would probably place them joint first on his list.

The breast enlargement cost just short of £5,000, but there were other costs to bear. My mother had to stay with us for an extra two weeks after the operation because I literally couldn't lift my arms higher than my waist: the pain was too great. I couldn't pick my kids up, or even give them a proper cuddle, which was also tough. I had to remain relatively still for at least ten days, unable to exercise. My breasts felt like they would burst at any given moment, given the pain that seared through them. Again I questioned whether I had done the right thing, but when the discomfort subsided and I saw my perfect pair of breasts in the mirror, I confirmed to myself that the short-term agony had been worth it.

I can empathize with people who become addicted to surgery. It's almost instant gratification and often solves a lifetime of self-loathing. I think that if you've the money to do it, then why the hell not enhance what you have? It infuriates me when people deny they have had plastic surgery. I wouldn't judge people if they'd had a nip and tuck, removed the bump from their nose, or had implants inserted into their arse cheeks. I believe that adults should be able to do whatever they want to their bodies if it makes their life better: ultimately, we have just one life and it's senseless to live it in unhappiness. Furthermore, I recognize that happiness is a state of mind, and that vanity is like a disease, but I didn't want to take antidepressants or have counselling sessions to get over my small-boob anxieties. I wanted to change them, and I believe that we should all be entitled to fix ourselves in whatever sensible and controlled manner we see fit.

There are huge risks with surgery. There are also worrying implications for future generations if all women turn to body enhancement: we'd lose our idea of what is real. However, I did it, and I'm much happier because of it. I'm not a grow-old-gracefully kind of person. Fuck that. If I can look thirty when I'm seventy, damn right I'm going to do whatever it takes.

I had my teeth laser-whitened a few years ago and

wore a brace for many years as a child, so my teeth are as straight as a board and I'm happy in the mouth department. I'm not content with the wrinkles section of my face, though.

One cosmetic procedure I have become well and truly hooked on is Botox. I love it. Around three years ago I began having it in my forehead as my frown lines were getting deeper and more visible by the day. Botox acted like a miracle cure. The area gradually begins to freeze, and since the muscles aren't working, the skin stretches out and the wrinkle lines disappear. Botox wears off, but I am a willing addict. It would be ignorant to think that injecting any foreign substance into your body is good for you but, sadly, I've been shallow enough to do it because it makes me look good and thus feel good.

I'm not alone in this but, interestingly, I know only a handful of other WAGs who have it done. This may be because most WAGs are young and have no money worries so there's no need for them to frown! Boob jobs among WAGs are much more common.

Threading is something I have also become a fan of. It's an alternative to waxing, where the therapist uses threads to effectively pluck out hair. I have my upper lip, lower lip and eyebrows threaded every couple of weeks. I love the shape it gives to my brows, but of course not the pain – my eyes still stream every time I have it. Again, no pain, no gain.

That's the only hair-removal procedure I have done as I had the rest of my unwanted body hair lasered off about five years ago. That permanent hair-removal procedure was the bitch of all bitches with regard to pain. The laser felt like I was being repeatedly poked with a burning hot rod every time it hit my skin. I was literally in agony at each of the seven sessions I had to endure to be hairless. The results were fantastic, though. It's amazing not to have to take a razor on holiday. I had my legs done and everything but a small strip of pubic hair on my lady bits. I even had my armpits lasered. At some point I'll get round to having my nipples done as the stray nipple hairs I get drive me mad! Those sneaky buggers appear from nowhere and are verging on being so long that I could plait them. Getting older and hairier is a hair-raising experience!

I find it annoying that culturally women 'should' be hairless yet men are allowed to be hairy beasts. My husband has an acceptable amount of hair on his chest, none on his back and a minimal amount on his legs. He gets a few stragglers in random places, like his shoulders, which I take great pleasure in plucking out and watching him wince. Every two weeks he has a wet shave in a proper old-fashioned barber's and a haircut with his favourite hairdresser, Lucy. His hair is short but his haircut never takes less than an hour; if Lucy could put her tongue back in her mouth and do her job I'm pretty sure it would take ten minutes.

I refer to my husband as 'metrosexual'. His collection of day and night creams is as extensive as mine. His washbag for training includes: moisturizer, deodorant, eye wash, Creed aftershave, shower gel, shampoo and conditioner, nail clippers, chewing gum and lip balm. He always smells so fresh. I like it that he takes care of himself. He's even partial to a manicure every now and again! I have a nail technician who comes to my house every few weeks to give me Shellac nails. It's always quite hilarious to watch him bashfully ask her, when she's finished my treatment, if she has time to sort his cuticles out. She paints a special 'man' varnish onto his nails, which is protective but not shiny. Throughout the whole treatment I can't help but whisper, 'Oooh, suits you, sir!' He usually responds by rolling his eyes at me and telling me where to go!

I love our holidays and being in the sun, but I am dead against sunbeds. As with smoking, the dangers are obvious and well known. It's simple: if you subject your skin to too much UV light you dramatically increase your chance of skin cancer. There are a few WAGs I know who use sunbeds regularly, especially in March and April in preparation for the summer holiday they have booked with their footballer. I guess they think being tanned as opposed to the palest around the pool in Dubai is worth the risk.

I don't, so the only option is to fake it. Over the years I have tried practically every fake tan available on the market. I always end up coming back to St Tropez. I find it lasts the longest, has the best natural colour and sinks in reasonably quickly. My only problem is that it stinks. My husband hates the smell and more often than not we end up sleeping in separate beds on fake-tan nights.

Generally my beauty regime is quite simple and low maintenance. I have tried all the products, from the ridiculously expensive like Crème de la Mer, to the mildly expensive like Clinique, but I always end up back with good old baby wipes to remove my makeup and Elizabeth Arden day and night cream. It's as simple as that. No frills, no real expense. If it works for me, that's what I'll use, whatever the label on the product. I don't think there's any point in forking out over a hundred quid just to say I use Crème de la Mer when really it made my skin oily. These days I rarely even treat myself to a facial as I can't face the break-out of spots afterwards. In my opinion, moisturizing and drinking water is the key to good skin. There is no need to take out another mortgage for a miracle cream.

The exception to my rule on expenditure is make-up. I honestly believe that with make-up products you get what you pay for. The amount of money I have spent on MAC, Dior and Chanel make-up is embarrassing. However, they are my favourites, they last the longest and they are good quality. Dior Airbrush foundation is amazing. You just spray your face with it and instantly your skin is covered. I absolutely adore the colours of eye shadows and blushers on the MAC counter – the choice is phenomenal. I always use Dior mascara too as it never smudges or gives me panda eyes, and the waterproof one is great for holidays. I have quite a collection of Chanel lipsticks and lip glosses as they last the longest and feel the nicest. My favourite scent is Chanel Mademoiselle. It's got a sweet and feminine aroma, which, if I may say so, sums me up too.

I detest tattoos on a woman, but a lot of WAGs have tats. One has three butterflies next to her lady parts. A few WAGs have their kids' names tattooed on the inside of their wrists; this seems like a craze of late. Shockingly, another WAG I know has barbed wire going round her arm, Pamela Anderson style. She has claimed she did it when she was eighteen and drunk. She is currently in the process of having it lasered off, although there will always be a mark on her arm.

I feel the same with piercings. One in each ear lobe can be very pretty, and earrings are fabulous fashion accessories, but nipple, clit, nose and other ear piercings are big no-nos for me. I had my belly button pierced when I was sixteen, and although I haven't worn a ring for at least ten years, I still have an annoying hole just above my belly button.

Last year I went on a girly weekend to Essex with a couple of my friends from home. We wanted to experience it *TOWIE* style so we booked a table at Sugar Hut, shopped in the boutiques owned by the stars of the show and even got a vajazzle in a salon. It was hilarious when we all compared our blinging vaginas back at the hotel. I must say it was nice to treat myself down there for once. Other than having a quick trim every now and again, my lady bits rarely get any attention, from me that is! When I showed the vajazzle to my husband, he just shrugged his shoulders and said, 'That looks nice, I guess.' I wouldn't rush to have another done. They're pretty pointless unless you're into regularly flashing people your nether regions. The gems didn't last long either so all in all they're great for a laugh with the girls but a total waste of time in reality.

The only beauty tip I take from the Essex girls is full lashes. I'm a big fan of eyelash extensions because my lashes are naturally quite short and they instantly add length and fullness. They are quite high maintenance: since they are individually glued on to natural lashes, in-fills are needed every couple of weeks to replace those that naturally drop out. However, the procedure is so relaxing that it's no big deal.

I feel I've put my poor husband through a lot with my grooming experiments and obsessions. The eyelashes, the tans, the painful procedures I moan about – sometimes I think he deserves a medal for putting up with me. Maintaining, or bettering, my appearance has cost him a fortune. I see it as his investment. If he keeps me well maintained now, he'll reap the benefits when I'm older. Hopefully he'll still fancy me when I'm eighty. If all else fails, if my beauty regimes and treatments stop taking effect, then I shall not hesitate in calling my plastic surgeon. I shall, without a doubt, grow old healthily, but gracefully? No chance! Us WAGs have a reputation to keep up, after all!

Chapter Eighteen

WAGs do not and should not feel they have to work hard to hold onto their man. They do not need to be dutiful housewives or answer the front door in stockings and suspenders to ensure that the only playing away their partner will do is at the next away match. No woman should feel insecure in her relationship. She should be adored and chased and held onto tightly. After all, a good woman is hard to find . . . and a hard man is good to find.

My footballer can be found hard in many of his waking moments. He has an insatiable sexual appetite. If I were to detail to a therapist his persistent overtly sexual behaviour, tendency to beg for sex, and masturbation timetable, since he claims he *needs* to ejaculate at least three times per day or he may explode, he'd most certainly be defined as a sex addict.

However, I understand him as a whole person and I do not take his minor sexual indiscretions out of context. Fortunately, my husband and I have over-whelming sexual chemistry, and I can meet his demand with my supply. Even when our relationship has hit rocky patches, our sex life has remained on good ground. It feels like we have an innate biological connection, that our sexual compatibility is not just because of our emotional attachment to each other but because our bodies chose each other as mates. I have a high sex drive and so does he, although his is almost off the scale. He'd have sex or masturbate all day if he could.

I have always assumed his high sex drive is because he's an athlete. On a daily basis he has to push his body to a high state of cardiovascular arousal and his brain reacts by releasing opioids, or happy hormones, into his endocrine system. What that may translate into is that he generally feels energized, healthy, happy . . . and horny.

I know other WAGs who, like me, have to feign headaches regularly just to get a night off, but when we have gossiped about our men and compared notes, some of the girls have claimed that their husband's sex drive is almost non-existent. The pressure of the beautiful game, or the sheer exhaustion of it, may get the better of them. While they may perform well on the pitch, their bedroom performance doesn't get anywhere near man-of-the-match status. Interestingly, the footballers I know of who allegedly have a low sex drive present an entirely different public image of themselves. As the saying goes, it may well be the quiet ones that we women have to look out for, or avoid.

When it comes to sex a footballer is like any other man and a WAG is like any other woman. Some of us obsess about it, some of us can take it or leave it, and some of us pay for it. My husband and I fall into the first category. When I'm pregnant, I fall into the second. We know a few too many footballers who fall into the third. I even know a WAG who has paid for sex.

A general difference between footballers and other men with regard to sex that can be evidenced is that sex is on offer to footballers from women who aren't their wives or girlfriends much more frequently. Not that it is normal for women to offer sex to men.

WAGs have to face the fact that their man is like a lighthouse in a booze-fogged atmosphere, a beacon that serves to guide single girls to where the fame, fit bodies, free drinks and finance are. And, whatever the footballer's age, as long as he remains rich, famous and handsome, he will remain attractive to women of all ages. Even the most butt-ugly of footballers can pull. Furthermore, WAGs do not get any younger, but the women who fawn around their men do. This knowledge can lead to paranoia in even the most secure WAG. For other WAGs, like me, it can lead to competitiveness.

The female attention my man has basked in throughout his life will not cool anytime soon. He's a well-known public figure, handsome, fit and rich. That he's a footballer increases his longevity on the pulling scene. Knowing my man is adored by other women invokes a sense of pride in me; it affirms that what I see in him is recognized by others. However, it also makes me want to compete with him, to show him that for every woman who looks at him, a man is looking at me.

When we go out for the evening together, the first thing I do is ensure that I am dressed to impress. When you have a footballer for a husband, regardless of how many years you have been together and how many awful states he's seen you in, you make sure that when you go out in public you look the very best you can. WAGs have to be confident in public settings, be alert to the paparazzi and feel comfortable, despite the stares of other people. Wearing a killer outfit fulfils such requirements. You also have to remind your footballer of how beautiful you are outside your gym outfit and pyjamas; that you would be any man's prized possession. Finally, WAGs aim to ward off other women from their partner while simultaneously attracting looks from other men, a delicate skill given that the warding-off has to be done without inciting bad feeling, and the enticing without any serious suggestion.

The other competitive tactic that I employ on an evening out with my man is that I am myself. It may seem odd to suggest that 'being myself' is a tactic, but it is. When you allow yourself to be free, to dance, sing and have fun, and I don't do such things by halves, you become naturally attractive to the opposite sex and naturally intimidating to any potential female rivals! It's an easy 'win'.

Like any relationship, we have to work at ours to keep the spark alive. I have watched some marriages collapse because couples have taken each other for granted and forgotten to make time for each other, or not stuck by each other when the going's got tough.

On my wedding day I meant the promises I made in my vows: I'm in this marriage for life and I don't want it to be boring. I won't let it be.

To avoid the rot setting into our relationship, ever since we've had our children my husband and I have reserved a babysitter at least one night every two weeks to allow us to go out together on a 'date night'. We go to the cinema or to a nice restaurant for a meal, or do something a little more active, like bowling. We've also surprised each other with some romantic gestures.

On one summer date night, when we lived near to the coast, my husband led me to the beach, to a secluded area where the sand met the rocks. There were two wooden chairs and a small table set for two. He invited me to sit down, then apologized that he had to make a quick call. His call, spoken in hushed tones, lasted no more than a few seconds, and less than five minutes later a young guy appeared, dressed in a waiter's outfit, with white wine in a cooler in one hand and a basket of bread in the other. My husband had arranged for a romantic picnic on the beach, alone. There were no prying eyes, no autograph requests and no camera lenses anywhere near us.

The beach waiter then served us a delicious seafood dinner and we dined as the sun went down. To this day I still do not know how or where the food was cooked: there wasn't a restaurant for miles.

One of the special date nights I arranged was an evening picnic in a wood. The setting was absolutely beautiful; the late spring sun illuminated the trees with a warm glow and bluebells covered the forest floor, like a delicate carpet. As my husband chomped down the party sausages and finger sandwiches I'd packed, and as I ate in a distinctly quieter fashion, our surroundings were serene. We saw a deer peek out from behind a tree, then bolt into the distance, and a few birds flapped around the canopy that the trees formed, but no other people seemed to be around.

That gave my husband an idea. He suggested, rather unromantically, 'Shall we have a quick shag?'

I feel obliged to have sex on date nights. Most of the time I want it as much as him, but on the odd occasion that I don't I still go through with it. I think my husband would feel rejected if I didn't have sex with him after a nice evening together. I'm not sure men would be so obliging of women if there were a comparable situation. So I agreed to his eloquent proposal in the bluebell wood.

My husband loves me to strip for him and I love to tease him so I knelt next to him on the picnic blanket and slowly got naked. He didn't take off his clothes. This often happens: sex begins when I'm naked and he's fully dressed. He lay back, opened the zip of his jeans, took his manhood out and I climbed onto him. I straddled him and we began to have frantic, fast sex, with me doing all of the work. Suddenly, when I was reaching a sexual crescendo, moments away from orgasm, a loud gunshot echoed through the forest.

I froze. Instantly my body stopped playing its beautiful music. My husband, however, was oblivious to my fear. He begged me to continue. 'Ssh,' I said. He grabbed my backside and tried to make me go on by pushing and pulling my arse, as if I was a machine that had temporarily lost power. Another gunshot echoed. My husband still tried to force my arse into a mechanical shag. Then a stag bolted past us. It ran by so close that it flicked earth onto our picnic blanket and its hoofs skimmed my husband's outstretched feet. His brain then registered the gunshots. 'Deer stalkers,' he whispered. 'Let's go!'

As I scrambled for my clothes and he hurriedly stuffed the remnants of our picnic back into the cooler box, a beagle barked and ran towards us, and a man with a large hunting rifle shouted and chased after it. Fortunately the hunter's shouts brought the dog to a standstill before it reached us, but we were in clear view of the man and I had not yet put my top back on. From the look on his face and his body language, it was clear that he acknowledged it would be inappropriate for him to walk any closer to us, but he looked angry. 'This is private land,' he bellowed. Then he turned on his heels and stomped back in the direction he'd come from, with the dog in tow.

I was mortified. I must've looked like a cheap tart in my lacy red bra. Yes, red – the shame! Nevertheless, my man appreciated the effort I'd gone to and, like all date nights, he knew that when we got home we'd have sex.

Sex isn't just reserved for our date nights: it's an important aspect of our relationship and we make a point of not allowing our sex life to get monotonous or formulaic. I know some women who book sex into their diary as if it's a chore that can be compartmentalized between 'Drop kids at school' and 'Hang washing out'. We try to keep our sex life evolving. We trust each other enough to try new things together, and we're both physically confident, which aids any adventure.

We use food in sex quite often. We've licked and sucked every sweet substance we have in our cupboards off each other's bodies, from chocolate spread to strawberry jam to sweet chilli sauce. The latter gave us both an interesting sensation. We've covered each other in whipped cream and poured champagne into every skin crease and crevice possible. I particularly enjoy giving him a blow-job with a mouthful of fizz: it makes the experience much tastier.

I also dress up for him. I've worn the classic nurse outfit, maid outfit and naughty-schoolgirl outfit. We don't find it embarrassing, as some people may do. It's just a bit of fun and foreplay, especially as we're both natural jokers. I particularly like to enact the dominant female role – it gives me a false sense of power! When I dress in my PVC halter-neck teddy suit lingerie that my husband spontaneously bought me, I play the dominatrix role and he is my subordinate. We don't go very far with it – he would never crawl around the room or howl like a dog upon my command, but he does let me spank, pinch and bite him. It can be quite a buzz! The fun has continued afterwards, too, because it provides me with great stories to tell my friends, which always gains their howls . . . of laughter.

He's asked me to do some slightly odd things too, namely to dress up in his football kit, including his football socks. It's become a normal request but when he first asked me to do it I thought it was a strange fantasy. After all, the only other people he sees in his kit are his team-mates, so a voice in the back of my mind wondered whether he wanted to imagine having sex with one of his team-mates instead of me! I've since heard that a lot of men want their women to dress in their work shirts, or wear a tie around their neck when they have sex, so I guess what my man wants me to dress up in is semi-normal. Although, if ever he asks me to perform headers and keepy-uppees in the bedroom, I *will* begin to worry.

Like most men, my husband is easily turned on by sexy lingerie. I have an extensive underwear selection that falls into the categories of pretty, racy, vintage and pornographic. Unsurprisingly, he particularly likes the last variety: the crotch-less knickers, peep-hole bras, the bondage-like leather jump-suits and generally the items most uncomfortable for me to wear.

Every day my husband tugs my jeans down and pulls my top up to see what underwear I have on. He has come to understand that if I'm wearing matching underwear it'll be on when the kids go to bed. If it's mismatching, I'm a no-go area. Such non-verbal communication works well for us and, luckily for him, I'm usually very coordinated in the underwear department.

I've lived up to my childhood nickname of 'Miss Knickerless' too. On a few poignant occasions I've removed my knickers and told him moments before he's been about to take part in something professional, like a TV interview. I've only ever done it in places where he can't act upon it immediately, to tantalize and torment him. Like when I went with him one of the times that he appeared on *A Question of Sport*. He knew I had no underwear on, and my husband has the type of mind that obsesses about this, regardless of the pressure he is under from other angles. I was in the front row of the audience, behind the cameras, with a clear view of him at the desk with his team. Even though I had a knee-length dress on, I resisted the temptation to perform a Sharon Stone!

However, whenever my husband looked in my direction for prolonged periods of time, like when he paused for thought or when it wasn't his turn to speak, it excited me to wonder if the beads of perspiration on his forehead were just because of the studio lights. When the recording finished, we hurried our good-byes and rushed out to our car. My husband confessed that he'd found it difficult to focus on the quiz because every time he looked at me his mind flipped to sex. That was exactly the result I had wanted.

My man *really* likes risqué sex, sex in public places. He's explained the thrill as a response to the pressure of being in the public eye and under the watchful gaze of the manager. He's said that having sex somewhere unsafe, where you could be seen by someone else, is like a rebellion, a reclaiming of his privacy. I don't think of it that deeply. For me, sex in dodgy places is simply fun.

We've shagged and fucked and screwed and made love in a multitude of public places and, thankfully, never, so far, been caught. That is, unless the lorry driver who got a glimpse of me giving my husband a blow-job while he was driving along the M1 counts. We've had sex on beaches, in fields and forests, in public toilets and dark alleyways, and in and on our car. We've christened every bonnet of every car we've ever owned, and there's a bit of a ceremony to it. We decided that it has to happen within the first twenty-four hours of ownership. Generally on the first night-time drive together, we find a dark country lane with lay-bys or even just on our drive, and screw on the warm bonnet. It's amazing that we've never been caught. Maybe that's due to my husband's perfected quick-shag timing – he can come in two minutes if need be – or maybe it's down to the fact that you see what you want to see and no one really expects to look out of the window at ten o'clock at night to see two people at it on their car.

We employed the assumption that people are not overly perceptive on a flight back from Las Vegas when we joined the Mile High Club. My husband and I had wanted to have sex on a plane more to cross it off our public-places-to-do-it list than anything else, although the thought excited us. The risk of getting caught by a stewardess or passenger was high. After five days of partying and gambling we had booked a night flight with seats in economy. It was an unusually quiet flight, so we had a row of three between the two of us.

After we'd watched a film and noticed that most of the other passengers had turned off their cabin lights, we turned off ours and lay across the seats with the aim of sleeping, or at least resting. I lay on my side with my back against the seats, and my husband lay to face me. I hooked my leg over his thigh, to allow him more room, and he pushed his pelvis into me to get closer. I then felt that he was hard. Before that point I had always assumed that people who had sex on aeroplanes must have done it in either the toilet or in first class as they were the only places I could think of where there'd be at least some space and privacy. But then I realized it could be possible in our seats.

I gave him a wide-eyed look when he again thrust towards me, because it certainly wasn't the seatbelt that I felt jab me in the stomach. He responded with a sexy smile. He then grabbed the blankets from the floor and carefully laid them over us. He momentarily held one of the blankets up and gestured for me to look; he had covertly undone his trousers. I felt a rush of fear and excitement! I touched him under the covers. He then touched me. As my leg was angled over his thigh, the blanket had formed a tent-like structure so no movement could be seen through it.

Then, in one swift move, he tugged my trousers halfway down my thighs. It was extremely erotic to be semi-naked and aroused on an aeroplane! Apart from the low hum of the aircraft, the occasional cough or a clatter from the stewardess's tray, it was silent in the cabin. All we could hear was our own breathing, hot and heavy, as we gently touched each other. Then my man wriggled down in the seat so that his feet touched the wall of the cabin and he angled himself so that we could sneakily have sex. It felt incredible, but I had to hold my breath so as to not make a sound. It was intense. We remained in that position for a few moments and secretly shagged whenever we could be sure that there was no one in the aisle near us. When we heard some of the cabin crew begin to move their trolley up the aisle towards us, we realized we weren't brave enough and stealthily adjusted our clothing.

While sex is just sex, my inner goddess high-fived me for having had sex on an aeroplane; at the time I thought it was quite a cool thing to do. We had joined the Mile High Club and it was more exciting than I'd thought it would be. However, we haven't always got it right when it's come to acting out our fantasies. There were two memorable occasions when my attempts went very wrong.

One happened when I had the not-so-bright idea to surprise my husband on his return home from training. It was midweek and he was due back at one p.m. I felt a little frisky and I knew he'd satisfy my womanly desires! When he called to say that he was on his way home, I stripped naked and stuck on a pair of heart-shaped nipple tassels. I had never thought in a million years I'd wear them, but their time to shine had arrived. I then poured myself a glass of champagne to give the scene even more boudoir appeal, and lay down on the sofa in the lounge, leaving the door open.

With the aid of a compact mirror, I ensured that my

body was positioned to make me look perfectly slim and alluring, my breasts pert and buxom and the nipple tassels taking centre stage. I thought I looked awesome. That might have been because I'd consumed two glasses of champagne in the short time it had taken me to get into position.

When I heard my husband's keys twist in the door, I called out, 'I'm in the lounge.' I had heard him talking, but because his mobile phone is generally locked firmly to his ear, I presumed that he was on a call. What I didn't expect was to see him and a team-mate walk into the lounge! I freaked out, jumped up, spilled champagne all over myself, grabbed the nearest cushion and cowered behind it on the sofa like a naughty child.

Fortunately my husband's friend walked out of the lounge quicker than he'd walked in, so while he did get a good look at me in my birthday suit, he saved me any further embarrassment. I heard him laugh as he shut the front door. My husband thought it was hilarious too. After a third glass of champagne, the shame left me and I was able to see the funny side of it too. The nipple tassels have not had an outing since.

The other time things went disastrously wrong was when I attempted to re-create a scene from *Sex in the City* that we had fantasized about. In an early episode, Samantha had lain on her kitchen table, her body covered with sushi, and waited for her man to walk through the door, then eat it off her. My husband loved the idea, and along with Chinese, sushi was his favourite food.

One evening when he'd gone out to meet his agent, I drove to Marks & Spencer and bought a shopping basket full. I raced home, took the sushi rolls out of their packaging and laid them on the kitchen table. It seemed that the packaging had taken up most of the room in the basket as when I looked at it, I wasn't sure it would cover my body in the way I had hoped.

I darted out into the back garden and picked some handfuls of mint, chives and lavender, then took my clothes off, lay down on the table and painstakingly arranged the sushi and fragrant foliage over myself. It was not an easy task. I leaned on my elbows and placed the sushi in a creative pattern on my pelvic area. Then I edged backwards, relying on my stomach muscles to support me, in order to lie a little flatter and make a trail of sushi from between my legs up to my breasts. Despite my crunch sessions at the gym, my stomach muscles were unreliable. As I had lain tense for so long to try to get the sushi to look as if it snaked up through my midriff and sternum, my torso shook, my stomach muscles spasmed and everything fell on to the floor.

I had to start again, and again, and again. Eventually, after much perseverance and dusting down the sushi rolls, I had managed to create the look I wanted. I had sushi in a heart shape around my vagina, and a trail of sushi curled up the middle of my body to my chest, where I had carefully balanced three small sushi rolls on each nipple. I had used the plants I had picked from the garden to dress the sides of my body, and I'd ripped some of the leaves off the stalks and scattered them over me as a garnish.

Then I waited. I waited for quite a long time. I became desperate for the toilet. However, I was resolute that I would not give in to my bodily needs until my man ate at least one sushi roll off me.

I soon discovered that while I could control my instinct to pee, I couldn't control my reflex to a small beetle that began to crawl over my chest. I screamed, bolted upright, flicked away the beetle and jumped off the table, sending everything plummeting to the kitchen floor. I ignored the mess and instead hopped from one leg to the other, frantically brushing myself down, as if thousands of fire ants were crawling over me. As fate would have it, the scene that greeted my husband as he walked through the kitchen door was of me naked and jumping on the spot, like a madwoman, with leaves and squashed sushi at my feet. It was not the food fantasy I had planned. It was one of *Ramsay's Kitchen Nightmare*.

Before my husband could even complete his opening line of 'What the fu—' he burst out laughing. He quickly registered what I'd tried to do and that it had somehow gone wrong. I felt like an idiot, but I was so relieved to dash to the downstairs toilet.

When I returned to the kitchen, he had taken his top off and was lying on the kitchen table with sushi on his chest. He also had a load of sushi stuffed into his mouth and was chewing, as he said, 'Well, go on, then!' We had our kitchen-table sex despite my failed plan, and after I'd checked that the surface was clear of insects.

While we WAGs occasionally gossip to each other about sex, like most girlfriends do, we don't give away all of our secrets. I certainly wouldn't tell them about my top tips. Although from the WAG grapevine I've heard some interesting stories about not-so-innocent ways in which other footballers and their partners keep their sex life alive. Apparently some top Premiership players and their WAGs have formed a small, discreet swinging circle. My WAG friend told me that one of the couples has a huge Jacuzzi in their house, 'big enough for at least ten people', where the sex parties are mainly held. The group of footballers and WAGs drink a lot of alcohol, then cram into the hot tub to have sex with a different partner, or many different partners. She said they've been doing it for years.

I'm not sure I believe the swinging rumours: it could simply be gossip made up by bitchy WAGs, or grossly exaggerated by the Chinese-whispers effect. My husband and I have certainly never been invited to join such activities and, knowing him, if he'd been asked, he wouldn't have been able to stop himself putting it to me.

Chapter Nineteen

*G*irls are damn good at being bitches. That's a fact. We are all born with the bitch gene. For some of us, the gene is more dominant, and for others it is only used in unavoidable situations. WAGs have exceptionally high levels of the bitch gene and are not afraid to use it because, quite frankly, WAGdom is a WAG-eat-WAG world.

It doesn't take a rocket scientist to understand that if you put any group of girls into a small room there will be a whole array of hormonal shit going on. The Players' Lounge is a melting pot of giggling, gossiping, back-stabbing, wandering eyes and, refreshingly, some genuinely great friendships. The latter is unfortunately a rarity in WAGdom. WAGs are great acquaintances, and I have loads of them, but lifelong friends whom I would take a bullet for? They're in short supply.

I'm the sort of girl who needs the type of friends who will crack up at my rip-roaring farts and tell me if I've got a piece of spinach covering my tooth. I want friends I can laugh and cry with, who can bond with my kids and keep my secrets. Most of the WAGs I've met just wouldn't be up for that. They'd take much greater pleasure in letting me sit through a whole game with a huge bogey on show, laughing among themselves and arguing about who should be the one to tell me, resulting in no one actually telling me. And, yes, I know this from experience.

I can say with conviction that the majority of WAGs are nothing but rivals. They strive to be the first to have the newest Miu Miu clutch, the latest Louboutins or the one-off Hervé Léger dress. They don't hold back in showing off. The number of pictures I've seen of WAGs on social network sites with new 'exclusive' purchases, in an attempt to (a) rub it in to other WAGs and (b) claim to be the first one to own the item, is quite laughable.

I once had a fabulous oversized bag given to me for a birthday present by a friend from home. It wasn't expensive: only seven pounds in a sale. I loved it, though, and couldn't have cared less how much it cost as it was given with love by my good friend. It was from a well-known high-street shop in which the majority of WAGs would never dream to be seen, let alone wear its clothes or accessories.

One Saturday after my birthday I took the bag to a game. I'd filled it with toys for my kids. As soon as I walked into the Lounge, the WAGs all commented on it.

'What a gorgeous bag!'

'The colour is fabulous!'

'It's amazing!'

Their faces were a picture when I said, 'Well, girls, if you want one, it's just been reduced in Primark right now from twelve pounds to seven.' Needless to say, no one rushed out to buy it.

I love breaking the mould of a WAG and going against the grain every now and again. The other WAGs probably slagged me off behind my back, in disgust that I would cheapen myself with such low-quality wares on my arm, but in all honesty, I couldn't give a damn. It's not all about the price tag.

WAGs don't trust each other; they're not friends; they feed off one another. Each and every Players' Lounge hosts an ecosystem of WAGs.

At the top of the food chain are the Queen WAGs: they are the oldest and most experienced of the creatures and usually headed by the team captain's wife. This group are often the most hostile, territorial and bitter variety of WAG since they feel they rule the roost by virtue of the time they've spent at the club, and the respect-your-elders concept. Age is a bone of contention with this group, so Queen WAGs are identified by their arched eyebrows, frozen foreheads and mutton-as-lamb dress sense.

Every club has a 'murder' (as with crows) of Queen WAGs. Their courtiers, those whom they feed off, are the Bitchy WAGs, or, if I were to be very un-PC, the Chav WAGs. These creatures provide a constant stream of drama and gossip for the Queen WAGs' entertainment, and reinforce the Queen WAGs' superiority via much arse-licking and false-flattery. To retain their status, Bitchy WAGs often intimidate or bully those lower down the food chain.

The Bitchy WAGs can be identified by their blinding

bling, Burberry and blacked-out cars. They often dress the same since they all share the same stylist, shop at Harvey Nicks store or thoughtlessly purchase the same 'new in' items on net-a-porter.com. The WAGs lower down the food chain particularly enjoy it when members from this group make the ultimate faux pas by arriving at the same event in the same clothes, sometimes in an identical dress with the same shoes *and* handbag.

The Bitchy WAGs feed off the Model WAGs. Indeed, the Bitchy WAGs are only higher on the food chain than the Model WAGs because they fight their way there, sometimes literally, in dodgy, sticky-carpeted, late-night establishments. The Model WAGs are unsurprisingly the prettiest WAGs. They can usually be identified as the tallest, skinniest WAGs, who wear the most expensive and high-fashion clothes. They will often wear the largest and darkest sunglasses – whatever the weather.

The Model WAGs are, of course, often recognizable from the pages of gossip magazines and tabloid news-papers, attention that their superiors, the Queen and Bitchy WAGs, yearn for. The Model WAGs also act as the bait on a WAGs' night out to attract the fittest men who will stroke the Queen/Bitch WAGs' egos, and sometimes stroke them in a more literal manner. It's not just footballers who have illicit liaisons.

My friend told me that when Peter Crouch joined the club her husband played for, the Queen WAGs and Bitchy WAGs were absolutely desperate to get Abbey Clancy on a night out. Even though they didn't know her and had barely spoken a word to her, she was the light and they were the moths: they invited her to everything and anything.

She eventually agreed, and it was billed as the WAG event of the season. The WAGs were hurrying out to buy their outfits and to book the best table in the club to prepare themselves for the anticipated barrage of media and male attention the evening would undoubtedly bring. When Abbey Clancy didn't turn up, their night must have been ruined.

The Model WAGs can also get a rough deal from the other WAGs for being temptresses. Many WAGs worry that Model WAGs will be husband-stealers.

Below the Model WAGs are the Foreign WAGs. It could be argued that the Foreign WAGs have a better command of English than some of the WAGs above them, given the thick accents that bark out in the Players' Lounge. The ability to speak another language does require a degree of intelligence that not all WAGs are blessed with, so Foreign WAGs should perhaps be in a more elevated food-chain positioning. Foreign WAGs can be identified via their accents, their large Italian handbags and purposeful separation from the WAG majority. Basically, they're the group in the corner of the room. The Foreign WAGs stick together, probably through their shared dislike for us natives, but at least they have some sense of solidarity.

I've often wondered whether the Foreign WAGS choose to speak their own languages to avoid the politics of WAGdom. If that is their tactic, then fair play to them; 'No comprende' would have been a great get-out from listening to all the bitching, gossiping and moaning that my ears have endured. So, in general, Foreign WAGs are left to their own devices, partly because very few of the others can be bothered to communicate with them and partly because they don't want to be communicated with.

Hovering near the bottom of the WAGdom food-chain are the Girl-Next-Door WAGs: those who are quite normal and thus don't fit in. Girl-Next-Door WAGs are often the childhood sweethearts of their partners. Think Melanie Slade: she's got a friendly look, she's not overly glamorous, but she's . . . nice. She has been with Theo Walcott for all of her courting days. She never gets anything but positive press as she is not outrageous or controversial. She keeps herself to herself, her head down and her nose clean. Girl-Next-Door WAGs are rarely seen on a WAG night out.

I have purposefully left out two types of WAG in my food-chain analogy, for I cannot consider them predator or prey. First, there are the Private WAGs. They keep a low profile and rarely take notice of, or care for, their WAG contemporaries. Put simply, they don't give a shit. They neither need nor want to belong in WAGdom, and they certainly don't care for making friends with any other WAGs.

Last, and most important, there are the down-to-earth, everyday, great company WAGs, a.k.a. my friends. They are the ones who don't give it large and who are not draped head-to-toe in designer gear as daywear. They are the WAGs who will ask how you are and be genuinely interested in the response.

They are the WAGs with whom I want to arrange coffee mornings where conversation flows naturally. They are the few women in WAGdom I can identify with. These Friend WAGs are supportive, empathetic and genuine. I have three of them.

Ultimately, the underlying reasons for why WAGs do all of this, why they compete, distrust and judge each other, is because of their, our, collective fear: adultery. The threat of that shame and heartbreak, and for some the loss of income, wreaks havoc on a girl's mind, behaviour and, sadly, her friendships.

WAGs can be good friends, but the best friends I have aren't WAGs. They are the normal girls who don't need stilettos, Botox, famous friends or fast cars to make them cool and attractive. My friends are naturally beautiful, from the inside to the outside.

The word WAG has been said to stand for 'Waste and Gunk', 'Want All Glamour', 'Wants Always Gets', 'Wannabes and Gold-diggers', 'Whores and Gadflies', 'Witches and Ghouls' and 'What About Gucci?'. Positive definitions for WAGs do not seem to exist. But while some WAGs epitomize their negative stereotype, the majority do a great many good deeds for which they are not publicly recognized; most good-hearted WAGs don't do those deeds for attention.

In fact, I do not know one WAG who has not contributed to charity, and by contribution I don't mean a donation of a fiver on Red Nose Day. It's an unwritten rule in the world of football that we, footballers and WAGs, have a responsibility to assist charities, and it's an obligation that is willingly undertaken by most. We give a lot of our time, energy and money to charitable causes. Rightly so, too! We are in privileged positions with regard to our finances and free time, especially us WAGs.

Charity work fits perfectly with a WAG's lifestyle because most WAGs don't need to earn money and can thus work for free. Voluntary work offers a flexibility that can meet the demands of our partner's football schedules. WAGs can also exert some power over the media so we can assist charities in raising their public profile. Also, a WAG's phonebook is full of useful contacts: businessmen and -women, celebrities, agents and reporters could all open doors of opportunity that may otherwise have been closed or hidden to a small, local charity.

WAGs have a unique position in the world of sport and thus have access to some of the most influential sportspeople and venues, all of which can be of benefit for fundraising. WAGs frequently provide amazing charity-auction prizes in the form of signed football shirts, bespoke memorabilia, exclusive sport experiences and even luxury holidays. For example, for one small charity auction I was involved in, I managed to get my contacts to donate as auction items front-row and backstage tickets to the West End theatre production of *Phantom of the Opera*, box seats to see Beyoncé perform at the Manchester Evening News Arena and a week-long golfing vacation at Gleneagles. Those three items alone raised thousands of pounds for the charity yet I had gone to barely any effort to secure them: all I'd done was phone a few people and speak in my sweetest voice.

It's a great shame that WAGs' generosity goes largely unrecognized by the media yet our occasional reckless behaviour is sensationalized. I actively support as many charities as I can. I have a long list of monthly direct debits that go out to different organizations, some local and others global, and I cannot walk past a fundraiser, busker or beggar without making a donation. I've often arrived home from a shopping trip with numerous copies of the same *Big Issue* magazine. I have run in races, modelled in fashion shows, climbed a mountain, skydived, played in a televised football match, been auctioned as a WAG-slave and appeared on a well-known primetime television show, all in the name of charity.

Also, like many other WAGs, I regularly donate my and my family's old clothes to charity shops. As WAGs are notorious fashion victims, our wardrobes can never be big enough, so clothes are frequently discarded. They are often worth hundreds of pounds and raise good money for the respective charity. On many occasions when I've dropped off a bag, I've indulged in a little rummaging through the rails and bagged a designer bargain of my own. I once bought a pair of Jimmy Choo shoes and an Yves Saint Laurent dress from the British Red Cross shop on the King's Road in London. I paid pennies for the two items in relation to what they would have cost at full price. It's also a great feeling to give to charity and get a designer dress in return.

Moreover, since I've been a WAG I've become intimately involved with an independent cancer charity local to the city my husband and I met in. We are both patrons. Over the years we have organized many special fundraising events for it and personally donated thousands of pounds to the cause. Instead of wedding gifts we requested that our guests make a donation to our charity; our happy day raised £20,000 for it. Our family and friends have gradually become more involved with the charity, and its local support has increased tenfold since we first became involved, due in no small part to the hard work of those who run it.

Most football clubs make regular concessions for charities and many make it easy for charitable organizations to approach them. For example, every month Stoke City offers a range of football-related donations, from match and meal tickets to signed memorabilia, and invites charities to enter a monthly draw to win them. The winning charities are then randomly selected at the end of each month.

A large number of the footballers and WAGs I know are closely involved in low-key charities close to their hearts. Some have even set up their own fundraising initiative in response to a personal tragedy. The Luey Jacob Sharp Foundation was set up by Billy Sharp in memory of his first-born son, who died of gastroschisis. Billy now spends every spare hour outside his football schedule organizing events to raise money towards care and cures for the condition, and awareness in other parents and parents-to-be.

Shay Given and ex-wife Jayne organize Fashion Kicks, a ticketed fashion show to raise funds for cancer sufferers, in memory of Shay's late mother who died of the disease. The annual event is in association with Selfridges and attracts a wealth of celebrities; tables sell for thousands and an astounding amount of money is raised in that one evening.

James Milner created a foundation that promotes healthy living through football. He's contributed to charity since he started his professional career as a sixteen-year-old. After working with the NSPCC he has channelled his efforts into helping children better themselves through sport.

The list of WAGs who devote much of their life to charity work is endless, and many of them commit themselves to charities that represent suffering they have personally witnessed or experienced. Julie Neville gives a lot of financial and public support to the Royal Manchester Children's Hospital where her daughter, who has cerebral palsy, has been regularly treated. Coleen Rooney is associated with the Royston Blythe charity that supported her younger sister Rosie, who suffered and sadly died from Rett's syndrome.

Ironically, charity is one of the rare areas in life within which WAGs show genuine unity. WAGs support WAGs in their charitable efforts. I have been to many charity lunches, dinners, fashion shows and children's football matches where the WAG organizer has been reliant on the attendance of her fellow WAGs to boost publicity and increase the money raised.

Therefore, while the word charity is not synonymous with 'WAG', I believe it should be. Giving to charity plays a central role in most WAGs' lives, and if the media would emphasize this element in their stories, then perhaps other people would be more inspired to volunteer their time and money to a good cause, and the negative public perception of WAGs would change. There's more to us WAGs than shoes and handbags, sunbathing and scandals.

In fact, with regard to our charity work, WAG should stand for 'Worthwhile and Generous'.

Chapter Twenty

*O*nly the other night, I heard my husband say on the phone to his team-mate, 'Mate, you got to take every game as it comes. Play every one as if it's your last and enjoy each and every minute, because it'll be over before you know it.' He hasn't always been so wise and inspirational. Back in his younger, carefree, live-life-on-the-edge years, his ethos would have been more along the lines of 'Party hard, train hard, play well, splash the cash and don't worry about a thing.' Luckily he grew up at some point during our relationship.

It's common knowledge that being a professional footballer is a short-lived career and, as a result, the wages are astronomical. All footballers know that the end is nigh. But retirement is the dreaded word that we WAGs fear.

When the full-time whistle blows, all the WAG can do is hope and pray that it is a decision her man has made for himself and not because he has failed to secure a contract with a club or because of a debilitating injury. I have witnessed friends endure both scenarios. Their husbands have felt unprepared and therefore not ready for retirement, and the WAGs have had to pick up the pieces. They've had to rethink the future for their families and motivate their man to seek a new career.

If a footballer feels fulfilled enough to retire, if he's earned enough money to sustain the life he and his family have become accustomed to and if he's achieved all of his career dreams, he will accept his retirement gracefully. The problem is that football is all that my – and every other – footballer knows. My man has lived and breathed it from a very young age. The majority of footballers have no previous trade, career or worthwhile academic qualifications. My husband, despite his intelligence, has only his GCSEs to prove his intellectual worth, which wouldn't get him very far on their own.

Without football, footballers are quite frankly fucked if they haven't earned enough money while playing. That's how most of them see it anyway. There are relatively few coaching, managing and presenting jobs up for grabs, certainly not enough for everyone who's left the game. So, unless a footballer has millions of pounds in the bank as a result of a top-flight career and can live off it for the rest of his life, he's pretty screwed as to what to do next in life's grand journey.

We have a good friend who rose through the ranks at a top club. He showed great potential at a young age and was obviously headed for stardom; he scored goals left, right and centre. However, his dreams were shattered at the tender age of twenty-two when a tackle resulted in his knee being totally shattered. It was so bad that even after many corrective surgeries he was told that he would never play again.

His insurance pay-out covered his injury, but it was by no means enough to live off for the rest of his life. He had to do something else, but he had no idea or motivation as to what that could be. He had to sell his penthouse apartment and move in with his parents, and initially spent most of his days watching television in a heap on their sofa. Some nights he didn't even make it up to bed as he couldn't be bothered to walk up the flight of stairs, so he slept on the sofa too. He slipped into depression. He alienated himself from his team-mates because they were constant reminders of what he once was and what he had lost, and he hid away from his old friends because he felt he had failed in life. He went from hero to zero practically overnight.

My husband went to his parents' house on a few occasions but each time his mother gave an excuse for why he couldn't come to the door, or lied to say that he was out. My husband knew he was there, but he also recognized that his friend just couldn't face seeing him. He still hasn't seen him after all these years. Apparently his dad eventually got him a job as a scaffolder. I sincerely hope that time has done its marvellous thing of healing and that life for him now is rosier, albeit vastly different.

Miraculously my husband has had quite a straight run in his career. He has had a few knocks and injury set-backs here and there, but if nothing major happens in the next few years, he'll slot into the lucky group of footballers who retire due to age alone.

But when we see the threat of retirement looming over our footballers' heads, we have to prepare ourselves for being ex-WAGs. No one wants to be an ex, let's face it. Ex-girlfriend, ex-wife, ex-WAG: the title says that something has been lost. Even though at times being a WAG is a royal pain in the arse, I'll miss being in the thick of it when it ends. I'll miss the games, the dramas, the scandal and, yes, seeing the other WAGs. It's all I have ever known through my adult life, and although there have been ups and downs, I feel that I have grown and changed immensely within WAGdom. I've lived an exciting life that has definitely opened my eyes and been a learning experience, that's for sure.

Ex-WAGs don't go to football matches, and unless they've sold themselves to the media, they're rarely seen in any of their WAGdom haunts. Even if my man pursues a post-playing career path in management, I'm pretty sure that my days of being in the thick of it all will be over once he hangs up his boots. The wives of football managers seem to live discreetly and quietly.

As I become more of a seasoned WAG, I often reflect on how incredibly different life is now in WAGdom compared to my early days in the wonderland. I'm a totally different person since I became a WAG. For starters, I've grown a much thicker skin: the bitchiness and back-stabbing that goes on in WAGdom has ensured it developed fast. I have come to appreciate the simple things in life, and I place more and more value on the good people around me than on wanting to fit in with everyone. I used to feel cheated in the early days of being a WAG, as if my freedom had been snatched from me, but now I can see the end of the tunnel, I realize that my independence is yet to come.

WAGdom today is a much more competitive environment than it used to be. It seems that every WAG wants to be the top WAG. The lower-profile WAGs arse-lick the higher-profile WAGs and can be seen to trample upon anyone who gets in their way as they climb their ladder of self importance. Most WAGs want to be invited to high-profile events, nights out, lunches and functions laid on by the media.

It seems that WAGs today are much more fame-hungry than they used to be. They aren't happy being in the shadow of their footballers. Everyone secretly wants to be the next Wayne and Coleen or, the ultimate couple, David and Victoria. Sadly, this is where the new generation's immaturity and naivety shine through. Instead of using a talent or implementing hard work to get where they want to go, they choose to behave like idiots in front of the camera or rant on social networks to cause such a commotion that they get noticed.

I, on the other hand, will not miss the public exposure that WAGdom has brought, not one little bit. There's enough negativity within the stereotype of a WAG as it is: it's time to change it for the better, not feed the fire. When I became a WAG there were no WAGs jostling for the spotlight. The press didn't refer to us with nasty nicknames, and the wives and girlfriends of footballers were not generically disrespected. We led relatively normal lives with virtually no backlash.

I envisage the derogatory connotations of WAGs will get worse. The explosion of reality television shows, and public acceptance that outrageous and ignorant behaviour leads to fame and fortune, has put WAGs in a good position to exploit their dark side and get the exposure they desire.

I predict footballers dating normal girls will become a rarity in years to come. WAGs are getting younger, prettier and bigger-busted, due in no small part to the media's projections of what young women should aim for, which usually translates to a fit body and a fit man with money.

There are so many more actresses, page-three girls and members of girl bands dating footballers, these days. Footballers seem to feel that these kinds of women are better suited to them because they now consider themselves more as celebrities than sportsmen. It's a fearful prospect for us normal WAGs because of the pressure to look great and remain looking young. Footballers receive so much adoration that they don't think very often about life's deeper issues or look for depth in a woman.

Also, the turnover of WAGs in the Players' Lounge has increased. Perhaps this is something to do with our throwaway generation and the explosion in mobile technology and social media: footballers are much easier to contact and to pull. Some WAGs we only see once or twice before their relationship with their footballer ends; this puts us seasoned WAGs off trying to bond with unfamiliar girls. We can watch them go through their petty fall-outs and dramas and identify with their insecurities and bitchiness from afar.

In addition, it's not only that the new WAGs can disappear in a flash: it's often the case that seasoned ex-WAGs seem to vanish off the face of the planet too. When footballers retire, the percentage of their marriages that fail is shocking. I have seen and heard it happen too many times, and even to some of the couples whom I considered the strongest. I can only imagine it happens because the WAG and the footballer pull in two different directions when they have to leave the world of football. The stress of retirement must take its toll on both partners.

Since retirement can be sudden, huge financial worries may occur with the footballer's loss of earnings. Sometimes couples have no choice but to sell their home, downsize, take their kids out of private school, and often move to an entirely different location. The lifestyle changes dramatically.

A couple of WAGs I know have not managed to come to terms with the upheavals that their partners' retirement has caused. They constantly bickered with their men over the future and, given that they felt more entitled to a say in their family's life choices, the footballers found their diffused power, or lack of control, difficult to handle. Eventually the WAGs felt resentment towards their footballer, and probably vice versa. These WAGs' marriages unfortunately resulted in divorce. I cannot help but think that they were married for the WAG lifestyle, since true love weaves a path around any road blocks.

I love my husband unconditionally, and I would not care if his retirement meant that we had to move to a smaller house or drive a smaller, cheap car. The loss of material possessions and a non-lavish lifestyle are not things I fear. I have always perceived them as a short-term perk of our privileged circumstances. I dread uprooting my kids from yet another school, but the stability of our family is worth a hundred times more than the familiarity of a classroom.

Fortunately, my husband has always had his head screwed on with regard to future finances. He has always paid the maximum amount into his PFA (Professional Footballers' Association) pension. We have an impressive property portfolio and he has invested wisely in various shares and businesses. We are mortgage-free, which sets us up in a very strong position when he ends his career.

However, he doesn't know what he wants to do when he has to exit the beautiful game. He's looking forward to the time when he can take the kids to school and generally be around the family more, and he can't wait to be able to play golf whenever he wants to. Whether or not the novelty of a life of leisure will wear off is unknown, but right now, unlike many of his football peers, he has no intention of going into coaching or management. He would like to try his hand at punditry as he has dabbled in it and enjoyed it. He particularly admires Gary Neville, who has taken to presenting like a duck to water.

So we are looking ahead to a comfortable future, financially at least. The emotional side of retirement remains the uncontrollable variable in our projections.

My biggest concern is how my husband will adapt to not being in a lads' environment, not being part of a team, with the banter and camaraderie that he has become so accustomed to. In a nutshell, I worry that being with just me and the kids will not be enough for him. I worry he will miss it all so much that he will feel like he hasn't got anything to get up for in the morning. I worry that he won't be able to adapt to normal life, that he won't be able to, or want to, fit into our mundane family routines and rhythms.

I'm terrified that he will change from being the person I married. I'm unsure who he will be once football and the limelight are taken away from him. I can't help but look at all the failed marriages of retired footballers, then listen to the voice in my mind that says ours won't survive. I hope and pray that won't be the case. At this moment, in the words of my very own footballer, I'm taking every game as it comes and enjoying every minute of being a WAG . . . because it'll be over before I know it.

However, a part of me believes that when it is over, my real life can begin. I have many hopes and dreams that remain unfulfilled because only time can allow them to be achieved. My ultimate yearning is for my children to gain good qualifications, then go out into the big wide world. I want my children to want to work, to provide for themselves and to feel confident in their own abilities. I don't want them to lead the dependent life I have led thus far, or the restrictive life my husband has led. We have both had to answer to the world of football since we were teenagers, and regardless of the thrills it has brought us, it has not always cultivated the best in who we are, or who we can be.

I want my children to have freedom in their decision-making and life-plans, and I don't want them to experience the extreme conformity that we've had to adhere to. Ultimately, I want them to realize that who they are on the inside, their hearts and minds, will get them to the places they want to be. They don't have to follow the bright lights to gain self worth or independence because, as the cliché goes, fly too close to the light and you get burned. My husband and I have definitely got burn marks. I hope my children stay out of the public eye too: it's corrupting, intrusive, and can turn the most secure people into paranoid wrecks. I'd hate my offspring to be afflicted by such pressures.

Other dreams I have for the future are for me to have my own career. I've been building a business in my spare time and seeking advice from those around me on how to establish myself in the field I studied all those years ago. The path to developing business acumen feels long, but I'm determined to get there, to stand on my own two feet, and perhaps to be able to buy my husband some treats instead of him always splashing the cash on me.

I haven't had the chance to live out my own life-plans yet, so when he retires, it'll be my turn. I vowed to live in the shadows only as long as my husband was basking in the sunshine, and he's had enough to last him a lifetime. I know that freedom from WAGdom is around the corner, and it'll soon be my time to shine.